THE ANALYSIS OF PORTFOLIO MANAGEMENT PERFORMANCE

An Institutional Guide to Assessing and Analyzing Pension Fund, Endowment, Foundation, and Trust Investment Performance

G. Timothy Haight
College of Business and Economics
Towson State University

Stephen O. Morrell
Andreas School of Business
Barry University

McGraw-Hill
New York   San Francisco   Washington, D.C.   Auckland   Bogotá
Caracas   Lisbon   London   Madrid   Mexico City   Milan
Montreal   New Delhi   San Juan   Singapore
Sydney   Tokyo   Toronto

332.6
H149a

Library of Congress Cataloging-in-Publication Data

Haight, G. Timothy (date)
    The analysis of portfolio management performance : an
institutional guide to assessing and analyzing pension fund,
endowment, foundation, and trust investment performance / G. Timothy
Haight, Stephen O. Morrell.
        p.   cm.
    Includes index.
    ISBN 0-7863-0800-1
    1. Portfolio management.   2. Investment analysis.   3. Trusts and
trustees.   4. Charitable uses, trusts, and foundations.
5. Endowments--Management.   6. Pension trusts--Management.
I. Morrell, Stephen Otis, 1949– .   II. Title.
HG4529.5.H34   1997
332.6—dc21   96-51723

McGraw-Hill

A Division of The **McGraw·Hill** Companies

Copyright © 1997 by the The McGraw-Hill Companies, Inc. All rights reserved. Printed in the
United States of America. Except as permitted under the United States Copyright Act of 1976, no
part of this publication may be reproduced or distributed in any form or by any means, or stored in
a database or retrieval system, without the prior written permission of the publisher.

1 2 3 4 5 6 7 8 9 0 DOC/DOC 9 0 9 8 7

ISBN 0-7863-0800-1
Printed and bound by R.R. Donnelley and Sons Company.

This publication is designed to provide accurate and authoritative information in regard to the subject
matter covered. It is sold with the understanding that neither the author or the publisher is
engaged in rendering legal, accounting,or other professional service. If legal advice or other
expert assistance is required, the services of a competent professional person should be sought.
                    *—From a Declaration of Principles jointly adopted by a Committee
                    of the American Bar Association and a Committee of Publishers.*

McGraw-Hill books are available at special quantity discounts to use as premiums and sales
promotions, or for use in corporate training programs. For more information, please write to the
Director of Special Sales, McGraw-Hill, 11 West 19th Street, New York, NY 10011. Or contact
your local bookstore.

Dedicated with love to my mother, Virginia Kathryn, father, Chester Dale Haight, to my wife, Ann, and to our three children, Jason, Tim, and Stephanie.

Tim Haight

To my daughter Kelly, as well as other people who are important to me: mother, Linda, and Lennie.

Steve Morrell

University Libraries
Carnegie Mellon University
Pittsburgh PA 15213-3890

Brief Contents

Contents

Chapter 3

Investment Overview   65

Chapter 4

Alternative Investment Vehicles   85

Preface

Investment professionals manage the vast majority of financial assets, including those of individuals, households, businesses, and nonprofit organizations. Properly monitoring, analyzing, and evaluating the performance of investment professionals has become increasingly important as the dollar amounts entrusted to professional managers continue to grow, and the range and complexity of the investments they make continue to expand. Very few books, however, provide investors with the necessary tools, understanding, knowledge, and information to judge the performance of professional investment managers.

The Analysis of Portfolio Management Performance is intended to provide the reader with the essential knowledge and skills to properly evaluate how professional investors do their jobs. Specifically, this book is intended for those individuals who either employ money managers or are responsible for safeguarding the investments of others. The latter category includes all individuals serving on investment committees of retirement funds, endowments, and similar investment sponsors who have a fiduciary responsibility to ensure that their fund managers are performing in a prudent manner.

This book will equip the reader with all the tools required to properly evaluate investment performance of the fund as well as the manager. Topics such as establishing an investment policy statement, investment approaches, and style and return-risk measurements are essential reading material for those charged with investment oversight. The latest methods of measuring return and risk are explained in depth in this book as well.

The Analysis of Portfolio Management Performance explains how to evaluate total portfolio performance as well as its fixed income, equity and reserve components. Evaluation techniques using benchmarks such as indexes and universes are presented in a clear and understandable fashion. Furthermore, this book examines how to decide between employing the services of an outside investment professional versus managing the funds internally. Finally, this book will provide guidance for selecting money managers and for conducting investment committee meetings.

ACKNOWLEDGMENTS

This book was written with the help of many individuals who have given invaluable assistance. First, we are indebted to our families and loved ones who have sacrificed so much in allowing us to spend the time necessary to research and write this book. Without their help and understanding, this work could not have been accomplished. We would also like to express our gratitude to McGraw-Hill, a constant source of encouragement throughout the project. Specifically, we wish to thank Steve Sheehan, Kevin Thornton, and Maggie Rathke for their efforts on behalf of this book.

Several individuals provided valuable assistance throughout the process. In particular, we would like to thank Glenn Ross, Mercantile-Safe Deposit and Trust Company, who served as a valuable resource throughout the entire project. We very much appreciate the time and energy that he devoted to us.

We would also like to thank Professor Donald L. Rosenberg, Towson State University, and John White, Baltimore Life Insurance Company-retired, for their helpful comments and suggestions. Many other individuals and organizations made significant contributions to the book. We would like to thank William H. Amoss, Maryland State Senator; Brother John Campbell, S. M., Chaminade-Madonna College Prep; Michelle Corriveau, Barry University; Marvin Diaz-Lacayo, M.D., Total Quality Advisors; Bret D. Erickson, Frank Russell Company; Terri Geske, Capital Management Sciences; Gil Hammer, Wilshire Associates; John Levitz, Smith Barney; Mark Lindblom, Morgan Stanley; John W. Mockoviak, First Virginia Bank; and Paul J. Yakoboski, Employee Benefit Research Institute, who provided valuable information for this book.

G. Timothy Haight
Stephen O. Morrell

CHAPTER 1

Investment Sponsors

INTRODUCTION

Understanding the characteristics and purposes of investment sponsors is the starting point in the analysis and evaluation of portfolio managers. *Investment sponsors* is the term used to refer to organizations and individuals who undertake the responsibility for establishing, developing, arranging, monitoring, evaluating, and overseeing investment programs for the benefit of, and on behalf of, other persons and groups. Investment sponsors establish investment programs for a wide array of purposes, ranging from the need to be competitive in the labor market (in the case of a corporate pension plan) to the desire to ensure the future financial viability of an institution (in the case of a university endowment plan).

Although the idea of sponsoring an investment program on behalf of others is certainly not a new one, the number and variety of such programs have soared in the past 50 or so years. There are at least three reasons for the explosive growth in sponsored investment plans. First, the generally healthy growth of the U.S. economy in the post–World War II period has resulted in a rising dollar amount of individual saving as well as sizable increases in grants, gifts, bequests, and the like to charities, foundations, and other investment sponsors. Second, continued development, enhanced efficiency, and innovations in U.S. financial markets have reduced the transaction costs of implementing sponsored investment programs. Finally, significant changes in the tax code (discussed later in this chapter), in conjunction with more competitive labor markets, have especially spurred an increase in the number of corporate-sponsored investment programs.

INVESTMENT OVERSIGHT RESPONSIBILITIES

Plan sponsors generally select a committee and entrust them with carrying out the investment mandate established by the organization. The responsibilities charged to these committees may be as simple as placing a few thousand dollars of excess cash in a savings account or certificate of deposit. For others, the investment decision may be more complex. Many of these organizations have sizable amounts of money to invest and are exposed to a wide array of investment choices.

COMMITTEE COMPOSITION

The investment committee oversees the entire investment process. Its responsibilities include developing and/or revising a comprehensive investment policy statement, selecting and evaluating investment managers, periodically reviewing the investment performance, and accomplishing the administrative duties associated with the fund's activities. Committee members are required to carry out these duties and obligations in a prudent manner.

It is important that the committee composition is such that these responsibilities can be carried out in the appropriate manner. Individuals selected should have the educational background and/or investment management experience to properly discharge their duties. Specifically, the committee should be composed of individuals knowledgable in investments, portfolio evaluation, economics, and plan administration. In many instances, the committee may seek representation from the portfolio's intended beneficiaries.

Since committee members are often required to commit a considerable amount of time and effort to managing the fund, prospective candidates should be made aware of what will be required of them prior to being invited to serve on the investment committee. The investment policy statement should address meeting attendance by its committee members. Individuals who attend meetings only occasionally should reconsider their commitment to fellow committee members and to the fund itself.

A formal orientation program should be available to new committee members to provide them with an opportunity to acquaint themselves with the goals and objectives of the fund, the investment strategies and styles of its managers, any constraints placed upon the portfolio managers, prior investment performance, and any additional information that will assist them in carrying out their duties. In short, a well-organized orientation program will provide new investment committee members with a clear understanding of their roles and responsibilities.

The duties and responsibilities of the investment committee are significant. The committee must identify the main purpose or goal for investing. They must make sure that these goals are translated into investment objectives. These goals, objectives, and additional constraints must be carefully articulated in the investment policy statement.

The committee must also establish investment guidelines. Specifically, the committee must identify those asset classes deemed appropriate for investment purposes and must establish allocation ranges for each asset type. Along these lines, the committee will be required to specify the level of risk that is acceptable as well as how and at what interval performance results will be evaluated.

The proper evaluation of investment performance will be influenced by the return benchmarks selected. These return benchmarks provide a standard against which the actual performance of the fund will be judged. The committee will be responsible for ensuring that the measures used are appropriate given the goals, objectives, constraints, and risks agreed upon by its members. In selecting an appropriate benchmark, the committee must carefully choose among a host of indexes and universes for all components of its portfolio.

The committee must decide who will be responsible for investing the organization's assets. The committee must first determine if an outside manager is appropriate. If so, the committee must carefully screen prospective managers and choose the one best suited to manage the investments. Subsequently, the committee must continually monitor the performance of its manager to safeguard the sponsor's interests.

Individuals charged with overseeing an organization's investment activities take on a major responsibility. They are ultimately responsible for the success or failure of the funds under their supervision. As fiduciaries, these individuals have an obligation to ensure that investments are managed in a prudent manner. It is extremely important that they fully understand the fundamentals associated with monitoring and evaluating investment performance.

TAX CONSIDERATIONS

There are two primary types of investment sponsors: tax-exempt sponsors and taxable ones. Tax-exempt sponsors include private foundations, public charities, and qualified retirement plans. Trusts, corporations, partnerships as well as wealthy individuals are examples of taxable investment sponsors. Whether they are tax-exempt or taxable investment sponsors, each has unique needs and features that shape the group's investment philosophy, investment goals, and investment objectives.

TAX-EXEMPT ORGANIZATIONS

According to Section 501(c)(3) of the Internal Revenue Code, organizations may qualify for exemption from federal taxation if they are established and function exclusively for one of the following purposes: charitable, religious, educational, scientific, literary, testing of public safety, fostering national or international amateur sports competition, and prevention of cruelty to children or animals.[1] These organizations can be formed as corporations, trusts, community chests, funds, or foundations.[2] Individuals and partnerships, however, are not eligible for tax-exempt status.

By far, the most numerous of the tax-exempt organizations—and the largest in terms of total assets—are the public charities. To be classified as a charity for tax-exempt purposes, the organization must be organized and operated for the benefit of the public interest.[3] To be considered tax-exempt, religious organizations must meet two guidelines:

- Religious beliefs of the organization must be truly and sincerely held.
- Religious organizations' practices and rituals must not be illegal or contrary to clearly defined public policy.[4]

Scientific and literary organizations, as well as others seeking tax-exempt status, must also meet prespecified guidelines.

Table 1–1 presents selected types of tax-exempt organizations as determined by the Internal Revenue Code. Column 1 lists the IRS code section, while column 2 describes the organizations covered by the code section. Column 3 reports the corresponding activities of these organizations, while column 4 lists examples of organizations that fall within each section of the code.

Over the years, tax-exempt organizations have grown tremendously. According to the Internal Revenue Service, the total assets of tax-exempt organizations (excluding private foundations) were estimated to be $1.019 trillion as of 1990.[5] This represents a significant increase from the 1975 asset level of $176 billion.[6] Charitable, religious, educational, and scientific organizations held almost 85 percent of these assets, followed by credit unions, which accounted for almost 12 percent of the total in 1990.[7]

Table 1–2 displays the 10 largest tax-exempt organizations ranked on the basis of total assets as of 1991. As the table reveals, the Teachers Insurance and Annuity Association of America's total assets were more than $55.6 billion in 1991. Among colleges, Harvard College was ranked highest, with total assets exceeding $7.5 billion.

TABLE 1-1

Selected Types of Tax-Exempt Organizations, by Internal Revenue Code

Internal Revenue Code Section	Description of Organization	Type of Activities	Examples of Qualifying Organizations
501(c)(3)	Religious, educational, charitable, scientific, literary, etc.	Activities of nature implied by description of class of organization	Catholic church, Harvard College, United Way, libraries
501(c)(4)	Civic leagues, social welfare organizations, and local associations of employees	Promotion of community welfare, charitable, educational, and recreational activities	Lions Clubs, Rotary Clubs, National Rural Electric Cooperatives, and volunteer fire departments
501(c)(5)	Labor, agriculture, and horticultural organizations	Educational or instructive, the purpose being to improve conditions of work or to improve products and efficiency	Major League Baseball Players Association, International Ladies Garment Workers Union, and United Auto Workers
501(c)(6)	Business leagues, chambers of commerce, and real estate boards	Improvement of business conditions of one or more lines of business	National Football League, Academy of Motion Picture Arts and Science, and American Bar Association
501(c)(7)	Social and recreational clubs	Pleasure, recreational, and social activities	New York Yacht Club, Metropolitan Club, and sorority and fraternity chapters
501(c)(8)	Fraternal beneficiary societies and associations	Provides for payment of life, sickness, accident, or other benefits to members	Independent Order of Odd Fellows, B'nai B'rith, Loyal Order of Moose, and Polish Union of America
501(c)(9)	Voluntary employees' beneficiary associations [including federal employees' voluntary beneficiary associations formally covered under 501 (c)(10)]	Provides for payment of life, sickness, accident, or other benefits to members	IBM Medical and Dental Plan Trust, U.S. Steel and Carnegie Pension Plan, and National Education Association Members Insurance Trust

Source: Internal Revenue Service, "Charities and Other Tax-Exempt Organizations, 1991," *Statistics of Income Bulletin, 1994–1995,* vol. 14, no. 3, p.31.

TABLE 1–2

Top Ten Tax-Exempt Organizations Ranked by Total Assets
Reporting Year 1991
(in millions of dollars)

Name	Total Assets
1. Teachers Insurance and Annuity Association of America	$55,576
2. College Retirement Equity Fund	45,518
3. Common Fund for Nonprofit Organizations	9,523
4. Harvard College	7,597
5. Howard Hughes Medical Institute	7,369
6. Kaiser Foundation Hospitals	4,650
7. Yale University	4,443
8. Stanford University	4,308
9. Shriners Hospitals for Crippled Children	3,327
10. Princeton University	3,270

Source: Internal Revenue Service, "Charities and Other Tax-Exempt Organizations, 1991," *Statistics of Income Bulletin, 1994–95*, vol. 14, no. 3 , p. 29.

Private Foundations and Charitable Trusts

Typically, private foundations are supported by a relatively small number of financial benefactors and/or contributors. In fact, private foundations are prohibited from receiving more than one-third of their annual receipts from either their members or the public. Private foundations are subject to an excise tax on their net investment income. Furthermore, specific rules and regulations are imposed upon these organizations. Precisely, private foundations are

◆ Restricted from self-dealing activities between the foundation and its substantial contributors and other disqualified persons.

◆ Required to annually distribute income for charitable purposes.

◆ Limited as to their holding of private businesses.

◆ Prohibited from entering into investments that jeopardize the carrying out of exempt purposes.

◆ Restrained from making expenditures that do not further its exempt status.[8]

The tax deductions of individuals for contributions to a private foundation are limited to a maximum of 30 percent of the contributor's adjusted gross income, and in some cases, the limitation can be as low as 20 percent. In contrast, contributors to public charities are allowed to take write-offs limited to 50 percent of their adjusted gross income.

Private foundations held approximately $192.2 billion in assets as of 1992. Securities investment accounted for roughly 75 percent, or $144 billion, of total assets as of this date.[9] The investment portfolios of private foundations were allocated in the aggregate as follows: $30.5 billion in U.S. and state government obligations; $95.2 billion in corporate stocks; and $18.7 in corporate bonds.[10] Chart 1–1 displays in percentage terms the asset mix of private foundations in 1992.

Charitable trusts are also nonprofit organizations. This organization is usually supported and controlled by either an individual or family. A charitable trust, as defined by Internal Revenue Code Section 4947(a)(1), is not tax exempt.[11] Charitable trusts are much

CHART 1–1

Private Foundations
Investment Mix 1992

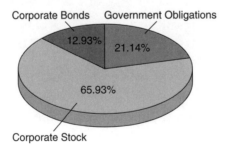

Corporate Bonds   Government Obligations
12.93%   21.14%
65.93%
Corporate Stock

smaller both in terms of numbers and assets controlled than private foundations. In 1992, there were 42,428 private foundations, while there were only 2,932 charitable trusts.[12] The fair market value of assets held by charitable trusts was $3.1 billion.[13] Nonexempt charitable trusts are required to pay an annual tax on income that is not distributed for charitable purposes.[14]

Qualified Retirement Plans

Congress has enacted tax legislation to create a variety of qualified retirement plans to assist workers saving for their retirement. The legislation has allowed contributions toward retirement to be invested without the income being subject to current federal income taxes. In fact, depending on circumstances, the contributions made may be treated as deductible items for tax purposes. Individuals are subsequently taxed when distributions are made from a qualified retirement plan. Qualified retirement plans can either be offered by the employer or established by the employee. Retirement plans are available in both the public and private sectors. Public retirement programs are offered at the federal, state, and local levels.

Table 1–3 reports the total financial assets held by private trusteed, private life insurance, and state and local plans from 1976 to 1994. Private trusteed plans accounted for $2,350.9 billion in assets as of 1994. The assets of these plans are managed by a trustee, who is appointed by the plan sponsor. The total qualified retirement assets managed by private life insurance companies were $738.9 billion, while state and local financial retirement assets were $1,176.4 billion at the end of 1994.

The 1994 asset distribution of private trusteed plans is presented in Chart 1–2. The highest percentage of assets is concentrated in equities, followed by bonds and other assets. Less than 10 percent of assets were held in cash.

Private Sector Plans

Pension plans are designed to provide income for employees during their retirement. Broadly speaking, these plans fall into either

TABLE 1–3

Total Qualified and State and Local Financial Retirement
Assets (in billions of dollars)
(1976–1994)

Period	Private Trusteed	Private Life Insurance	State and Local
1976	$ 251.9	$ 85.8	$ 120.4
1977	271.7	97.5	132.5
1978	326.2	111.6	152.0
1979	386.1	131.7	167.8
1980	469.6	158.2	196.6
1981	486.7	182.5	222.8
1982	653.9	219.9	260.9
1983	797.1	251.7	305.5
1984	857.8	290.8	350.4
1985	1,087.6	346.7	398.7
1986	1,282.2	409.7	476.6
1987	1,359.2	458.7	523.8
1988	1,421.8	516.4	609.0
1989	1,705.6	572.5	766.8
1990	1629.2	636.1	820.4
1991	2,055.9	678.1	941.1
1992	2,213.3	694.7	1,058.7
1993	2,449.9	738.9	1,151.2
1994	2,350.9	738.9	1,176.4

Source: "Quarterly Pension Investment Report," *Employee Benefit Research Institute,*
10, no. 1 (July 1995), p. 41.

one of two categories: defined benefit (DBP) or defined contribution (DCP) plans. Employees who are covered by defined benefit plans receive a prespecified benefit from the plan during their retirement years. In contrast, under a defined contribution plan, the employees' benefits at retirement are a function of the amount contributed and the investment performance of the plan.

CHART 1-2

Private Trusteed Plans

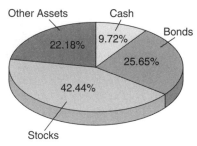

Source: Employee Benefit Research Institute.

Table 1–4 reports the distribution of private trusteed funds based on plan type. In addition to defined benefit and defined contribution plans, the table also reports the asset holdings of multiple employer plans.

Defined Benefit Plans In contrast to defined contribution plans, where the employees' retirement earnings are affected by investment performance, defined benefit plans call for retirees to receive postretirement payments based on specific, predetermined criteria. As an illustration, the dollar payments to the retiree are often determined by formulas that are based on years of service to the organization and pay level over a specified time period. For example, a defined benefit plan may stipulate that employee annual retirement benefits are based on the employee's average salary during the last three years of employment, multiplied by the employee's number of years of service, divided by 30 years. If the employee's salary over this period averaged $40,000 and the employee worked for the organization for 27 years, the employee's annual retirement benefit would be $36,000 (i.e., $40,000 \times 27 \div 30$).

The 1994 asset distribution of DBPs is presented in Chart 1–3. The highest percentage of assets is concentrated in equities followed by bonds, and other assets. Less than 10 percent of assets were held in cash.

TABLE 1–4

Distribution of Private Trusteed Assets (in billions of dollars) (1983–1994)

Year	Defined Benefit	Defined Contribution	Multiple Employer	Total
1983	$ 514	$ 255	$ 85	$ 854
1984	531	290	97	918
1985	648	385	123	1,157
1986	751	460	154	1,365
1987	759	524	170	1,454
1988	752	563	177	1,492
1989	882	686	230	1,798
1990	848	651	225	1,723
1991	1,032	834	267	2,133
1992	1,071	956	289	2,316
1993	1,156	1,096	313	2,565
1994	1,090	1,060	299	2,448

Source: "Quarterly Pension Investment Report," *Employee Benefit Research Institute* 10, no. 1 (July 1995), p. 10.

CHART 1–3

Defined Benefit Plans

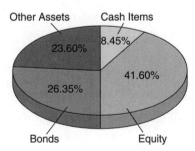

Source: Employee Benefit Research Institute.

Table 1–5 reports the percentage distribution of assets for single-employer defined benefit funds. As the table reveals, the largest asset type held by these plans were equity securities. From 1983 to 1994, equities ranged from 38.4 percent to 44.7 percent of all investment assets held by defined benefit plans. The second largest holding during this period was in bonds. These ranged from a low of 26.4 percent in 1994 to a high of 30.4 percent in 1990. The table also reports the cash and other assets holdings during this period.

To fund such plans, employers are required to make annual contributions to them. The annual contribution is, in part, based on the estimated future liabilities (pension payments to participants) of the fund, the current size of the fund's assets, and the assumed return on those assets. In essence, the plan's assets represent the source

TABLE 1–5

Single Employer Defined Benefit Plan Investment Mix

Year	Equity (%)	Bonds (%)	Cash Items (%)	Other Assets (%)
1983	44.7	27.1	9.2	18.9
1984	41.9	29.5	10.4	18.1
1985	44.4	28.5	9.8	17.3
1986	43.6	28.3	11.0	17.1
1987	39.2	29.2	12.5	19.0
1988	42.3	29.0	13.5	15.1
1989	40.2	28.2	12.9	18.7
1990	38.4	30.4	12.6	18.6
1991	41.6	28.4	10.2	19.7
1992	41.8	27.8	9.4	21.1
1993	41.2	27.0	9.3	22.5
1994	41.6	26.4	8.5	23.6

Source: "Quarterly Pension Investment Report," *Employee Benefit Research Institute* 10, no. 1 (July 1995), p 14.

of payment to the retirees, while the present value of future pension liabilities is the cost stated in terms of today's dollars. A comparison of the assets and liabilities will reveal one of three outcomes:

1. If the assets exceed the present value of liabilities, then the plan is overfunded.
2. If the assets are less than the present value of the liabilities, then the plan is underfunded.
3. If the assets equal the liabilities, then the plan is fully funded.

The actual determination of the plan's funding status requires certain assumptions regarding future employment costs and future investment returns on the plan's assets. These assumptions are crucial in determining if the plan has sufficient funds available to meet its obligations. Thus, the funding requirements are, in part, related to the investment performance relative to those assumed. If, for example, the plan's assets achieve investment results superior to those assumed, then the required future contributions to the plan will be less than anticipated. In contrast, if investment performance is significantly less than assumed, then the employer will be required to increase the amount of contributions to make up for the shortfall. Regardless of the plan's asset performance, the employee will receive the same benefit at retirement. Thus, the employee's retirement benefits are not tied to investment performance. This is a cost borne by the plan's provider.

Defined benefit plans are expensive to administer and must meet nondiscrimination regulations. To properly administer these plans, the services of a plan actuary are required. The actuary is responsible for developing the model measuring the plan's funding status and the resulting annual contributions required by the sponsor. The actuary also assumes the responsibility for the regulatory filings associated with the DBP.

In 1974 the Employee Retirement Income Security Act (ERISA) established the Pension Benefit Guaranty Corporation (PBGC) to safeguard employee pension benefits by:

- Encouraging the continuation and maintenance of private pension plans.
- Protecting pension benefits in ongoing plans.
- Providing timely payments of benefits in the case of terminated pensions plans.
- Making the maximum use of resources and maintaining premiums and operating costs at the lowest levels consistent with statutory responsibilities.[15]

The PBGC insures more than 58,000 privately organized defined benefit pension plans covering more than 41 million workers.[16] As of 1995, the annual insurance premium ranges from $2.60 per worker for the multiple-employer plan to $19 per participant plus $9 for each $1,000 of underfunded vested benefits for the single-employers' plan.[17] For plans terminated in 1996, the PBGC provides retirees up to a maximum protection of $31,704.60 per year.[18]

Defined Contribution Plans   The defined contribution plan requires the employer to contribute a specific amount of money to the worker's retirement account. These plans include 401(k) plans, money purchase, and profit-sharing plans. Unlike the defined benefit plan, the employer is not guaranteeing a specific periodic amount at retirement. Rather, the amount of contribution and the investment performance of these funds over the investment period will determine the benefits to be received by the employee at retirement.

The 1994 asset distribution of DCPs is presented in Chart 1–4. As in the case of defined benefit plans, the highest percentage of assets is concentrated in equities. Bonds and other assets represent 22.64 percent and 21.89 percent of the fund's holdings, respectively.[19]

Table 1–6 presents the distribution of assets for single-employer defined contribution plans. As the table reports, the asset distributions are similar to those found in defined benefit plans. Again, the largest investment type is equities, followed by bonds.

CHART 1-4

Defined Contribution Plans
Asset Mix 1994

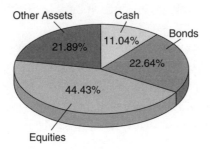

TABLE 1-6

Single-Employer Contribution Plan Investment Mix

Year	Equity (%)	Bonds (%)	Cash Items (%)	Other Assets (%)
1983	39.4	22.1	14.9	23.7
1984	39.6	22.9	15.0	22.5
1985	37.9	24.3	14.8	23.0
1986	38.4	23.2	15.0	23.3
1987	37.7	22.8	15.1	24.4
1988	41.3	24.7	16.7	17.4
1989	42.7	23.8	15.6	17.9
1990	38.5	26.2	17.1	18.1
1991	41.6	24.5	14.2	19.6
1992	42.8	23.6	13.7	20.0
1993	43.9	22.2	12.3	21.6
1994	44.4	22.6	11.1	21.9

Source: "Quarterly Pension Investment Report," *Employee Benefit Research Institute,* 10, no. 1 (July 1995), p. 22.

There are at least two advantages to a DCP from the employer's viewpoint: (1) these plans are less expensive to administer than DBPs, and (2) the benefits are directly related to the investment performance of the plan's assets. Thus, the employer does not have to make up for shortfalls due to weaker than expected investment performance.

Alternative Contributory Plans

Several alternative retirement plans are available to many employees. Employees may be eligible to participate in 401(k) or profit-sharing plans, as well as a number of other retirement plans that are available to individuals who meet certain requirements. Each of these plans is designed to assist participants in funding their retirement years.

401(k) Plans   401(k) plans are another source for retirement funding. These plans contain more than $670 billion dollars invested by approximately 22 million workers. 401(k) plans give the participant the option of either receiving cash contributions (i.e., salaries) or having these contributions placed in the plan. The latter form of contribution to the plan reduces the participant's taxable income. In addition, many organizations match the contributions of the participants. This allows the organization to reward those individuals who contribute to their retirement. However, there are upper limits to the amount of contributions that can be deducted. Additionally, to receive favorable tax treatment as a qualified retirement plan, participants must meet certain distribution, vesting, and other requirements. Furthermore, a minimum number of employees must participate in the plan.

Profit–Sharing Plans   Profit-sharing plans are also used by employers to provide retirement benefits to their employees. Typically, the employer makes contributions to the plan based on the business's profits using a predetermined formula. The employer can make contributions in excess of the profit earned during any tax year. Contributions to this plan must be substantial and of a recurring nature in order to receive favorable tax treatment.

Salary Reduction Simplified Employee Pension Plan The Salary Reduction Simplified Employee Pension (SARSEP) is available to organizations with fewer than 25 employees. To qualify under SARSEP, at least one-half of all eligible employees must contribute to the plan. The total contributions from both employer and employee cannot exceed 15 percent of annual compensation up to $150,000. Furthermore, the employee's maximum contribution is established annually (i.e., $9,240 in 1995). Additionally, the SARSEP is subject to nondiscrimination testing. For this purpose, highly compensated employees cannot receive contributions exceeding 125 percent of the non-highly-compensated employees' contributions.

The Small Business Job Protection Act, signed in August 1996, repeals SARSEPs as of January 11, 1997, and establishes a new simplified plan, discussed next.

Savings Incentive Match Plan for Employees Established by the Small Business Job Protection Act of 1996, the Savings Incentive Match Plan for Employees (SIMPLE) provides employers with a new alternative to meet their employees' retirement needs. SIMPLE plans are available to employers who meet the following requirements: (1) 100 or fewer employees, (2) employee earnings of at least $5,000 in compensation the previous year, and (3) no employer-sponsored retirement plans. Under the plan, employers must meet certain matching contribution requirements. This plan can be in the form of an IRA or 401(k) plan.

Individual Retirement Accounts Individual retirement accounts (IRAs) are available to those covered by other plans as well as those who are not covered by a retirement plan. Under this plan, individuals are allowed to contribute up to $2,000 per year toward retirement. Married individuals with nonworking spouses are entitled to contribute $4,000 per year into an IRA. For those individuals who are not covered under other qualified retirement plans, the annual contribution is tax deductible.

Individuals who are a part of employer-maintained retirement plans may be able to deduct a portion or all of their IRA contributions, depending on their adjusted gross income level. Single individuals with adjusted gross incomes below $25,000 ($35,000 for married individuals) are permitted to fully deduct their annual contribution. Single taxpayers with adjusted gross income (AGI) between $25,000 and $35,000 (between $35,000 and $45,000 for married filers) are permitted to partially deduct their annual contributions; no deduction is permitted if a single taxpayer has an AGI greater than $35,000 ($45,000 for married individuals). Regardless of the current deductibility, all income within an IRA grows on a tax-deferred basis.

Contributions into an IRA can continue until the taxpayer reaches age $70^1/_2$. Distributions may begin after the participant reaches age $59^1/_2$. Distributions must start after the participant reaches age $70^1/_2$ (actually, distributions begin on April 1 following the time the participant reaches age $70^1/_2$.) In addition, there is a 10 percent penalty for premature IRA withdrawals. Effective in 1997, the 10 percent penalty will not apply for distributions used to pay medical expenses in excess of 7.5 percent of AGI or to pay health insurance premiums by certain employees separated from employment.

Simplified Employee Pension Plans   Many of the preceding retirement plans are costly to administer. To extend the benefits of retirement savings to smaller organizations, Simplified Employee Pensions (SEPs) were created. The employer's contributions are made annually at the employer's discretion directly to employee-participants' accounts. SEPs are more desirable than IRAs in regard to the maximum deferral of income. Under a SEP, employers' contributions can be up to 15 percent of earned income or $30,000, whichever is less, and the amount contributed is excluded from the employee's gross income. By comparison, if an individual is self-employed, a maximum of only 13.04 percent of earned income can be deferred. To meet the qualification standards, a SEP cannot be discriminatory.

Public Sector Retirement Plans

Qualified retirement plans are available to federal, state, and local government employees. These public sector retirement plans represent a significant amount of investable funds. The following sections report the relative sizes of these plans along with their investment mixes.

Federal Supplemental Retirement Plans   In addition to the retirement benefits available to federal government employees, federal workers can participate in a supplemental contributory plan. The Thrift Savings Plan was authorized by Congress as part of the Federal Employees' Retirement System Act of 1986. The Thrift Savings Plan is a defined contribution plan. Under the plan, eligible federal employees are permitted to contribute a portion of their pay to the fund on a tax-deferred basis. As of March 31, 1996, accounts totaled $37.3 billion with approximately 2.2 million federal employee participants.[20]

Thrift Savings Plan participants can direct their savings into three distinct funds (see Chart 1–5). Fund G consists of short-term, nonmarketable U.S. Treasury securities created specifically for the fund. Fund C is directed into the Wells Fargo Equity Index Fund. This fund is designed to track the Standard & Poor's (S&P) 500 Index. Finally, participants can direct their contributions to Fund F, the Wells Fargo U.S.17 Debt Index Fund, which is designed to track the Lehman Brothers Aggregate Bond Index.[21]

State and Local Retirement Plans   State and local government retirement funds represent a significant amount of investment assets. In fact, state and local retirement assets grew from $104.8 billion in 1975 to $1,176.4 billion in 1994.[22] This represents an average increase of more than 13 percent per year. Thus, on an annual basis,

CHART 1-5

Thrift Savings Fund
Investment Mix March 31, 1996

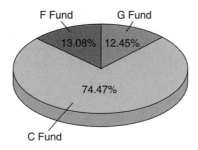

F Fund   G Fund

13.08% 12.45%

74.47%

C Fund

state and local retirement assets have grown faster than their private trusteed and private life insurance counterparts.

The investment practices of state and local government retirement funds have been much more conservative than the corporate defined benefit and defined contribution plans presented earlier. Table 1–7 reports the annual asset mix of state and local government funds from 1975 to 1994. As the table reveals, bonds represent the largest single asset class investment during this period. In fact, only in 1993 did the percentage invested in equities exceed the percentage invested in bonds.

The data contained in the table indicate a shift in the asset allocation mix over this period. In 1975, 67 percent of available state and local government retirement funds were invested in bonds, while only 25 percent were placed in equities. By 1994, the allocation between stocks and bonds narrowed. During this period the percentage invested in bonds decreased substantially, while the percentage invested in equities steadily grew. Also noteworthy was the gradual increase in the cash and equivalent category. This category grew from 1 percent of fund assets in 1975 to 6 percent by 1994. Still, state and local governments invested far more conservatively (as measured by asset mix) than their private sector counterparts.

TABLE 1-7

State and Local Government Assets Investment Mix

Year	Equity (%)	Bonds (%)	Cash Items (%)	Other Assets (%)
1976	25	67	1	6
1977	23	70	1	6
1978	22	71	2	6
1979	22	70	2	6
1980	23	69	2	6
1981	21	70	2	6
1982	23	68	3	6
1983	29	60	4	7
1984	28	61	5	6
1985	30	58	6	5
1986	32	57	6	5
1987	32	57	6	5
1988	36	52	5	7
1989	39	48	4	9
1990	36	48	4	12
1991	41	46	5	8
1992	42	44	5	9
1993	44	42	5	9
1994	43	45	6	6

Source: "Quarterly Pension Investment Report," *Employee Benefit Research Institute*, 10 no. 1, (July 1995), p 45.

TAXABLE INVESTMENT SPONSORS

The investment sponsors discussed so far are able to either defer taxes (qualified retirement plans) or avoid them completely (public charities). Even private foundations can avoid significant taxation if they follow IRS guidelines. However, for some sponsors, their investment choices must be made with a clear understanding of the tax consequences. As you will see in the following sections, taxes can play a significant role in affecting investment results. Taxable investment sponsors such as trusts, corporations, partnerships, and individual investors all fall into this category.

Trusts

A trust is a legal entity formed to hold assets for the benefit of another. The creator of a trust is referred to as the settlor or grantor. Trusts can be formed during an individual's lifetime (inter vivos) or by provisions of a will (testamentary). The trustee carries out the fiduciary responsibilities as specified in the trust agreement. The beneficiary of the trust is the one who derives the benefits.

A trust can be formed for a variety of reasons. Frequently, a trust is formed to give beneficiaries income or the use of assets placed within a trust without transferring the asset's legal title to the recipient. There can be several reasons for this arrangement. For example, the grantor may want to provide for his children but does not believe that they will be able to manage the assets prudently. In this instance, the grantor can establish the trust by appointing a trustee to manage the trust according to the grantor's requirements.

Likewise, a grantor may want to establish a trust to provide support for a loved one for the remainder of his or her life and thereafter contribute the assets to a charity. In this instance, the trust assets would be turned over to the charity after the death of the beneficiary. This type of trust is referred to as a remainder trust.

Trusts are treated as a separate taxable entity. Taxable income distributed to beneficiaries of the trust is taxed to them at their own individual or group tax rates. Undistributed taxable income results in a tax liability at the trust level. The tax code provides for special treatment of undistributed trust income. Table 1–8 presents the applicable tax rates for undistributed income for trusts. Trusts are allowed a standard deduction and can be classified as either simple or complex. For simple trusts, a deduction of $300 is permitted. For

TABLE 1-8

Trust Marginal Tax Rates On Undistributed Income
(1996)

Taxable Income Range	Tax Rate (%)
$0–1,600	15
1,600–3,800	28
3,800–5,800	31
5,800–7,900	36
7,900 and above	39.6

complex trusts, the deduction is $100. Undistributed taxable income is also subject to the alternative minimum tax.

As shown in the table, the tax rates range from 15 percent to 39.6 percent. These rates are applied to lower income levels than those of individuals. Thus, there is a substantial exposure to taxes for a trust that chooses not to distribute income. In some circumstances, beneficiaries are taxed on income accumulated by trusts under what are called "throwback" rules.

Corporations

Corporations must recognize the unique tax consequences associated with holding different types of financial assets. Specifically, income from corporate bonds would be taxed at the corporation's marginal tax rate, while there may be significant tax incentives to hold other types of financial assets. For example, corporations have an important tax incentive to purchase and hold equity securities issued originally by other domestic corporations. Corporations purchasing such securities are entitled to deduct at least 70 percent of any dividend income received. Furthermore, if the corporation owns at least 20 percent of another domestic corporation's stock,

TABLE 1–9

Corporate Marginal Tax Rates
(1996)

Taxable Income Range	Tax Rate (%)
$0–$50,000	15
$50,000–$75,000	25
$75,000–$100,000	34
$100,000–$335,000	39
$335,000–$10,000,000	34
$10,000,000–$15,000,000	35
$15,000,001–18,333,333	38
$18,333,334 and above	35

the deduction increases to 80 percent of the dividend income received. Finally, if a corporation owns at least 80 percent of another corporation's stock, then it receives a 100 percent deduction.

While capital gains are also taxed at the corporation's marginal tax rate, capital losses are only deductible to the extent that they offset capital gains. Additional losses may not be applied against ordinary income. However, they can be carried back (three years) or carried forward (five years) to apply against prior or future capital gains. These tax rates appear in Table 1–9.

Partnerships

A partnership exists when two or more individuals form a noncorporate entity for the purpose of conducting business to make a profit. From a tax perspective, the partnership does not pay taxes. It merely serves as a conduit through which profits and losses pass along to the individual partners. Partnerships are categorized as either general or limited partnerships. In a general partnership, there is only one class of partner and each partner is liable for the debts and obligations of the partnership.

A limited partnership has two classes of partners: general and limited. General partners are responsible for carrying out the duties of the partnership. Limited partners usually supply most of the partnership's capital but do not participate in the activities of the partnership. While the general partners have unlimited liability, the limited partners' liability is usually limited to the amount invested and/or pledged.

Individuals

Individuals may also establish investment portfolios for a variety of investment objectives. These can range from accumulating capital for some future expenditure to providing additional current income. Thus, the characteristics of these portfolios depend on the goals and objectives of the individuals establishing the portfolio.

Individual tax rates associated with investment activity depend on whether the investor has income and/or capital gains or losses. Interest and dividend income are taxed at the individual investor's marginal tax rate. Currently (November 1996), these tax rates are 15 percent, 28 percent, 31 percent, 36 percent, and 39.6 percent, depending on the amount of taxable income and the filing status of the taxpayer. However, capital gains are subject to a maximum of 28 percent. Both short-term capital losses (assets held up to one year) and long-term capital losses (assets held more than one year) can be used to offset capital gains. However, deductions for capital losses against ordinary income are limited to $3,000 per year.

SUMMARY

Investment portfolios are managed for a wide variety of participants. They include retirement plans, profit sharing, endowments, foundations, trusts, and individuals. Each of these groups has specific objectives or requirements that determine the nature of the portfolio's holdings. Certain organizations have been granted tax-exempt status. The investment sponsors include qualified retirement plans, charities, and private foundations. Each of these sponsors must meet certain requirements to maintain their preferential tax status. Qualified retirement plans allow their participants to defer taxes until they start receiving benefits. Among the investment sponsors subject to taxation are trusts, corporations, partnerships, and individual investors. Each of these must consider the impact of taxes when making their investment decisions.

REFERENCES

1. "Tax-Exempt Status for Your Organization," *Internal Revenue Service Publication 557*, p.14.
2. *Ibid.*
3. *Ibid.,* p. 21.
4. *Ibid.,* p. 23.
5. Daniel F. Skelly, "Tax-Based Research and Data on Nonprofit Organizations, 1975–1990," *Statistics of Income,* Figure D, p. 85.
6. *Ibid.*
7. *Ibid.*
8. "Tax-Exempt Status for Your Organization," *Internal Revenue Service Publication 557*, p. 24.
9. "Private Foundations and Charitable Trusts, 1992," *Statistics of Income,* p. 152.
10. *Ibid.,* Table 1.
11. *Ibid.,* p. 152
12. *Ibid.*
13. *Ibid.*
14. *Ibid.,* p. 153.
15. "Report to the Congress—Fiscal Year 1994," *Pension Benefit Guaranty Corporation,* cover.
16. *Ibid.*
17. "FACTS, Pension Insurance Premium," *Pension Benefit Guaranty Corporation* (March 1995).
18. Press Release, *Pension Benefit Guaranty Corporation* (1996).

19. "Quarterly Pension Report Employee," *Benefit Research Institute*, 10, no. 1, (July 1995), p. 22.
20. "Highlights for Thrift Savings Plan Participants," *Federal Retirement Thrift Investment Board* (May 1996), p. 4.
21. *Ibid.*, pp. 3–4.
22. "Quarterly Pension Report Employee (First Quarter 1995)," *Benefit Research Institute*, 10, no. 1 (July 1995), p. 41.

CHAPTER 2

Investment Policy Statement

INTRODUCTION

Investment policy statements specify the overall objectives of portfolios and the guidelines to be followed in reaching these goals. These statements should articulate the fund's investment philosophy, investment goals, return objectives, and the acceptable risk levels consistent with these goals and objectives. Additionally, they should explicitly disclose any constraints to be placed upon the investment manager, identify asset classes that are acceptable investments, and establish guidelines for asset allocation within these classes. Furthermore, investment policy statements should identify the investment strategy and/or strategies to be used to achieve the portfolio's goals and objectives. Finally, these policy statements should spell out the methods to be used in the evaluation of investment managers and the frequency that the portfolio and its managers will be evaluated.

A well-written investment policy statement can be used as a blueprint to provide guidance for those with oversight responsibility as well as investment managers and beneficiaries. It should promote better communication between the parties and therefore minimize misunderstanding. The policy statement specifies what is to be accomplished, the strategies to be employed, and the basis for assessment. In short, the investment policy statement is an important tool in carrying out the fiduciary responsibility for those monitoring and managing the fund.

INVESTMENT PHILOSOPHY AND GOALS

The investment philosophy determines the overall portfolio goals. The investment philosophy explicitly identifies the reasons for investing, which may include providing for a secure future, funding scholarships, and providing a steady source of income for a particular cause, as well as many other purposes. After the reasons for investing have been identified, then investment goals are set that are consistent with the portfolio's investment philosophy. This is accomplished by translating the investment philosophy into goals.

It is important that the policy statement explicitly state the portfolio's philosophy and identify the specific goals that will accomplish its purpose. Investment goals may be stated in terms of growth, income, or preservation of principal. An individual who desires to save for retirement would normally identify growth as a goal. In contrast, retired workers would more likely desire high current yield from their investment portfolios and would choose income as a goal.

INVESTMENT RETURN OBJECTIVES

Once the investment goals have been determined, they are then translated into investment return objectives. These return objectives should be quantifiable and time specific and must be consistent with the investment goals and philosophy of the portfolio. The return objectives can be stated in absolute and/or relative terms. For example, a growth-oriented equity portfolio may set a return objective of 12 percent per year. It may also set as an objective an annual rate of return of 2 percent over an index such as the S&P 500.

The actual target return must be set after proper consideration of the portfolio's goals, its permissible holdings, and the range and quality of the investments to be made by the fund. The investment objectives of the fund should be clearly stated so that the portfolio managers as well as those monitoring the fund have a thorough understanding of its goal.

RISK TOLERANCES

A crucial responsibility of the investment committee is to establish an acceptable level of risk for the investments they are charged with overseeing. *Risk* refers to the likelihood or probability that the actual investment outcomes will be different than the desired or expected ones. In particular, risk is the probability that the specified return objectives will not be met.

For most investors, risk is undesirable, implying that higher risk should only be accepted if it is accompanied by the expectation of higher returns. Therefore, there must be reasonable consistency between the return objectives and the level of risk tolerance. Specifically, if the investment committee deems that a low tolerance for risk is appropriate, then they cannot also seek unreasonably high returns. The investment policy statement should clearly specify the degree of risk the investment sponsors are willing to assume for the investment portfolio in total and for each component.

CONSTRAINTS

The policy document should explicitly state any requirements that might affect the management of the portfolio. For example, if the fund is required to make disbursements on a periodic basis, this constraint must be addressed in the performance objectives. Furthermore, the portfolio must be structured in such a way that these disbursements do not hinder the investment performance. This document should deal with the issue of whether investment managers have full discretionary authority over the purchase and sale of securities.

The investment policy guidelines are sometimes used to address social issues. Prior to the elimination of apartheid, it was common for policy statements to prohibit investment in firms that conducted a significant part of their business with South Africa. In addition, policy statements may prohibit investing in tobacco, liquor, or another such industry.

INVESTMENT STRATEGY

The investment strategy is the plan(s) and methods that will be employed to realize the investment return goals. Strategies can be active, passive, or a combination of the two. Active strategies seek to achieve returns that exceed those of the relevant market indexes. Various investment styles might be utilized to generate such returns. Among the approaches that could be used are value investing, market timing, or perhaps contrarian investing.

In contrast, a passive strategy involves designing a portfolio that seeks to match the returns of a predetermined index or group of indexes. For example, the investment committee may decide to structure the portfolio in such a way that it tracks the performance of the S&P 500. Under this approach the committee would periodically "adjust" the portfolio so that it replicates the targeted index. Each of these approaches will be examined in later chapters.

IN-HOUSE OR OUTSIDE MANAGEMENT

One of the most elementary issues to be addressed by the investment policy statement is who will manage the portfolio. Broadly speaking, the portfolio can be managed either by the investment committee or by an outside investment manager. There are several questions to ask prior to making this decision. First and foremost, is the level of expertise sufficient within the committee? If the expertise is there, are the members willing to invest the time necessary to properly manage the investment portfolio? What are the relative costs of inside versus outside management? Are there any conflicts of interest? Who will evaluate the investment performance? The investment policy statement should specifically deal with the sensitive issue of using in-house versus outside investment managers.

INVESTMENT POLICY

The policy statement should establish the classes of assets in which the portfolio will be invested, guidelines for asset allocation among these classes, and specify the types of securities to be held. These considerations should be addressed for equities, fixed income securities, cash and equivalents, and other financial and nonfinancial assets that are permissible investments in the portfolio as well.

SECURITY TYPES AND RISK CHARACTERISTICS

Equities

Equities are ownership claims in a corporation. The ownership claims or shares originate when the corporation is formed, and additional claims or shares may be created and issued during the life of the corporation. The shares give to their owner the right to vote on issues of corporate control and governance. Generally, each share of stock provides its owner with one vote. Some corporations, however, might issue several different classes of common stock, and each class might have different voting rights.

The equity claims in a corporation are residual in nature. That is, the shareholder's claims on the corporation's earnings and assets come last, after the claims of all other parties have been satisfied. In essence, an ongoing corporation must first pay all of its contractually obligated expenses (such as interest on debt, taxes, wages, and salaries) before any earnings can be distributed as dividends to shareholders. If the corporation is in liquidation, then all liabilities must first be satisfied before the distribution of any remaining assets is made to shareholders.

A shareholder's legal liability for the corporation's obligations is limited to the shareholder's initial investment. Limited liability protects the personal assets of shareholders from claims made on the corporation.

Equity securities can be classified along a number of dimensions, including the market capitalization of the company (i.e., the number of shares of stock multiplied by the price per share), the corporation's industry, the market on which the shares are traded, and the financial characteristics of the company. A number of financial characteristics have been developed to help classify equity securities. Earnings growth rates, the percentage of earnings paid as dividends, the ratio of stock price to earnings, and a host of other financial features are often used to classify stocks. These characteristics can be used by the investment committee to set investment policy guidelines for permissible stock holdings.

As stated earlier, the investment policy statement should contain explicit guidelines as to the permissible levels of risk exposure within the equity portfolio. Risks from investing in equities arise from a number of sources. Risks may be firm specific or particular to a company's industry. They can arise from regulatory and tax changes, economic trends and cycles, and cycles and trends in financial markets. Along these lines, the statement should require that equities are well diversified. It should specify a maximum investment amount permitted in any individual equity issue. The limit can be on the basis of market value and/or cost. For example, a policy statement may limit the amount of funds concentrated in a single investment to 5 percent (cost basis) or 8 percent (market value) of the total portfolio. Avoiding stock concentration is a necessary diversification strategy, although it may not solve the diversification problem entirely. Additional constraints may be needed. For example, a portfolio may have a concentration in one or a few industries or sectors, such as a portfolio with 4 percent interests in Citibank, Bank of America, Banc One, and J.P. Morgan. The investment performance of a portfolio with a large concentration in these banks could be adversely affected by some unanticipated economic event. It is for this reason that the equity portion of the portfolio should be diversified among many unrelated industries. The policy statement should state this explicitly.

Since many investment opportunities are appearing in foreign markets, the policy statement should address the extent to which global diversification is appropriate. Guidelines in terms of foreign investment should include the overall level of investment as well as the degree of concentration within each market.

The portfolio's exposure to market risk is another issue that should be addressed in the policy statement. The level of market risk is typically measured by the portfolio's beta. The *beta* indicates the responsiveness of the portfolio to movement in the overall equity market. Portfolios can be designed to assume more risk than the market (i.e., beta > 1), the same risk (beta = 1), or less than market risk (beta < 1). The portfolio's desired exposure to market risk will depend on its return objectives. If the objective is to match the market, then a portfolio with a beta of 1 would be appropriate. By establishing a beta of 1, the portfolio is assuming a risk level equivalent to the market. Likewise, if the portfolio's objective is to outperform the market, then a portfolio's beta > 1 would be appropriate. This strategy would increase both the expected return and risk of the portfolio. Additionally, if the portfolio's objective is to assume less than market risk, then it would be appropriate to design a portfolio having a beta < 1. In this instance, both the expected return and risk would be below market levels. The investment policy statement should establish ranges for beta consistent with the portfolio's overall return/risk objectives.

Fixed-Income Securities

The investment policy statement sets guidelines as to the types and characteristics of the fixed-income securities. Fixed-income securities or bonds are notes of indebtedness. Issuers of bonds include the U.S. government, agencies of the federal government, domestic and foreign corporations, foreign governments, and state and local governments. Bonds are now issued with a seemingly ever-growing array of features, but the typical bond possesses the following:

1. *Stated maturity*—The length of time until principal is repaid.

2. *Principal or par value*—The amount the bondholder receives at maturity.

3. *Coupon payment*—The periodic interest received by the bondholder, computed by multiplying the coupon rate of interest by the principal value.

The suitability of each type of fixed-income security must be evaluated in terms of the portfolio's goals.

One important consideration that must be addressed in the policy statement is the amount of risk to be assumed within the fixed-income component of the portfolio. Chapter 9 details these risks.

Cash and Equivalents

The cash and equivalents component of the portfolio is typically used to provide income, add liquidity and stability to the portfolio, and provide a reserve for purchasing securities at attractive prices. It is characterized by short-term maturity, high-quality instruments. Typically, U.S. Treasury bills, commercial paper, certificates of deposit, and various other money market instruments are categorized as cash and equivalents. Quality ratings for cash and equivalents are presented in Table 2–1.

TABLE 2–1

Credit Quality Ratings

Standard & Poor's	Moody's	Interpretation
A-1+	—	Extremely strong
A-1	P-1	Very strong
A-2	P-2	Strong
A-3	P-3	Satisfactory
	NP	Not prime
B	—	Adequate
C	—	Doubtful
D	—	Close to default

The investment policy statement should also specify the acceptable risk level for cash equivalents. For example, the investment policy guidelines may prohibit investing in cash and equivalents with a rating below A1 by Standard & Poor's or P1 by Moody's.

ASSET ALLOCATION GUIDELINES

The single most important determinant of a portfolio's performance is the asset allocation decision. The investment policy statement must explicitly spell out the portfolio's acceptable asset allocation range. *Asset allocation* refers to the distribution of the fund's investments among permissible investments such as equities, fixed-income securities, and cash and equivalents. The asset allocation guidelines specify the maximum and minimum percentages that may be invested in each of these categories. Rather than a precise percentage, these guidelines specify a range within which each asset type must fall.

Table 2–2 presents a hypothetical asset allocation guideline for Fund XYZ, a balanced portfolio. The asset allocation guidelines found in the table specify the acceptable range for each investment category. For example, the guidelines specify that the amount to be invested in cash and equivalents should be between 0 and 25 percent of the total portfolio value. Likewise, investment in equities can range from 40 percent to 70 percent of the funds. Finally, fixed-

TABLE 2–2

Fund XYZ Balanced Portfolio Asset
Allocation Guidelines

Investment Type	Range (%)
Cash and equivalents	0–25
Equity securities	40–70
Fixed-income securities	15–50

income securities are required to represent between 15 percent and 50 percent of the portfolio's market value.

The selection of specific ranges for each asset type depends on the portfolio's investment objectives and the ranges of expected returns and risk for each asset class. For example, portfolios with a growth emphasis and no annual distribution requirement would have a higher upper limit on investment in equities and a lower range for fixed income securities. This type of portfolio would have an asset allocation range similar to that shown in Table 2–3.

A portfolio whose objective is growth would be heavily invested in equities. As Table 2–4 illustrates, under these circumstances the investment portfolio would be made up primarily of equity securities (i.e., 70 percent to 100 percent) with considerably less invested in fixed-income securities.

The asset allocation for an investment portfolio whose objective is to produce current income would be heavily weighted toward fixed-income securities. Table 2–4 depicts the asset allocation guidelines for such a portfolio. As shown in the table, the current income needs would be met by investing primarily in fixed-income securities. In this illustration, the investment range in fixed-income securities would be between 50 percent and 80 percent, while the range for equities would be considerably less. Furthermore, the

TABLE 2–3

XYZ Portfolio Growth Objective Asset Allocation Guidelines

Investment Type	Range (%)
Cash and equivalents	0–20
Equity securities	70–100
Fixed-income securities	0–10

equity component would likely be invested in high-dividend-yield common and preferred stocks. Nevertheless, the predictability associated with the payment of a debt obligation's coupon rate along with its higher current yield relative to equities is reflected in the fixed-income securities' higher allocation percentage.

Thus, the asset allocation decision is not arbitrary. The actual mix among equities, fixed-income securities, and cash and equivalents will be influenced by the overall objectives of the portfolio. The proper asset allocation ranges cannot be determined without considering the portfolio's investment objectives.

Although the upper and lower limits are set by the fund's policy, the individual portfolio manager has the responsibility of determining the actual mix at any given point in time. Many managers use fixed-income securities to add stability to the fund while using the equities component to generate high returns. It is well recognized that over time, equities will outperform fixed-income securities. However, it is also accepted that this higher return comes with higher risk. The total fund's performance is the result of asset allocation within the measurement period as well as among the individual securities held during this time. Once the decision is made regarding the appropriate range for each of the asset categories, criteria must be established to determine the appropriate investment holdings in each of these groups.

TABLE 2-4

XYZ Portfolio Current Income Objective
Asset Allocation Guidelines

Investment Type	Range (%)
Cash and equivalents	0–20
Equity securities	0–25
Fixed income securities	50–80

EVALUATION OF PERFORMANCE

The investment policy statement should specifically identify the benchmarks that will be used to evaluate performance results. This is accomplished by designating indexes, composite indexes, and/or universes to serve as the comparison reference. Under this approach, the investment policy guidelines would require that the portfolio maintain a return relative to an index or achieve specific ranking within that universe. These investment performance measurement tools are presented next.

Using Indexes as an Evaluation Tool

If the investment committee decides to employ indexes, then the investment policy statement should specifically identify the index or indexes that will be utilized for comparison purposes. Indexes can be used to evaluate a fund's equity, fixed income, cash and equivalent holdings, real estate, collectibles, municipals, commodities, and various other asset types. Since these indexes are used to provide the investment committee with a benchmark of the portfolio's performance, extreme care should be used in identifying the most appropriate index among those available.

Most indexes are constructed using either a price-weighted or value-weighted method. With a *price-weighted index*, the price of each stock in the index is added up and then divided by the number of separate stocks in the index. For example, if the index included 10 stocks, then at the end of each trading day, the prices of the 10 stocks would be added together, and the total would then be divided by 10. This average of the prices would be reported as the numerical value of the index. To simplify measurement and evaluation, the starting value of the index is assigned a numeric value of 100. Additionally, the divisor of the index is adjusted to account for stock splits or additions to or deletions from the number of stocks in the index. The Dow Jones Industrial Average (DJIA), which measures the stock prices of 30 large U.S.-based corporations, and the

Nikkei 225 average of large Japanese company stocks are examples of price-weighted indexes.

One shortcoming of price-weighted indexes is that higher priced stocks are, via the method used to construct the index, assigned more weight or importance than lower priced stocks. Value-weighted indexes correct for this shortcoming. *Value-weighted indexes* are constructed by adding the market capitalization of each stock in the index and then dividing this total by the number of stocks in the index. The relative importance of each stock in the index is based on the total market value of the company's stock and not just on the price of one share of the company's stock. Stock market indexes such as those published by the Standard and Poor's Corporation, for example, are based on value-weighted methods.

Equity Indexes

There are numerous equity indexes available for evaluating portfolio performance. These indexes can be categorized according to geographic territory (domestic, global, country) or investment industry styles. Equity funds that primarily invest within the United States may be evaluated using indexes such as the S&P 500, S&P 100, DJIA, Russell 2000, Value Line, and the Wilshire 5000. These indexes are intended to be representative of the U.S. equity markets or segments of it and are presented in Table 2–5.

Over the past several years there has been a great deal of interest in global investing. Portfolio managers are increasingly taking advantage of foreign equity securities. In fact, the percentage of equity foreign holdings by investment sponsors has increased steadily over the last decade. The index used to evaluate these portfolios should be representative of the markets in which these investments are found. Indexes are available for evaluating funds with global, regional, or country orientations. Table 2–6 presents a sample of these global equity indexes. The global and regional markets reported in the table can be used to evaluate global and/or regional equity funds.

TABLE 2-5

Major U.S. Equity Indexes

12-Month High	12-Month Low		Weekly High	Weekly Low	Friday Close	Friday Chg.	Weekly %Chg.	12-Month Chg.	12-Month %Chg.	Change from 12/9	Change from %Chg.
Dow Jones Average											
6471.76	5032.94	30 Indus	6471.76	6346.91	6471.76	123.73	1.95	1422.92	28.18	1354.64	26.47
2296.20	1882.71	20 Transp	2273.63	2242.91	2265.34	43.89	1.98	231.38	11.38	284.34	14.35
235.68	204.86	15 Utilities	235.40	233.37	235.40	.49	.21	21.26	9.93	10.00	4.44
2035.82	1655.55	65 Comp	2035.82	2004.11	2035.82	34.90	1.74	350.29	20.78	20.61	20.23
706.28	564.39	Global U.S.	706.28	695.46	706.28	10.08	1.45	139.29	24.57	124.85	21.47
New York Stock Exchange											
394.66	320.40	Comp	394.66	389.66	394.66	4.64	1.19	74.26	23.18	65.15	19.77
498.36	402.96	Indus	498.36	492.68	498.36	5.08	1.03	95.40	23.67	85.07	20.58
266.69	236.63	Utilities	260.93	258.84	260.93	1.87	.72	21.72	9.08	8.03	3.18
353.72	294.40	Transp	353.72	349.18	352.76	5.50	1.58	49.66	16.38	50.80	16.82
351.19	263.70	Finan	351.19	345.26	351.19	6.95	2.02	83.39	31.14	76.94	28.05
American Stock Exchange											
614.99	526.60	Amex Index	590.77	584.18	590.77	5.36	.92	59.50	11.20	42.54	7.76
672.45	528.23	MajorMKt	672.45	663.42	672.45	9.75	1.47	142.43	26.87	136.85	25.55
Standard & Poor's Indexes											
723.11	571.55	100 Index	723.11	711.56	723.11	10.52	1.48	149.21	26.00	137.19	23.41
748.73	598.48	500 Index	748.73	737.02	748.73	11.11	1.51	148.76	24.79	132.80	21.56
878.54	702.07	Indus	878.54	865.30	878.54	11.87	1.37	172.63	24.45	157.35	21.82
547.90	464.94	Transp	547.90	541.17	545.91	7.94	1.48	67.53	14.12	66.90	13.97
213.83	184.66	Utilities	202.26	201.17	201.98	(.11)	(.05)	12.99	6.87	(.60)	(.30)
82.87	58.67	Finan	82.87	81.02	82.87	2.14	2.65	22.45	37.16	20.90	33.73
254.97	207.94	MidCap	254.97	252.39	254.97	2.44	.97	40.95	19.13	37.13	17.04
141.96	115.48	SmallCap	141.96	139.91	141.96	2.00	1.43	25.24	21.62	20.86	17.23
Nasdaq Stock Market											
1274.36	988.57	Comp	1274.36	1254.57	1274.36	12.56	1.00	244.19	23.70	222.23	21.12
818.51	534.42	100 Index	818.51	793.29	818.51	19.07	2.39	240.19	41.53	242.28	42.05
1193.13	908.41	Indus	1104.04	1090.44	1104.04	1.66	.15	160.75	17.04	139.36	14.45
1397.85	1196.03	Insur	1397.85	1384.41	1393.74	4.41	.32	189.53	15.74	101.10	7.82
1250.90	982.19	Banks	1250.90	1229.98	1259.90	23.51	1.92	268.71	27.36	241.49	23.92
232.57	189.64	Telecom	212.12	209.36	210.23	(3.50)	(1.64)	4.85	2.36	1.88	.90
572.01	441.77	NNM Comp	572.01	562.69	572.01	6.05	1.07	110.72	24.00	100.84	21.40
486.92	368.88	NNM Indus	448.66	442.86	448.66	1.21	.27	64.16	16.69	55.36	14.08
Russell Indexes											
396.67	318.24	1000	396.67	390.99	396.67	5.15	1.32	76.23	23.79	67.78	20.61
364.61	301.75	2000	349.92	345.94	349.92	3.40	.98	47.66	15.77	33.95	10.74
420.74	340.20	3000	420.74	414.84	420.74	5.33	1.28	78.50	22.94	68.83	19.56
363.16	296.45	Value	363.16	356.59	363.16	7.12	2.00	66.71	22.50	56.70	18.50
360.91	282.88	Growth	360.91	357.11	360.91	2.29	.64	72.06	24.95	66.51	22.59
369.91	302.32	MidCap	369.91	365.63	369.91	3.86	1.05	61.64	20.00	54.74	17.37
Others											
675.21	554.14	Value Line-a	675.21	666.73	675.21	8.53	1.28	116.41	20.83	105.30	18.48
373.20	373.64	Value Line-g	373.20	368.84	373.20	4.28	1.16	47.61	14.62	42.16	12.74
7210.59	5850.20	Wilshire 5000	7210.59	7118.49	7210.59	82.41	1.16	1317.98	22.37	1153.38	19.04
463.41	452.83	Wilshire SC	459.77	452.83	459.77	6.46	1.43	71.83	18.52	60.16	15.05

a-Arithmetic Index. g-Geometric Index.

Source: *Barron's*, November 25, 1996.

TABLE 2-6

Global and Regional Indexes

National and Regional Markets	US Dollar Index	Day's Change %	Pound Sterling Index	Yen Index	DM Index	Local Currency Index	Local % chg on day	Gross Div. Yield	US Dollar Index	Pound Sterling Index	Yen Index	DM Index	Local Currency Index	52 week High	52 week Low	Year ago (approx.)
Australia (78)	219.30	2.2	193.85	154.11	170.76	182.39	1.4	4.19	214.65	189.95	151.09	167.70	179.81	219.30	183.46	183.46
Austria (24)	184.78	0.4	163.33	129.85	143.88	143.81	0.0	1.99	184.08	162.90	129.58	143.82	143.75	195.04	168.36	170.47
Belgium (27)	228.80	0.0	202.24	160.79	178.16	174.14	-0.3	3.83	228.74	202.42	161.02	178.71	174.71	229.11	197.59	200.88
Brazil (28)	179.09	-0.4	158.30	125.85	139.44	339.76	-0.3	1.80	179.77	159.09	126.55	140.45	340.77	189.70	129.15	129.15
Canada (116)	194.69	1.2	172.09	136.82	151.60	189.20	1.2	1.91	192.37	170.24	135.41	150.30	186.92	194.69	144.35	145.77
Denmark (30)	340.41	0.6	300.89	239.21	265.05	266.36	0.2	1.73	338.50	299.56	238.28	264.47	265.74	340.41	276.89	281.68
Finland (24)	239.31	1.2	211.53	168.17	186.33	226.83	0.9	2.21	236.35	209.16	166.37	184.66	224.70	239.34	171.73	217.25
France (93)	211.77	0.2	187.18	148.81	164.89	168.27	-0.2	2.90	211.43	187.10	148.83	165.19	168.57	211.77	167.70	181.54
Germany (59)	188.55	0.7	166.67	132.50	146.81	146.81	0.3	1.66	187.30	165.75	131.84	146.33	146.33	188.59	159.60	161.26
Hong Kong (59)	497.44	1.1	439.69	349.56	387.32	493.81	1.1	3.13	492.19	435.57	346.46	384.54	488.60	497.44	357.56	357.56
Indonesia (27)	221.11	-1.4	195.44	155.38	172.16	317.20	-1.4	1.62	224.18	198.38	157.80	175.15	321.60	—	—	—
Ireland (16)	318.27	-0.2	281.33	223.66	247.82	266.48	-0.5	3.43	318.80	282.12	224.41	249.07	267.68	319.32	249.80	258.59
Italy (58)	83.53	1.0	73.84	58.70	65.04	93.42	0.0	2.22	82.68	73.17	58.20	64.59	93.46	84.53	67.22	70.23
Japan (480)	143.25	0.9	126.62	100.66	111.54	100.66	0.8	0.76	141.94	125.61	99.91	110.89	99.91	164.68	137.62	145.51
Malaysia (107)	589.95	0.6	521.47	414.57	459.36	572.57	0.5	1.10	586.27	518.82	412.69	458.05	569.50	589.95	428.31	428.31
Mexico (27)	1209.27	0.1	1068.89	849.78	941.58	10431.80	0.0	1.06	1207.74	1068.79	850.15	943.59	10431.80	1325.65	878.35	878.35
Netherland (19)	324.50	-0.1	286.83	228.03	252.57	248.80	-0.5	2.97	324.93	287.54	228.72	253.86	249.99	325.84	260.87	260.87
New Zealand (15)	92.42	0.1	81.69	64.94	71.96	69.10	0.4	4.02	92.32	81.70	64.98	72.13	68.82	94.35	75.94	78.45
Norway (35)	282.21	0.7	249.45	198.31	219.73	241.80	0.4	2.09	280.15	247.92	197.21	218.88	240.89	282.21	222.24	226.56
Philipines (22)	198.15	0.3	175.14	139.24	154.28	259.11	0.3	0.61	197.55	174.82	139.06	154.34	258.43	—	—	—

Figures in paranthese show number of lines of stock.

Source: *The Financial Times*, November 22, 1996.

Copyright, FTSE International Limited, Goldman, Sachs and Co. and Standard & Poor's. 1996. All rights reserved. "FT/S&P Actuaries" is a joint trademark of The Financial Times Limited and Standard & Poor's. CONSTITUENT CHANGE 11/21/96: Name change: Melville Corp to CVS (USA). Latest prices were unavailable for this edition. Market closed 11/20/1996: Mexico. The FT/S&P Actuaries World Indices are owned by FTSE International limited, Goldman, Sachs & Co. and Standard & Poor's. The indices are compiled by FTSE International and Standard and Poor's in conjunction with the faculty of Actuaries and the Institute of Actuaries. NatWest Securities, Ltd. was a co-founder of the indices.

TABLE 2-6

(Continued)

National and Regional Markets	US Dollar Index	Day's Change %	Pound Sterling Index	Yen Index	DM Index	Local Currency Index	Local % chg on day	Gross Div. Yield	US Dollar Index	Pound Sterling Index	Yen Index	DM Index	Local Currency Index	52 week High	52 week Low	Year ago (approx.)
Singapore (43)	414.55	1.5	366.43	291.31	322.78	267.74	1.6	1.01	408.38	361.40	287.47	319.06	263.47	465.21	369.24	369.24
South Africa (44)	329.11	-1.3	290.90	231.27	256.25	335.57	-0.6	2.32	333.34	294.99	234.65	260.44	337.74	437.76	314.20	376.66
Spain (37)	198.13	0.6	175.14	139.23	154.27	189.06	0.2	3.16	196.95	174.29	138.64	153.88	188.70	198.13	153.59	153.59
Sweden (48)	406.71	-0.1	359.49	285.80	316.68	397.59	-0.3	2.14	407.14	360.30	286.59	318.09	398.88	409.12	294.19	316.23
Switzerland (37)	250.23	-0.1	221.18	175.84	194.83	196.38	-0.2	1.51	250.39	221.58	176.25	195.62	196.85	254.34	219.29	228.12
Thailand (45)	121.63	0.1	107.51	85.47	94.71	119.93	0.0	2.86	121.53	107.55	85.55	94.95	119.89	193.95	112.17	147.63
United Kingdom (213)	267.46	-0.2	236.41	187.95	208.25	236.41	-0.3	4.02	268.09	237.24	188.71	209.45	237.84	268.09	222.43	226.10
USA (624)	302.41	0.2	267.30	212.51	235.47	302.41	0.2	1.98	301.67	266.97	212.35	235.69	301.67	302.41	243.34	144.77
Americas (795)	276.84	0.3	244.70	194.54	215.56	232.70	0.3	1.97	276.06	244.30	194.32	215.68	232.04	276.84	222.53	222.82
Europe (720)	232.86	0.1	205.82	163.63	181.31	196.22	-0.2	2.94	232.62	205.86	163.75	181.74	196.56	232.86	194.31	197.10
Nordic (137)	350.10	0.3	309.45	246.02	272.60	299.21	0.0	2.08	349.16	308.99	245.78	272.79	299.19	350.64	261.13	282.02
Pacific Basin (876)	160.50	1.0	141.87	112.79	124.97	114.35	0.8	1.22	158.94	140.65	111.88	124.18	113.44	177.01	153.87	154.80
Euro-Pacific (1596)	190.53	0.5	168.41	133.89	148.35	145.21	0.3	2.10	189.52	167.72	133.41	148.07	144.77	190.57	172.18	172.33
North America (740)	296.04	0.3	261.68	208.03	230.51	295.02	0.3	1.98	295.18	261.22	207.78	230.62	294.16	296.04	237.55	238.65
Europe Ex. UK (507)	209.10	0.3	184.82	146.94	162.81	171.58	-0.1	2.33	208.48	184.50	146.75	162.88	171.70	209.10	174.81	177.10
Pacific Ex. Japan (396)	311.47	1.2	275.31	218.88	242.52	268.05	1.0	2.78	307.86	272.44	216.71	240.53	265.43	311.47	245.02	245.02
World Ex. US (1811)	192.62	0.5	170.26	135.36	149.98	150.65	0.3	2.09	191.63	169.58	134.89	149.72	150.17	192.62	173.24	173.26
World Ex. UK (2222)	223.20	0.5	197.29	156.85	173.79	189.90	0.4	1.83	222.16	196.61	156.39	173.57	189.23	223.20	192.21	192.21
World Ex. Japan (1955)	271.32	0.3	239.82	190.66	211.26	254.84	0.2	2.35	270.59	239.46	190.47	211.41	253.40	271.32	222.93	222.93
The World Index (2435)	227.01	0.4	200.66	159.53	176.76	192.24	0.3	2.04	226.11	200.10	159.17	176.66	193.69	227.01	195.17	195.17

Figures in paranthese show number of lines of stock.

Source: *The Financial Times*, November 22, 1996.

Copyright, FTSE International Limited, Goldman, Sachs and Co. and Standard & Poor's. 1996. All rights reserved. "FT/S&P Actuaries" is a joint trademark of The Financial Times Limited and Standard & Poor's. **CONSTITUENT CHANGE 11/21/96:** Name change: Melville Corp to CVS (USA). Latest prices were unavailable for this edition. Market closed 11/20/1996: Mexico. The FT/S&P Actuaries World Indices are owned by FTSE International limited, Goldman, Sachs & Co. and Standard & Poor's. The indices are compiled by FTSE International and Standard and Poor's in conjunction with the faculty of Actuaries and the Institute of Actuaries. NatWest Securities, Ltd. was a co-founder of the indices.

Table 2–7 provides a list of indexes that can be used to evaluate performance results of funds that are invested within a given country. For example, the performance of a manager who invests in Japan could be evaluated using either the Nikkei 225 Stock Index or Tokyo Stock Exchange Index. Here, the evaluator can compare the returns of the individual fund with those achieved using the specific country's index.

TABLE 2–7

Country Indexes

Affarsvarlden All-Share Index (Sweden)
Australia Stock Exchange Fifty Leaders Index
Australia Stock Exchange All Ordinaries Accumulation Index
Bangkok SET Index (Thailand)
Belgian Stock Exchange Index
BEL 20Index (Belgium)
BSE National Price Index (India)
Canadian Balanced Index
DAX Equity Index
FT-Actuaries All-Share Index
FT-Actuaries British Government All Stocks Index
FT-Actuaries Europe & Pacific Index
Hang Seng-Hong Kong Index
IGPA General Index (Chile)
Kuala Lumpur Composite (Malaysia)
Madrid General Index (Spain)
Merval Price Index Argentina
IPC All-share Index (Mexico)
Milan Stock Index (Italy)
New Straits Times Index-Malaysia
New Zealand Stock Exchange-30 Index
Nikkei 225 Stock Index
Seoul Composite Index (South Korea)
Straits Times Index (Singapore)
Swiss Bank Corporation Stock Index
Tokyo Stock Exchange Index

There are additional equity indexes that can be used to evaluate the performance of investment professionals who employ varying management approaches and styles. The evaluator would choose one of these indexes if the investment professional was charged with investing in certain types of equity securities. For example, if the portfolio manager was instructed to invest in growth stocks, then an index representing growth portfolios would be chosen. Likewise, if the manager was charged with the task of investing in companies with relatively small capitalization, then an index such as the Burns Fry Smallcap Index or the Hoare Govett Small Companies Index would serve as a valid comparison benchmark. Some of the more common indexes that can be used to evaluate the investment results of these managers are listed in Table 2–8.

Fixed-Income Indexes

Indexes are also used to evaluate the fixed-income component of portfolios. The fixed-income index chosen should be representative of the portfolio's guidelines relating to credit risk, liquidity, interest rate risk, and maturity required. For example, if the policy statement prohibits investing in nongovernment securities, then an

TABLE 2–8

Equity Style Indexes

Small and MidCap Indexes	Growth Indexes
Burns Fry Smallcap Index	Hambrecht & Quist Growth Stock Index
Hoare Govett Small Companies Index	Russell 1000 Growth Index
Russell Midcap Index	Russell 2000 Growth Index
Standard & Poor's MidCap 400 Index	Wilshire Large Company Growth Index
	Wilshire Small Company Growth Index
Value Indexes	**Technology and Venture Capital**
Wilshire Large Company Value Index	Hambrecht & Quist Technology Stock Index
Wilshire Small Company Value Index	Salomon Brothers Primary Market Index (PMI)
	Venture Capital 100 Index

index using corporate securities may be inappropriate. Furthermore, if the investment policy statement prohibits investing in long-term bonds, an index should be chosen to reflect this constraint.

Table 2–9 lists corporate fixed-income indexes that are available for performance comparison purposes. The bond indexes in this table vary according to maturity and risk. The choice of an index should be based on the return/risk guidelines within the investment policy statement. The investment guidelines should be matched carefully with the characteristics of the index to be used for comparison purposes.

Table 2–10 presents the most common U.S. government bond indexes used to evaluate government bond fund managers. Since these financial assets possess virtually no default risk (although President Clinton's treasury secretary, Robert E. Rubin, may contest this assertion), the main consideration when deciding on the appropriate comparison index is its maturity, duration, and convexity characteristics. Thus, the evaluator should select an index based on the fund's return/risk objectives. The short-term indexes, such as the Salomon Brothers Treasury Bill Index (one year), would be less risky in terms of price fluctuations than the Lehman Brothers Treasury—Intermediate Bond Index due to its

TABLE 2-9

U.S. Market Corporate Bond Indexes

Lehman Brothers Corporate Intermediate Bond Index
Lehman Brothers Aggregate Bond Index
Lehman Brothers Corporate A Bond Index
Lehman Brothers Corporate AA Bond Index
Lehman Brothers Corporate AAA Bond Index
Lehman Brothers Corporate BAA Bond Index
Lehman Brothers Government/Corporate Bond Index
Salomon Brothers Broad Investment-Grade Bond Index
Salomon Brothers Corporate Bond Index-High Grade

TABLE 2-10

U.S. Government Treasury Indexes

Lehman Brothers Government Intermediate Bond Index
Lehman Brothers Government Long-term Bond Index
Lehman Brothers Government Bond Index
Lehman Brothers Treasury—Intermediate Bond Index
Lehman Brothers Treasury—Long-Term Bond Index
Lehman Brothers Treasury Bond Index
Salomon Brothers Treasury Bill Index (one year)
Salomon Brothers Treasury Bill Index

shorter maturity. Likewise, it would be expected to earn a lower return. In contrast, the Lehman Brothers Treasury—Long-Term Bond Index would be representative of both higher returns and risks. Here again, the investment policy guidelines should be used to determine which index is the most appropriate.

Fixed-income portfolio managers may also invest in mortgage-backed and/or convertible securities. Mortgage-backed securities generally provide returns higher than those paid by U.S. treasuries. Furthermore, they have distinguishing characteristics, such as prepayment considerations, that differ from the call feature associated with straight debt instruments. For example, if interest rates fall, homeowners refinance their existing mortgages. This results in mortgage-backed securities holders experiencing early principal repayments.

Convertible securities also differ markedly from other fixed-income securities. Typically, these instruments provide lower yields than straight debt instruments. Due to the conversion feature, convertibles are influenced by the changes in the underlying equity instruments. Table 2–11 presents a sample list of indexes appropriate for these types of funds.

Finally, many professional managers invest in fixed-income securities of nondomestic entities. Foreign investing can often pro-

TABLE 2-11

Mortgage and Convertible Indexes

Mortgage Indexes

    Lehman Brothers Asset-Backed Securities

    Lehman Brothers GNMA's Mortgage-Backed
        Securities Index

    Lehman Brothers Mortgage-Backed Securities Index

    Salomon Brothers Mortgage Securities Index

    Sciotia McLeod Residential Mortgage Index

Convertible Bonds Indexes

    First Boston Convertible Securities Index

    Froley, Revy 30 Convertible Bond Index

    Goldman Sachs 100 Convertible Bond Index

vide the investor with diversification benefits and attractive returns. For these types of investments, the investor's returns are not only tied to the issuing country's interest rates but also to changes in the currency exchange rate. Therefore, it is important to select an index that reflects the characteristics of these securities as well. Table 2–12 presents a list of foreign fixed-income indexes to conduct such an evaluation.

Benchmark Portfolios

Customized benchmark indexes may be appropriate for some funds. These indexes may be designed and developed by the fund managers in consultation with the investment committee. They appear best suited for portfolios that have highly specific return and risk requirements that are not closely tracked by existing indexes. For example, an endowment fund may have very near term income requirements as well as very long term planned withdrawal goals for its fixed-income portfolio. A customized benchmark may better reflect whether this goal is being achieved than a weighting of standardized ones.

TABLE 2-12

Global and Country Fixed-Income Indexes

Australian Treasury Notes
Commonwealth Bank Bond Indexes
J. P. Morgan Global Government Bond Index
J. P. Morgan Non-U.S. Government Bond Index
Lehman Brothers Eurobond Indexes
Lehman Brothers Eurobond High Grade Public Sector
   Indexes
Lehman Brothers Eurobond Japanese Corporate Indexes
Lehman Brothers Eurobond U.S. Corporate Indexes
Merrill Lynch Eurodollar Master Bond Index
Pictet Swiss Bond Index
Pictet Swiss Foreign Bond Index
Salomon Brothers Non-U.S. Government Bond Index
Salomon Brothers Swiss Foreign Bond Index
Salomon Brothers World Bond Index
Salomon Brothers World Government Bond Index

A type of customized benchmark that has received increasing attention is recent years is the so-called normal portfolio. These normal portfolios contain "a set of securities that contain all of the securities from which a manager normally chooses, weighted as a manager would weight them in a portfolio"[1] Normal portfolios appear to have the benefit of reflecting the style of the investment manager, allowing the investment committee to evaluate results independently of the manager's style. Universe comparisons can be made more readily. At the same time, the construction and maintenance of these indexes is an added expense.

The cash and equivalent component of a portfolio can also be evaluated in terms of an index. U.S. Treasury bills and other short-term money market indexes are readily available for performance evaluation purposes. Again, the index chosen must be consistent with the goals and objectives of the portfolio's cash and equivalent

TABLE 2–13

Cash and Equivalent Indexes

Commercial Paper Index
Payden & Rygel Treasury Note (one year)
Salomon Brothers Certificate of Deposit Index (three months)
Salomon Brothers Treasury Bill Index (three months)
Salomon Brothers Treasury Bill Index (six months)
Salomon Brothers US Dollar Euro-Certificate of Deposit
  (three months)
ScotiaMcLeod 30-Day Treasury Bill Index

component. Several indexes used for performance comparisons for these portfolios are listed in Table 2–13.

Composite Indexes

The indexes identified earlier are employed when the funds being evaluated are comprised exclusively of equities, fixed-income securities, or cash and equivalents. Unfortunately, funds that comprise all of these financial assets cannot be properly evaluated using only one of these indexes. For example, it would be inappropriate to evaluate the performance of a balanced fund using the S&P 500 or a similar index. It is important that the benchmark tool have similar characteristics to the fund that is to be evaluated.

This problem can be overcome by using a composite index approach. Under these circumstances, each component is "matched" with an index possessing the desired attributes as specified by the investment guidelines. These indexes are then used to develop a composite, which represents the weighted average of the individual component's returns. For example, if the portfolio consists of 60 percent equities, 25 percent in fixed-income securities, and 15 percent in cash equivalent, then the composite return would be found by multiplying each component's return by its proportionate weight within the portfolio. In turn, these results would then be summed up, to arrive at a composite return.

Using Universes as an Evaluation Tool

The use of indexes for comparison purposes provides the evaluator with many advantages. Indexes are readily available to the evaluators of investment managers, for example, and performance results can be updated rather easily. There are some drawbacks, however. A comparison of investment performance with that of an index may put the fund manager at a disadvantage or an advantage. Specifically, index performance is not affected by transaction costs and cash holdings, while the manager's performance results are affected by these factors. Furthermore, the indexes do not reflect the effect of fees charged by investment professionals. Finally, other investment constraints faced by the investment professional, such as required cash distributions, are not reflected in these indexes.

The utilization of investment universes can overcome many of the problems associated with using indexes as a means of evaluating investment performance. An *investment universe* is a grouping of portfolios with investment characteristics similar to the fund being evaluated.

Several services are available that rank a portfolio's performance relative to other portfolios with similar goals and objectives. This allows for a comparison of the portfolio's performance with portfolios managed by other investment professionals. Thus, the evaluator can tailor the universe to fit the requirements of the fund manager. The investment policy guidelines should state how fund performance is to be evaluated. Typically, the investment policy statement might set as an objective that the portfolio returns rank within the given quartile of the universe chosen over a given period of time.

PERIODIC REVIEW

The investment policy statement should specify how and when the performance of the portfolio will be evaluated. Performing a periodic review is an essential part of a committee member's fiduciary responsibilities. The performance of an investment portfolio can be monitored on a monthly, quarterly, or annual basis. At a minimum, the investment policy statement should require annual meetings with the portfolio's money managers. Chapter 12 presents an overview of the areas to be addressed during these reviews. The importance of conducting periodic reviews cannot be overstated.

SUMMARY

The investment policy statement provides guidelines to assist managers in achieving the investment goals and objectives of the portfolio. The document specifies the return objective as well as the risk level to be assumed. It provides guidance regarding the type of securities to be held, their risk attributes, and the level of diversification to be achieved. In short, the policy statement should provide all parties with the information necessary to carry out their fiduciary responsibilities.

The policy statement should identify the standard to be used for evaluation purposes. The evaluator can choose from a single index, a composite index, or a universe. The selection of the appropriate index or universe can only be made after the investment goals, objectives, and risk considerations are determined. The policy statement should also state how and when performance will be measured and evaluated.

Exhibit 2–1 is a sample investment policy statement.

REFERENCES

1. Frank J. Fabozzi, *Bond Markets, Analysis and Strategies*, 3rd ed. Upper Saddle River, NJ, Prentice-Hall, pp. 468–69.

E X H I B I T   2 – 1

SAMPLE INVESTMENT POLICY STATEMENT

PURPOSE

The purpose of this statement is to communicate a clear understanding of _____'s, investment philosophy, goals, and objectives, as well as the policies it seeks to implement to achieve these objectives.

This statement will outline an overall philosophy that is specific enough to guide investment expectations and decisions, but sufficiently flexible to allow for changing economic conditions and securities markets. The policy will provide realistic long term rate of return and risk tolerance objectives, as well as standards for evaluating investment performance. The policy will also establish the investment restrictions to be placed upon the management of the account and will outline procedures for policy and performance review.

INVESTMENT PHILOSOPHY

_____ seeks to invest the account for three primary purposes. The first purpose is to help ensure the fiscal soundness of _____ by accumulating a reservoir of financial resources. This purpose will be achieved, in part, by the total investment return on the account. The second purpose for investing the account is to help support the growth and development of _____ by enhancing either the operating budget or capital expenditures of the institution. This purpose will be achieved, in part, by either the current income from the account or withdrawals from the *corpus* of the account. The third purpose for investing the account is to provide a source for _____.

Within the account are monies, including endowment monies, the returns on which are earmarked for _____. The *corpus* of these specific restricted monies, however, cannot be withdrawn for any purposes.

Investments will be made for the sole interest and the exclusive purpose of providing the maximum return within the con-

Exhibit 2-1   Continued

straints described herein. The party or parties managing the account will use the care, skill, prudence, and diligence under the circumstances prevailing that a prudent man or woman would use in managing the portfolio under similar circumstances. The party or parties managing the account will satisfy the "prudent man" criteria by giving appropriate consideration to those facts and circumstances that, given the scope of its investment duties, it knows or should know are relevant to the particular investment course of action.

The portfolio must be structured over the long term with an intent first, to conserve principal and second, to enhance capital value. The party or parties managing the account will diversify the investments within the portfolio so as to minimize the risk of excessive losses, unless under the circumstances it is clearly not prudent to do so. It is also important for them to diversify among many types of investments, not just individual stock or bond issues (asset classes). Additionally, the party or parties managing the account will perform its investment responsibilities in accordance with the documents and instruments governing the account.

OBJECTIVES OF THE ACCOUNT

Expected Rate of Return

The objectives of the account should be pursued as a long-term goal designed to maximize the returns without exposure to undue risk as defined herein. Since fluctuating rates of return are characteristic of the securities markets, the greatest concern of the party or parties managing the account should be preservation of the purchasing power of the *corpus* of the account. Because short-term market fluctuations may cause variations in the account performance, the account is expected to achieve the following objectives over a three-year time period:

1. The account's total *minimum* expected rate of return will *exceed* the increase in the consumer price index by 5 percent annually (average growth of inflation plus 15 percent over three years).

Exhibit 2–1   Continued

2. The total expected return should be at least 10 percent (net of fees and transaction costs) annually.

While a long-term positive correlation exists between performance volatility (risk) and expected returns in the securities markets, the following short-term (annual) objective is established:

The portfolio should be invested to minimize the likelihood of negative total returns, defined as a one-year return worse than negative 10 percent. It is anticipated that such a loss will occur no more than 1 out of 20 years. Should such a negative return appear likely, a determination will be made as to the proper course of action to be taken.

Moreover, the account will seek to provide stable and predictable current income from interest and dividends from year to year to provide sufficient current funds to meet operating needs, as appropriate, as well as provide a "real" component of total return net of inflation as a base of value.

Risk Tolerance

A conservative level of risk, that is a low tolerance for risk, is desired for the account in light of the investment philosophy and return objectives. Preservation of the purchasing power of the account's principal is the dominant requirement, and investment decisions must recognize the primacy of this requirement.

However, there may be occasions when the expected return on an investment exceeds the estimated risks associated with the investment. As long as such investments do not materially affect the risk profile of the entire account, then such investments may be considered.

The conservative level of risk sought for the account (portfolio) refers to the aggregate (combined) risk of the total collection of securities (assets) included in the account. Portfolio risks will be measured by the variance or standard deviation of the expected return on the portfolio relative to benchmark standard deviations. Moreover, a conservative level of risk implies that the portfolio's standard

Exhibit 2–1 Continued

deviation will not exceed that of the benchmark's and, in periods of high market volatility, will be significantly less than that of the benchmark.

Funding Objectives and Liquidity

In addition to the constraints listed elsewhere in this document, the account is to be managed to achieve the following scheduled withdrawals:

1. An annual withdrawal of $_____ —adjusted for inflation— on or about June 1 of each year for _____ from the true endowment portion of the Fund restricted specifically for _____ .

2. An annual withdrawal of five (5) percent of the nonrestricted portion of the fund's annual gain for operating budget and/or capital expenditure purposes on or about August 1 of each year. The annual gain on the nonrestricted portion of the fund is defined as the sum of interest proceeds plus dividends plus capital gains that have accrued during the 12-month period from the most recent July 31.

3. The nonrestricted portion of the Fund can be used as contingency with a total not to exceed $10,000. Any such contingency allocation must have the prior approval of the Finance Committee.

4. Ninety (90) days prior written notice of such withdrawals will be required.

INVESTMENT STRATEGY

Asset Allocation

Research indicates that as much as 90 percent of portfolio return is accounted for by asset allocation as opposed to individual security selection, market timing, or other factors. Asset allocation, the

---

Exhibit 2–1   Continued

apportionment of the portfolio among asset classes, is therefore expected to account for a substantial portion of the account's total return. Moreover, existing asset allocations will be monitored, evaluated, and reviewed frequently in light of prospective market conditions to ensure the achievement of objectives.

Passive Strategy

Given the return and risk objectives for the account, it is anticipated they can be accomplished without the considerable time, effort, and expense required to consistently outperform relevant security market indices. Net of expenses, it is expected that the 10 percent annual return and low-risk tolerance objectives can be achieved via an investment strategy that seeks to match security market performance over a complete cycle.

However, at times investment opportunities may be present to earn potential returns in excess of the associated risks and/or expense associated with them. In order to take advantage of such opportunities, no more that 10 percent of the account can be used for such discretionary purposes.

Asset Classes

The assets within the portfolio will be allocated between cash equivalents, fixed income instruments, and equity securities. Subject to provisions listed below, these assets may include those of foreign companies and sovereign nations. Permissible investments include money market funds, insured certificates of deposit, commercial paper, U.S. Treasury obligations, federal agency obligations, corporate bonds, convertible corporate bonds, preferred and common stocks. Open-end mutual funds representing the above are also permissible investments.

The assets within the portfolio will be allocated among the following six asset classes as represented by the associated indexes.

Exhibit 2-1   Continued

These indexes will also serve as a benchmark for evaluating return and risk on the portfolio.

Equity Asset Classes	Index/Benchmark
"Large" company stocks	S&P 500
"Midsize"/"small" company stocks	NASDAQ Composite or Ibbotson-DFA index
International equities	E.A. F.E. index or M.S.C.I. index

Fixed Income Asset Classes	
Intermediate maturity government and Corporate bonds	Lehman Brothers Intermediate Government/Corporate Bond Index
Long-term bonds -Corporate -Government	Salomon Brothers Long-Term High-Grade Corporate Bond Index; or Merrill Lynch high 10+ Year Corporate Index. Lehman Brothers Long Term Treasury Bond Index, or Merrill Lynch U.S. Treasury 10+ Years Index.

Cash Equivalent	
Treasury Bills	90-day T-bills

RISK MANAGEMENT
Index/Benchmark

A conservative level of risk will be achieved and maintained primarily by an asset allocation mix and, when deemed appropriate, an asset reallocation mix among equities, fixed income, and cash equivalent securities. In addition, risk will be minimized by

  1. Diversifying properly the equity component of the portfolio via:

      (*a.*) Having at least 20 equity securities in the portfolio at all times so as to minimize nonsystematic "firm-specific" risk.

Exhibit 2–1   Continued

    (*b.*) To the extent practical including equity issues whose price changes are, ideally, negatively related or not strongly positively related.

    (*c.*) Properly diversifying across industries, sectors, and countries.

    (*d.*) Maintaining an equity portfolio risk that does not exceed that of a relevant benchmark.

    (*e.*) Only including securities or funds that are highly liquid as evidenced by their listing and active trading on established exchanges / secondary markets.

2. Diversifying properly the fixed income component of the portfolio by

    (*a.*) Including only corporate issues rated A or better by Standard and Poor's or Moody's to limit default risk.

    (*b.*) Including a maturity distribution that is appropriate, given market conditions and forecasts of market conditions, to limit reinvestment risk.

    (*c.*) Properly diversifying across issuers, industries, sectors, and countries.

    (*d.*) Including an interest rate distribution that is appropriate, given market conditions and forecasts of market conditions, to limit interest rate risk.

    (*e.*) Maintaining a bond portfolio risk as measured by duration and convexity that does not exceed that of a relevant benchmark.

    (*f.*) Only including fixed income instruments that are highly liquid as evidenced by their listings and active trading on established exchanges / secondary markets.

3. Ensuring, via disclosure from brokers and reading of prospecti, that cash equivalents are primary securities with maturities of one year or less.

Exhibit 2-1   Continued

Prohibited Investments

In addition to those investments discussed elsewhere in this document, the use of the following securities are strictly prohibited except for their use in reducing risk as so-called hedges. Any such use will require full documentation and disclosure to the Finance Committee as to how they will be utilized as risk-reduction devices, fees involved in using them, and an analysis of their daily performance. Such restricted investments include:

- Short-sales.
- Futures contracts on cash equivalents, equity, fixed income, and foreign exchange.
- Forward contracts on the above.
- Options on the above.
- Interest rate and foreign-exchange rate swaps.
- Swaptions.

INVESTMENTS AND QUALITY STANDARDS

Equities

To the extent consistent with its investment objectives and policies, the equity component of the portfolio will seek to maximize capital appreciation as well as the growth of dividends.

No more than 20 percent of the equity component may be invested in small capitalized companies that, while they may have been in existence for only a limited number of years, have achieved an important position in the markets served. These markets may be developing markets or meaningful segments of larger markets.

Purchase of equities shall be limited to those of good quality. Issues with limited marketability will normally be avoided.

Exhibit 2–1   Continued

The party or parties responsible for managing the account may invest up to 20 percent of the total portfolio's equity assets in securities of companies domiciled outside the United States. Securities of foreign companies traded on foreign stock exchanges may be purchased only with written permission of the Finance Committee.

Fixed Income

The management of the fixed-income component of the portfolio will be based on interest rate anticipation and will be conducted by altering the duration of the fixed-income component to maximize total return while, at the same time, minimizing volatility of principal. The parties responsible for managing the account may select from appropriately liquid corporate debt securities, obligations of the U.S. government and its agencies, and securities convertible to equities.

The parties responsible for managing the account will continuously monitor the yield curve as well as the spreads between various fixed income instruments to identify overvalued and undervalued securities.

The parties responsible for managing the account may, from time to time, use convertible securities in lieu of other fixed-income securities. Therefore, substituting convertible issues for straight corporate debt (assuming similar coupon rates and maturities) will be expected to furnish the yield and stability of a bond, but include the potential for capital appreciation through the ultimate conversion into the company's underlying common stock.

All convertible debentures will have at least $50MM outstanding and will be rated BBB or better.

No single industry group, as defined by Standard and Poors Corporation, shall constitute more than 20 percent of the equity portion, and no single equity shall represent more than 5 percent of the equity portion of the portfolio unless specifically approved by the Finance Committee.

Corporate bonds (excluding convertible debentures) shall be limited to publicly issued items, rated A or better by Standard and

---

Exhibit 2–1 Continued

Poor's or Moody's. They shall be debt of the issuers with at least $100MM in original face value amount to ensure adequate marketability and liquidity.

No single industry group, as defined by Standard and Poor's shall constitute more than 20 percent of the bond portfolio, and no single company shall constitute more than 5 percent of the total portfolio except direct or indirect obligations of the U.S. government.

The parties responsible for managing the account shall endeavor to maintain an appropriate distribution of fixed-income maturities consistent with the business cycle and interest rate forecast.

The parties responsible for managing the account are prohibited from investing in private placements and from speculating in fixed income or interest rate futures.

Cash and Equivalents

The parties responsible for managing the account may invest in commercial paper, Treasury bills, certificates of deposit, and money market funds to provide income, liquidity for expense payments, and preservation of the account's principal value. All such assets must represent maturities of one year or less at the time of purchase. Commercial paper assets must be rated A-1 or P-1 by Standard & Poor's or Moody's. The parties responsible for managing the account may not purchase short-term financial instruments considered to contain speculative characteristics (uncertainty of principal and/or interest). The parties responsible for managing the account also may not invest more than 5 percent of the account's market value in the obligations of a single issuer, with the exception of the U.S. government and its agencies.

Uninvested cash reserves should be kept to minimum levels. Within the limitations mentioned above, the parties responsible for managing the account have complete discretion to allocate and select short-term cash and equivalent securities.

Exhibit 2–1   Concluded

Other Assets

The parties responsible for managing the account will not purchase assets other than those mentioned above without written consent of the Investment Policy Committee. Investments not specifically addressed by this policy statement are forbidden without written consent.

MONITORING AND EVALUATING

Communications

The parties responsible for managing the account will receive periodic (monthly) portfolio valuations as well as a statement of transactions and income/additions/disbursements.

The parties responsible for managing the account will receive confirmations of all transactions.

Monthly performance reports and regular telephone conversations will be scheduled by the parties responsible for managing the account to review reports and to discuss the outlook for the economy and the securities markets.

Fiduciary Responsibility

In conformance to ERISA, the parties responsible for managing the account will manage the assets of the portfolio so that the assets are used exclusively to provide benefits for the account and the beneficiaries and to defray the reasonable expenses of administering the account.

CHAPTER 3

Investment Overview

INTRODUCTION

Professional investment managers are charged with the actual implementation of a sponsor's investment plan. Their job is to ensure that the investment sponsor's investment return objectives are met, while operating within the risk tolerance limits, time frame, tax status, and other constraints specified in the investment policy statement.

In light of the wide spectrum of investment sponsors, and the even wider variety of investment goals and objectives sponsors seek to achieve, professional investment managers can be assigned a considerable range of responsibilities. At one extreme, professional managers may be charged with a complete scope of duties—from helping to draft the investment policy statement, to making the asset allocation decisions, to the actual selection of securities in each asset class for a multibillion dollar fund. At the other extreme, professional investment managers may be responsible for security selection only within a relatively small subsector of an overall portfolio, for example, foreign equities.

CAPITAL APPRECIATION VERSUS CURRENT INCOME

Broadly speaking, investors can be classified as desiring growth, current income, and/or a combination of these two objectives. The investor's objectives will be reflected in the investment policy statement and in the investment characteristics of the portfolio being managed. For example, a trust that is required to make a pre-determined payment at a specified future date would engage a professional investment manager to invest in a portfolio consisting of equity securities expected to appreciate over the investment period. This trust may have little need for current income and may, therefore, be willing to accept little in terms of current income.

Most retired individuals, in contrast, prefer current income to the prospects of future capital appreciation. In fact, they may count on dividend and interest income to supplement their other sources of income. In these instances, investing in a portfolio that provides high current income is the most sensible course of action. These portfolios are characterized by investing in fixed-income securities and high-dividend-yield preferred and common stocks. The managers of these portfolios would be charged to look for stocks with above-average growth in dividends, a high dividend yield, and a consistent record of dividend payments. Furthermore, companies that pay out a significant portion of their earnings in the form of dividends are frequently stressed. Often the high dividend payout is possible since these companies' growth prospects are insignificant. This lack of growth contributes to lower price/earnings multiples than growth stocks and thus much higher dividend yields. Investors who desire high current income while minimizing their exposure to taxes would seek out portfolios consisting of municipal bonds and other tax-exempt instruments.

Many investment sponsors fall in between these two categories. For example, a pension plan generally requires current income in order to provide retirement benefits to qualified recipients as well as growth in the fund's value in order to meet future oblig-

CHART 3-1

Retirement Income Sources
$28,714 Annual Income or More

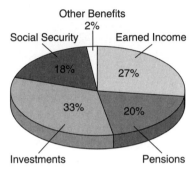

Source: Social Security Administration, 1990.

ations to retirees. Balanced portfolios that provide both capital appreciation and current income are available for these sponsors. These portfolios consist of both equities and fixed-income securities. The investment professional will manage the portfolio within a predetermined asset mix range. Typically, the portfolio manager is required to maintain a minimum percentage of assets invested in a fixed-income category. For example, the portfolio guidelines may specify that the fixed-income component is at least 25 percent of the total investment portfolio size.

As Chart 3–1 suggests, approximately 33 percent of retirement income is derived from investments. Therefore, if you are planning on retiring or are already retired, the performance of your investment portfolio will play an important role during these years.

ACTIVE VERSUS PASSIVE INVESTMENT APPROACHES

Investment professionals can take either an active or passive approach in investing their clients' monies. An active approach requires managers to identify investment classes and securities within these classes that are expected to achieve superior performance relative to a market benchmark index over a given investment horizon. On the other hand, a passive investment approach calls for the identification of a performance benchmark and the construction of a synthetic portfolio that will mirror the performance of that benchmark.

Often, an index such as the S&P 500 is chosen as the appropriate benchmark to be used to evaluate investment performance. In short, performance is based on the ability of the portfolio to achieve the investment results of that index. The investment objective would be to earn a return equal to this index. Obviously, a passive manager would not knowingly select securities that he or she believes will outperform the index. Rather, the manager is charged with achieving the same results.

Unlike passive investing, the active approach requires investment professionals to use their expertise in terms of the asset allocation and security selection decisions. To be sure, the performance of active managers has been under close scrutiny. Each quarter their performance is judged against a host of indexes and universes. Thus, these managers are not only expected to "beat the market" but their peers as well.

INVESTMENT STYLES—EQUITY MANAGERS

Investment managers who pursue active strategies have followed a variety of investment strategies and approaches. These approaches not only reflect *how* these managers invest but also *where*. Portfolios are categorized according to the investment manager's "style." While the classification of investment approaches often varies, they generally fall within the following categories:

- Capitalization.
- Growth.
- Value.
- Cyclical.
- Market.

- ◆ Sector.
- ◆ Contrarian.

Capitalization

In terms of total return, low capitalization stocks have historically outperformed higher capitalization stocks. An increasing number of professionals are investing in small *capitalization* stocks. The stocks of smaller sized companies are attractive investment vehicles to many professional investment managers who believe they have a comparative advantage in being among the first to identify small companies with exceptional earnings prospects. By being among the first to invest in such companies, professional managers believe their clients will enjoy substantial excess returns, adjusted for risk, on their portfolios.

Table 3–1 reports the annual total return for large and small company stocks as well as the annual inflation rate from 1926 through 1995. During this period, both large and small company stocks provided investors with returns exceeding the rate of inflation. As the table reveals, small company stocks provided investors with higher annual returns than the large company stocks. However, as indicated by the corresponding standard deviations, these returns were accompanied by greater risk. Small company stocks have historically provided returns about 40 percent greater (17.7 percent versus 12.5 percent) than those in large company stocks. The risk in small company stocks has historically been almost 70 percent higher (34.4 percent versus 20.4 percent) than those of larger company stocks.

The relationship between capitalization and performance is also shown when viewing the historic results of companies listed on the New York Stock Exchange (NYSE). Table 3–2 reports the annual returns of stocks traded on the NYSE from 1926 to 1995 according to decile. As the table indicates, lower capitalization stocks provided returns greater than their larger capitalization counterparts. The table also reveals that these stocks were more risky as measured by their corresponding standard deviations.

TABLE 3-1

Annual Total Returns, 1926–1995

Investment Category	Geometric Mean (%)	Arithmetic Mean (%)	Standard Deviation (%)
Large company stocks	10.5	12.5	20.4
Small company stocks	12.5	17.7	34.4
Inflation	3.1	3.2	4.6

Source: © Computed using data from *Stocks, Bonds, Bills and Inflation, 1996 Yearbook,*™ Ibbotson Associates, Chicago (annually updates work by Roger G. Ibbotson and Rex Sinquefield). Used with permission. All rights reserved.

TABLE 3-2

Firm-Size-Based, Annual Returns, 1926–1995

Decile	Geometric Mean (%)	Arithmetic Mean (%)	Standard Deviation (%)
1 (largest)	9.69	11.42	18.95
2	10.94	13.36	22.55
3	11.39	14.07	24.39
4	11.46	14.65	26.84
5	12.09	15.60	27.67
6	11.71	15.53	28.72
7	11.68	15.98	31.18
8	11.94	17.11	35.01
9	12.08	17.86	37.56
10 (smallest)	13.83	22.04	46.81
Mid cap 3–5	11.58	14.52	25.53
Low cap 6–8	11.80	15.98	30.56
Micro cap 9–10	12.63	18.97	39.84
NYSE total value Weighted index	10.23	12.20	20.30

Source: © Computed using data from *Stocks, Bonds, Bills and Inflation, 1996 Yearbook,*™ Ibbotson Associates, Chicago (annually updates work by Roger G. Ibbotson and Rex Sinquefield). Used with permission. All rights reserved.

Growth

Many professional managers strive for superior returns by focusing on growth investing. Their portfolios are concentrated in sectors, industries, and companies that are expected to grow much faster than the economy overall, resulting in earnings growth rates that exceed those in other sectors, industries, and companies. The equity securities in growth portfolios would be characterized by high returns on equity and accelerated growth in earnings. Historically, these securities have produced annual earnings growth rates well in excess of those achieved by the S&P 500 companies. Furthermore, these stocks tend to have high market-to-book value ratios. Current yields are low compared with the market since dividend payouts are low because earnings often must be reinvested into the company to fuel its growth.

Table 3–3 reports the style characteristics for three categories of growth indexes—large, medium, and small capitalization growth stocks—together with the style characteristics of the S&P 500 and the S&P Mid Cap indexes. The style characteristics listed in the table are price/earnings ratio, dividend yield, five-year earnings growth

TABLE 3–3

Style Characteristics, Growth Indexes

Market Indexes	P/E Ratio	Dividend Yield	5-Year EPS Growth Rate	ROE	Beta	P/B Ratio
Wilshire large growth	23.60	1.20	15.70	23.93	1.01	5.90
Wilshire mid growth	21.70	0.60	15.20	19.01	1.02	5.40
Wilshire small growth	20.00	0.30	13.90	17.24	0.79	5.00
S&P 500	19.30	2.20	10.18	20.71	1.00	4.26
S&P mid cap	18.05	1.61	9.48	13.36	1.22	3.72

Source: Trust Universe Comparison Universe Equity Style Metric Universe, Wilshire Associates Incorporated, second quarter 1996.

rate, return on equity, beta, and the market/book value ratio. As
mentioned earlier, growth stocks are characterized by relatively
high price/earnings, equity growth rates, return on equity, and
market price to book value. These stocks also possess relatively low
dividend yields.

The historic performance of growth indexes based on size is
reported in Table 3–4 for the 1978 to 1995 period. Column 1 represents the year, while columns 2, 3, and 4 represent the total rates of
return for the Large Growth Index, Mid Cap Growth Index, and
Small Growth Index, respectively. The final column reports the
total return for the S&P 500 over this time.

The highest total rates of return for this period were achieved
by the Mid Cap Growth Index (17.4 percent), followed by the Small
Growth Index (16.8 percent). The return for the High Cap Growth
Index of 16 percent outpaced that of the S&P 500, which achieved
an annual rate of return of 15.5 percent over this period.

Value

Value investment style, as the name implies, seeks to identify
stocks that are undervalued relative to an assessment of their fundamental worth. The managers use fundamental analysis to spot
companies that have significant strengths, such as consistent earnings, but are also characterized by relatively low market to book
values. These stocks may also have a higher dividend yield than a
growth stock, a lower return on equity, a lower equity growth rate,
and a lower beta. Managers would consider such stocks as undervalued or relatively cheap securities.

Table 3–5 reports the style characteristics of selected value
indexes for the quarter ending June 30, 1996. As the table reveals,
value stocks are characterized by a low price/earnings ratio, low
equity growth rates, a low return on equity, and a low
market/book value ratio relative to growth stocks. These stocks
provide investors with much higher dividend yields than growth
stocks.

TABLE 3-4

Growth Index Performance, 1978–1996

Year	Large Growth Index (%)	Mid Cap Growth Index (%)	Small Growth Index (%)	S&P 500 (%)
1978	9.5	20.8	26.6	6.4
1979	29.7	43.8	51.7	18.5
1980	41.3	43.7	52.3	32.4
1981	−10.7	0.8	−1.0	−5.1
1982	14.5	23.2	19.1	21.1
1983	17.4	22.0	22.6	22.4
1984	3.0	−4.6	−9.0	6.1
1985	33.0	30.2	26.5	32.0
1986	15.5	14.8	10.1	18.6
1987	4.7	−5.7	−8.9	5.2
1988	15.2	14.8	19.3	16.8
1989	35.2	22.0	18.9	31.5
1990	0.3	−13.0	−19.0	−3.2
1991	46.6	55.4	56.8	30.6
1992	5.9	12.3	13.2	7.7
1993	−0.5	15.8	18.0	10.0
1994	3.0	0.9	0.6	1.3
1995	37.9	39.0	35.2	37.5
1996 (2Q)	13.9	10.2	11.8	10.2
Annualized returns	16.0	17.4	16.8	15.5

Source: Trust Universe Comparison Universe Equity Style Metric Universe, Wilshire Associates Incorporated, second
quarter 1996.

A comparison of the value style characteristics to the S&P 500 is also worth noting. The S&P 500 is selling at a higher price/earnings ratio and a higher price/book ratio than the value index. These differences can be understood when viewing the relative growth rate of earnings and return on equity figures. For both measures, the S&P figures are higher than the value index.

TABLE 3–5

Style Characteristics, Value Indexes

Market Indexes	P/E Ratio	Dividend Yield	5-Year EPS Growth Rate	ROE	Beta	P/B Ratio
Wilshire Large Value	12.50	3.90	9.90	17.78	0.90	2.20
Wilshire Mid Value	12.50	4.10	8.70	13.23	0.82	1.80
Wilshire Small Value	12.80	3.80	6.90	12.14	0.79	1.70
S&P 500	19.30	2.20	10.18	20.71	1.00	4.26
S&P Mid Cap	18.05	1.61	9.48	13.36	1.22	3.72

Source: Trust Universe Comparison Universe Equity Style Metric Universe, Wilshire Associates Incorporated, second quarter 1996.

Table 3–6 reports the historic performance of various value indexes for the 1978 to 1995 period. Column 1 represents the year, while columns 2, 3, and 4 report the total rates of return for the Large Value Index, Mid Cap Value Index, and Small Value Index, respectively. Column 5 displays the total rate of returns for the S&P 500 during this period.

The Small Value Index achieved an annualized total rate of return of 19.7 percent followed by the Mid Cap Value return of 18.4 percent, while the Large Value Index earned a return of 16.4 percent. The relative returns of these value indexes are consistent with the findings of other studies reporting superior total return performance of smaller capitalized companies.

Cyclical

A cyclical style is characterized by an investment process that focuses on changing economic and market climates. The investment manager will attempt to time the market by identifying firms whose earnings are sensitive to changes in the business cycle of the economy. Industries that exhibit sensitivity to changes in the busi-

TABLE 3-6

Value Index Performance 1978–1996

Year	Large Value Index (%)	Mid Cap Value Index (%)	Small Value Index (%)	S&P 500 (%)
1978	6.8	9.9	11.6	6.4
1979	20.8	25.7	22.3	18.5
1980	21.8	20.1	18.6	32.4
1981	10.3	17.7	25.0	−5.1
1982	15.8	30.5	35.8	21.1
1983	25.4	32.7	42.3	22.4
1984	19.1	18.3	22.1	6.1
1985	30.2	38.7	43.9	32.0
1986	22.2	23.2	23.5	18.6
1987	3.6	−5.9	−3.1	5.2
1988	22.8	23.0	22.4	16.8
1989	25.1	21.5	18.1	31.5
1990	−7.6	−16.4	−19.4	−3.2
1991	25.6	48.5	49.0	30.6
1992	14.4	22.6	29.2	7.7
1993	3.5	12.8	14.1	10.0
1994	−4.3	−2.7	−2.0	1.3
1995	43.5	37.2	29.8	37.5
1996 (2Q)	5.4	3.8	4.7	10.2
Annualized returns	16.4	18.4	19.7	15.5

Source: Equity Style Portfolios, Wilshire Asset Management, second quarter 1996.

ness cycle would be attractive to this type of investment manager and would include interest-sensitive sectors such as consumer durable goods and manufacturer's capital goods such as automobile, housing, banking, aircraft, and machine tools industries. Thus, this investment approach is characterized by "sector rotation," that is, by identifying how industries will perform during different segments of the business cycle and acting accordingly.

Market

Market timing was an investment style that was quite popular at one time. This requires the manager to identify the troughs and peaks of market cycles and change the asset allocations to coincide with these shifts. Market timers rely heavily on technical analysis to signal when to get in and out of the market. The underlying concept is that historical price and volume data convey information concerning future movements in the market. Such signaling devices (e.g., the Dow Theory and the Elliot Wave Theory) have been around for years. After several studies illustrated the perils of being out of the market, this timing approach lost much of its following.

Investment managers who are market timers seek to identify major shifts in markets and adjust their portfolios to reflect the anticipated change. Their approach to adjusting a portfolio involves changing the asset allocation as well as selecting the types of securities that are likely to benefit from the anticipated market environment. Prior to a major upswing in the market, these managers are expected to shift funds out of cash and equivalents and into stocks in anticipation of a bull market. Likewise, if these managers believe that the end of a bull market is at hand, they would likely reduce the amount of equities in the portfolio while simultaneously increasing the percentage of cash and equivalents. The remaining equities within the portfolio would likely consist of securities that possess relatively low market risk.

Sector

Sector managers concentrate their holdings in a one or a few industries. This type of management style is not often found in the mutual fund industry. It allows investors to concentrate a portion of their holdings in a portfolio specializing in a particular industry. By focusing on one industry group, the managers can develop industry expertise and target the top prospects within that sector. The disadvantage is the lack of diversification. However, the investor may be able to gain diversification by investing simultaneously in other sectors.

In addition to reporting the performance of the S&P 500 as a whole, the relative performances of the index's sectors are recited. The index is usually broken down into the following nine sectors: consumer nondurables, consumer durables, materials and services, capital goods, technology, energy, transportation, utilities, and finance. The performance results of each sector are then reported. Table 3–7 presents the S&P 500 performance by these sectors for the year ended June 30, 1996.

During this period, the total rate of return for the S&P 500 was 26.1 percent. As the table shows, four of the nine sectors outperformed the index. The capital goods component led the way with a total return of 37.4 percent during this time. Of the five sectors that

TABLE 3–7

S&P 500 Index Sector Performance, Year Ended June 30, 1996

Sector	Return (%)
Consumer nondurables	30.8
Consumer durables	18.2
Materials and services	12.8
Capital goods	37.4
Technology	20.0
Energy	26.5
Transportation	25.3
Utilities	21.9
Finance	34.5
S&P 500	26.1

Source: *Management Summary*, Trust Universe Comparison Service, Wilshire Associates Incorporated, second quarter 1996.

achieved lower returns than the index, materials and services was the poorest performer with a total return of 12.8 percent for the year ended June 30, 1996.

Contrarian

The contrarian investment style attempts to recognize stocks that are either overlooked by others or that fall out of favor. An excellent example of a contrarian investment is the health care industry, whose stocks dropped during the discussions of President Clinton's health reform initiative in 1993. Health care stocks such as Bristol Myers, Merck, and Johnson and Johnson were deeply discounted by Wall Street based on expectations of lower profit margins and investment returns. These stocks have since rebounded.

Contrarians often seek out securities that have a small following and little if any institutional interest. Low P/E multiple companies, with their price selling near book value, would be candidates for contrarian investors. Companies with disappointing earnings or firms that are potential turnaround candidates would also fall within this category.

International Investing

A discussion of investment strategies would be incomplete without considering foreign investing. With the recent advances in foreign capital markets and heightened growth prospects around the globe, professional investors are identifying new investment opportunities. The improved opportunities to hedge in the foreign exchange arena greatly reduce the foreign exchange risk of foreign investing.

Investments can be made on a global, regional, or country basis. Furthermore, professional managers invest indirectly through mutual funds or directly by purchasing the securities of individual firms. Passive investing indexes can also be utilized by investment managers. Broadly speaking, professional managers classify international markets as either developed or emerging. Developed markets represent the industrialized countries. Emerging markets are made up of economies in various stages of development.

Table 3–8 reports the annualized total returns of the 20 developed markets during the 1989 to 1995 period. As shown in the table, the highest annualized rate of return was 21.8 percent achieved by

TABLE 3—8

Developed Markets, 1989–1995
Annualized Total Returns (percentages)

Country	Total Return (U.S.$)
Australia	7.622
Austria	9.654
Belgium	7.395
Canada	4.340
Denmark	7.278
Finland	−4.973
France	6.706
Germany	9.634
Hong Kong	21.800
Ireland	16.670
Italy	−1.977
Japan	−2.735
Netherlands	10.497
New Zealand	9.946
Norway	10.350
Singapore	17.506
Spain	4.415
Sweden	−0.152
Switzerland	16.543
United Kingdom	9.420

Source: Wilshire Associates.

Hong Kong. The lowest return was recorded by Finland (–4.973 percent).

Table 3–9 reports the performance of emerging markets over the same period. During this period Chile achieved an annualized total return of 39.350 percent, the highest of any emerging nation. Impressive returns were also achieved by other emerging nations during this period. Columbia and the Philippines recorded annual-

TABLE 3–9

Emerging Markets, 1989–1995
Annualized Total Returns (percentages)

Country	Total Return (U.S.)
Argentina	27.063
Brazil	–9.209
Chile	39.350
Colombia	34.824
Greece	13.982
India	9.967
Jordan	9.146
Korea	–0.867
Malaysia	20.705
Mexico	16.754
Nigeria	14.349
Pakistan	9.131
Philippines	33.454
Portugal	–0.146
South Africa	18.198
Taiwan	–3.928
Thailand	19.124
Turkey	18.638
Venezuela	–3.156
Zimbabwe	4.976

Source: Wilshire Associates.

ized returns of 34.8 percent and 33.4 percent, respectively, during the 1989 to 1995 period. However, several emerging nations posted negative returns. For example, Brazil's total return for this period was –9.21 percent.

FIXED-INCOME MANAGERS' APPROACHES

As in the case of equities where there are several approaches to managing monies, fixed-income professionals can utilize a variety of techniques in managing their investment portfolios. They can invest in U.S. Treasury issues, U.S. government agency issues, corporate bonds, publicly traded mortgages, mortgage-backed securities, municipal bonds, and preferred and convertible stocks. Each of these fixed-income investment alternatives has an impact on the portfolio's return and risk characteristics. In addition there are several decisions that a fixed-income manager faces. Chapter 9 discusses a variety of styles used by professionals. In the section below, we touch upon two factors that influence performance of the fixed-income portfolio: quality considerations and maturity. These and other issues will be more fully developed later.

Quality Considerations

The long-term performance of selected fixed-income securities is presented in Table 3–10. Column 1 represents the investment category, while columns 2 and 3 report the geometric and arithmetic means, respectively. Column 4 reports the standard deviation of each investment's return.

As one would suspect, long-term corporate bonds provided the highest return over the 1926 to 1995 period. Corporate bonds expose investors to credit risk or default risk. Thus, this premium over long-term government bonds is expected since this risk is not faced by holders of government bonds. In an effort to achieve higher returns, managers can choose lower quality issues. In doing so, the manager exposes the portfolio to higher risks. We will cover this in more depth in Chapter 9.

TABLE 3-10

Annual Total Returns,1926–1995

Investment Category	Geometric Mean (%)	Arithmetic Mean (%)	Standard Deviation (%)
Long-term corporate bonds	5.7	6.0	8.7
Long-term government bonds	5.2	5.5	9.2
U.S. Treasury bills	3.7	3.8	3.3
Inflation	3.1	3.2	4.6

Source: © Computed using data from *Stocks, Bonds, Bills and Inflation, 1996 Yearbook,*™ Ibbotson Associates, Chicago
(annually updates work by Roger G. Ibbotson and Rex Sinquefield). Used with permission. All rights reserved.

Maturity Considerations

In addition to the credit risk described earlier, the returns on fixed-income securities are subject to interest rate risk. Bond values and interest rates move inversely. Interest rate risk refers to the loss of market value due to increases in market interest rates. As a general rule, fixed-income securities with longer maturities have greater interest rate risk than securities with shorter maturities. Normally, yield curves are upward sloping, providing higher returns with longer maturities.

Often managers adjust the maturity of the fixed-income portfolio in anticipation of changes in overall interest rates. If interest rates are expected to rise, the managers shorten the fixed-income securities' maturities to minimize losses in value. If, on the other hand, rates are expected to fall, managers increase the maturities of the fixed-income securities in order to achieve capital gains.

S U M M A R Y

Investment sponsors are generally interested in growth and/or current income. In developing an investment strategy to assist investors in achieving their goals, professional managers must understand their clients' objectives, risk tolerance levels, investment time horizons, and tax status. Each of these elements must be explicitly considered as part of the investment process.

Professional managers can take either a passive or active approach when managing their sponsor's funds. Using a passive approach, the manager creates a portfolio that contains the same attributes as the index he is replicating. If successful, the portfolio will achieve investment results identical to the underlying index.

Active managers strive to beat the market rather than merely match it. To accomplish this, professionals use various approaches and tactics. For equity managers, these include the following: capitalization, growth, value, cyclical, market, sector, and contrarian investing styles. Managers will also invest within their home country or internationally. For the latter type of investing, one can choose an array of investment vehicles in foreign countries, regions, or on a global basis.

Fixed-income managers also have choices in how they are to meet their clients' needs. They can invest in U.S. Treasury instruments, U.S. government agency bonds, corporate bonds, mortgage-backed securities, publicly traded mortgages, municipal bonds, and preferred stock. Each of these has its advantages and disadvantages.

CHAPTER 4

Alternative Investment Vehicles

INTRODUCTION

Investment committees occasionally extend the types of permissible investment vehicles that the portfolio managers they employee can select beyond the traditional listing of common stocks, fixed-income instruments, and cash securities. Allocating part of the fund's portfolio to alternative investment vehicles may enhance its expected return and risk characteristics. Investment vehicles in addition to stocks, bonds, and cash and equivalents may provide the investment committee with such things as a wider choice and better matching of maturities, preferred cash flow streams, greater diversification, lower transactions costs, and higher expected yields.

Deciding whether to include alternative investment vehicles in the range of permissible investments should be based on two factors: (1) the investment objectives the committee has established for the fund, and the consistency of the return and risk properties of alternative investment vehicles with the fund's investment objectives, and (2) the investment committee's understanding of the characteristics of alternative investment vehicles. Without such an understanding, the committee cannot make informed decisions as to the utility of including these vehicles in the portfolio.

Several alternative investment vehicles are discussed in this chapter. They include hybrid securities, derivative contracts, real estate, international investments, commodities, and so-called collectibles. The chapter describes the important features of each vehicle.

HYBRID SECURITIES

Hybrid securities are those issued by firms that contain features of debt and equity instruments. The most common types of hybrid securities are convertible bonds, convertible preferred stock, and warrants that may be issued in conjunction with either bonds or stock.

Convertible Securities

Convertible securities provide the owner with the right to convert or trade the security into a specified number of shares of common stock of the issuing company. Convertible bonds give to their owners the right to exchange the bonds for a fixed number of shares of common stock anytime up to and including the maturity date of the bond. Convertible preferred stock provides a similar option to its owners except that the preferred stock does not have a specified maturity date. Warrants provide the owner the right, but not the obligation, to purchase a fixed number of shares of common stock of the issuing company directly from the company at a predetermined price for a specified period of time.

Hybrid securities appear to be issued most often by relatively high-risk corporations.[1] By issuing bonds with equity enhancements, bondholders may receive some protection from the high risk. If the company prospers, then the bondholders will benefit from the risk they have taken. Also, since the bondholders will have some prospective equity interest in the company, conflicts between bondholders and stockholders may be diminished.

Investment committees should be cognizant of several features of convertible securities. The *conversion ratio* specifies the number of shares of common stock that will be received for a convertible bond. For example, a convertible bond with a conversion ratio of 20 allows its owner to convert a bond with a par value of $1,000 into 20 shares of common stock. Once the conversion ratio has been set, then the *conversion price* is the ratio of the bond's par value to its conversion ratio. Extending our example, the $1,000 par value bond with a conversion ratio of 20 would have a conversion price of $50. Essentially, the conversion price is the price at which the bondholder can purchase the company's stock by giving up the bond. If the current market value of the bond is less than the market price of the company's stock multiplied by its conversion ratio, then converting the bond may be profitable. For example, suppose the current market value of the $1,000 par value bond was $900, and the company's stock was selling for $55 per share; by giving up a bond currently worth $900 the investor would receive stock worth ($55 x 20) = $1,100. In this example, as long as the stock was worth more than $45 per share, it would be profitable to convert the bonds. Issuers of convertible bonds are keenly aware of the likelihood of the bonds being converted to stock; therefore, when issuing convertible bonds, they typically set the conversion ratio so that the conversion price is at a considerable premium to the company's current stock price.

The value of a convertible bond has three components: the pure bond value, the conversion value, and its option value. The *pure bond value* is the value of the convertible bond as only a bond. This value, like most bond values, depends on the risk of the issuer and the general level of interest rates. If the company's stock price is very low relative to its conversion price, which would make conversion highly unlikely, then the pure bond value would set a lower limit on the value of the convertible bond.

If the bond is to be immediately converted into common stock, it would be worth its conversion ratio multiplied by the current stock price. This is the bond's *conversion value*. The conversion value sets a second, lower limit on the bond's value. As the issuing company's stock price rises, which makes conversion more likely, the bond will not sell for less than its conversion value. Otherwise, investors could buy the bond, immediately convert it to common stock at the conversion value, and then sell the stock at the higher price.

There is also an option value component to the value of a convertible bond. This *option value* arises because the owner of the convertible bond has the choice to either continue to hold the bond or convert it to common stock. These choices have value and generally result in the value of a convertible bond being greater than the pure bond value and conversion value.

Warrants

Warrants are similar to call options in that they give the owner the right, but not the obligation, to purchase shares of common stock at a predetermined price for a specified period of time. Moreover, like options, warrants are usually protected against dividends and stock splits. However, there are important differences between warrants and options. Warrants, when exercised, require the firm to issue additional shares of stock, thereby increasing the total number of shares outstanding. The firm also receives the proceeds from the exercise of the warrants. Options in contrast, do not originate with the firm and, therefore, do not result in an increase in the number of shares of stock outstanding and in additional capital for the firm when exercised. Additionally, warrants are often issued in conjunction with bonds and are used as so-called equity kickers. Generally, the warrants can be detached or stripped from the bonds after issue and sold separately.

Warrants are valued in a similar fashion to call options, with adjustment for the change in the number of shares outstanding after their exercise. Because of this adjustment, however, the gain on a warrant will be less than a gain on an identical call option of a firm without warrants.

Finally, it should be noted that convertible securities and warrants affect reported accounting statements. Because they result in a greater number of shares of stock, earnings are spread over more shares, thereby reducing reported earnings per share. Accounting conventions require firms with significant amounts of hybrid securities to report their financial results on a primary (unadjusted) and fully diluted (adjusted) basis.

DERIVATIVE CONTRACTS

A *derivative contract* is a contract whose value is derived from and dependent upon the value of an underlying asset or index of assets. Derivative contracts exist for a number of commodities, such as soybean and crude oil futures, as well as for a growing number of financial securities. Our discussion focuses only on financial derivative contracts.

In spite of a number of relatively recent, highly publicized losses associated with the use of financial derivative contracts, their use and importance have increased markedly in the last several years. Table 4–1 presents information on the size and composition of the market for financial derivatives.

TABLE 4–1

Financial Derivatives—Market Size and Composition
Notional Principal Outstanding (Billions of Dollars)

	1989	1990	1991	1992	1993	1994
Over-the-Counter Instruments	2,966	3,450	4,449	5,346	8,475	10,207
Interest rate swaps	1,503	2,312	3,065	3,851	6,177	N/A
Currency swaps	449	578	807	860	900	N/A
Other OTC instruments	514	561	577	635	1,398	N/A
Exchange Traded Instruments	1,767	2,290	3,519	4,633	7,761	8,838
Interest rate futures	1,201	1,455	2,157	2,913	4,943	5,757
Interest rate options	1,388	600	1,073	1,315	2,362	2,623
Currency futures	16	17	18	25	32	33
Currency options	50	57	63	71	75	55
Stock index futures	41	69	76	80	110	128
Stock index options	71	94	133	159	238	242

Source: Stephen O. Morrell, "Trends in the Market for Financial Derivatives," *Derivatives Risk Management Service* 1, no. 1, (February 1996).

Many portfolio managers routinely utilize derivatives in the management of their client's funds. Investment committees should, therefore, clearly articulate an appropriate policy regarding their use. Some committees may decide that such contracts are beyond the scope of the fund's investment philosophy, while others may conclude that derivatives are a highly effective, low-cost means of managing risk. In either event, an informed decision requires a basic understanding of the characteristics of derivative contracts.

Uses of Derivative Contracts

Derivatives are used for one of two fundamental purposes: speculation and risk management or hedging. *Speculation* refers to the purchase or sale of financial assets on the basis of information about expected price movements that is considered to be superior to that possessed by other market participants. For example, an investor who thinks that he or she has a superior ability to forecast equity price changes might employ stock index futures contracts to take advantage of his or her alleged skill. Beyond this type of investor, we assume that investment committees that include derivatives as permissible investments restrict their use to risk management purposes.

Risk management, or *hedging,* refers to the process of reducing a portfolio's risk. Properly structured, executed, and monitored derivative contracts can be used to reduce this risk by helping to reduce the variability of returns, which is accomplished by using derivative contracts to offset changes in either equity prices, interest rates, or foreign exchange rates. The idea is that the value of the derivative contract will move in the opposite direction from that of the underlying portfolio or security being hedged. Consequently, the change in the value of the derivative contracts will offset the change in the value of the investments being hedged. As a result, the returns on the portfolio will be less volatile than without the use of a hedging strategy.

Employing derivative contracts as part of a risk management strategy also entails some risks. Three such risks are worth noting. First, it may not be possible to completely or perfectly hedge the entire portfolio using derivative contracts. While the range of derivative contracts continues to expand at a brisk pace, the currently available derivative contracts do not perfectly correspond to all underlying financial securities. For example, interest rate futures contracts do not exist on corporate bonds rated Baa. A portfolio manager seeking to hedge the value of a portfolio of such Baa bonds against adverse price changes would be required to use a futures contract whose price movements were expected to be highly correlated with the Baa bonds. This cross-hedge may not provide complete protection against interest rate changes.

The second risk faced by users of derivative contracts is basis risk. *Basis* refers to the price spread between the value of the derivative contract and the current or spot value of the financial asset being hedged. Unexpected variations in this spread can result in an imperfect hedge.

The third type of risk derivative users may face is counterparty or default risk. *Counterparty risk* exists when there is some positive likelihood that the opposite party in the derivatives arrangement—for example, the seller of an equity option—may not execute their contractually stipulated part of the agreement. A variety of methods exist for reducing counterparty risk in derivative contracts. Clearinghouse organizations, which are comprised of member firms of exchanges on which derivative contracts are traded, may position themselves between buyers and sellers of futures and option contracts. Credit enhancements may be used to reduce default risk in interest rate swaps.

Types of Derivative Contracts

There are four basic types of derivative contracts: forward contracts, futures contracts, option contracts, and swap contracts. Variations on these basic contract types, such as options-on-futures and options-on-swaps, have been developed as well as new types of derivatives, such as credit derivatives. All four basic contracts exist for equities, fixed-income securities, and foreign exchange rates. Generic definitions of each contract type are given in the following paragraphs.

Forward Contract
A *forward contract* calls for the future delivery or receipt of a specified amount of a specified financial asset at a price agreed upon today.

Futures Contract
The definition of a futures contract is the same as that for a forward contract. However, they differ in that *futures contracts* are traded on organized futures exchanges, such as the Chicago Board of Trade. The exchange specifies the terms of the futures contract, such as its dollar size, maturity, and margin requirements, as well as its trading characteristics, such as limits on daily price changes and marking-to-market or daily settlements. Futures contracts can thus be viewed as standardized derivatives, while forward contracts are customized to suit the particular needs of their users.

Option Contract
Options contracts provide the holder with the right, but not the obligation, to purchase (call option) or sell (put option) a specified amount of a specified financial asset, at a predetermined price, within a specified period of time.

Swap Contract
A *swap contract* exists when parties agree to exchange cash flow streams for a specified period of time.

REAL ESTATE INVESTMENT VEHICLES

Investment committees considering real estate as a permissible investment vehicle for their plans have several alternative methods of making such investments. Committees may approve direct investments through which the portfolio managers either purchase land, commercial, and/or residential properties or lend directly to others for the purchase of real estate. Relatedly, a committee may permit investment in a real estate partnership as a limited partner.

Alternatively, portfolio managers may be permitted to purchase equity and debt securities of companies whose assets include substantial real estate holdings or whose value is significantly influenced by activity in real estate markets.

Finally, portfolio managers may be permitted to invest the fund's assets in shares of a *real estate investment trust* (REIT). REITs are a type of closed-end mutual fund. Closed-end funds issue a limited number of shares. The proceeds from the initial or original sale of these shares are then used to finance the REIT's holdings of real estate assets. Shares in the REIT are subsequently listed and traded on either organized or over-the-counter securities markets, providing a degree of liquidity for the investor. As is the case with all mutual funds, REITs may provide a way to lower the transaction costs of either investing in real estate or achieving diversification with it.

REITs are typically organized as either equity or mortgage REITs or as a combination of the two. As the term implies, an *equity REIT* holds ownership in real estate. Revenues are generated via the income from the real estate, usually in the form of rent. *Mortgage REITs* act as lenders and finance the acquisition of properties, the construction of facilities, or the longer term financing of projects. As lenders, mortgage REITs produce income from the interest received on the mortgages they hold. REITs also hold a special tax status based on the Real Estate Investment Trust Act of 1960, which authorized their foundation.[2] As long as certain stringent requirements are met, REITs are not subject to corporate taxes on their net income. A REIT's net income is, therefore, largely distributed to shareholders. This provision eliminates so-called double taxation, whereby corporate earnings are taxed first at the corporate tax rate and then at the individual tax rate for any dividends distributed to shareholders.

REITs generate returns for their investors via the net income they distribute to shareholders (1) by any capital appreciation in the value of the underlying assets they own (real estate and real estate mortgages) and (2) by management improvements that lead to a faster growth of net income.

The returns on REITs are also subject to a variety of risks, as explored more thoroughly in Chapters 6 and 9. Returns may be adversely affected by deteriorating economic and market conditions or by the prospects of higher risk-adjusted returns in other sectors of the economy. Moreover, the investment management of a specific REIT may be a source of risk, especially in a nondiversified portfolio. Additionally, committees considering REITs as an investment vehicle should monitor potential changes in the tax code that might jeopardize their special tax status. Finally, mortgage REITs are subject to risks associated with other fixed-income type securities, such as default, interest rate, reinvestment, and prepayment risks.

Table 4–2 presents data on REIT returns from 1972 through 1995. Data are depicted for returns by type of REIT and as a composite. A simple inspection of the data reveals several interesting points. First, all REITs have produced an annual average return of almost 11.50 percent from 1972 to 1995. Second, mortgage REITs have exhibited the greatest volatility or risk during this period. The range of returns on mortgage REITs has been from a low of about 45 percent in 1974 to a staggering high of about 63 percent in 1995. In contrast, the range of returns for equity and hybrid REITs, while also quite dispersed, has been less than that for mortgage REITs.

INTERNATIONAL INVESTMENT VEHICLES

U.S. securities are only a relatively small portion of the total investment universe. Securities of foreign companies and countries represent a large and increasing share of the total universe. The Global Finance World Market Index provides an illustration. This index, which includes government and corporate debt, equities, and commodities worldwide, has a market capitalization of almost $22 tril-

TABLE 4-2

Annual Total Returns—REITs, 1972–1995

Year	Equity (%)	Mortgage (%)	Hybrid (%)	Composite (%)
1972	8.01	12.17	11.41	11.19
1973	−16.52	−36.26	−23.37	−27.22
1974	−21.40	−45.32	−52.22	−42.23
1975	19.30	40.79	49.92	36.34
1976	47.59	51.71	48.19	48.97
1977	22.42	17.82	17.44	19.08
1978	10.34	−9.97	−7.29	−1.64
1979	35.86	16.56	33.81	30.53
1980	24.37	16.80	42.46	28.02
1981	6.00	7.07	12.23	8.58
1982	21.60	48.64	29.56	31.64
1983	30.64	16.90	29.90	25.47
1984	20.93	7.26	17.25	14.82
1985	19.10	−5.20	4.32	5.92
1986	19.16	19.21	19.75	19.18
1987	−3.64	−15.57	−17.58	−10.07
1988	13.49	7.30	6.80	11.38
1989	8.84	−15.90	−12.14	−1.81
1990	−15.35	18.37	−28.21	−17.35
1991	35.70	31.83	39.16	35.56
1992	14.59	1.92	16.59	12.18
1993	19.65	14.55	21.15	18.55
1994	3.17	−24.30	4.00	0.81
1995	15.27	63.42	22.88	18.31

Source: National Association of Real Estate Trusts.

lion. U.S. securities comprise about 55 percent, or roughly $12 trillion of this total. The picture is even more dramatic when only the global equity markets are considered. In 1984, U.S. equities accounted for more than 50 percent of the total world equity market capitalization of approximately $7.0 trillion dollars. By 1994, when world equity market capitalization had increased to some $12.6 trillion, the percent represented by U.S. equities had dropped to about 35 percent.

The striking advance in world market capitalization is a reflection of fundamental changes in the global economy. Dramatic economic and political transformations are occuring in China, Latin America, India, parts of Africa, and the former Soviet Union. Reductions in trade barriers are stimulating international commerce and economic growth throughout the world. External sources of capital, especially in the so-called emerging markets, are required to fuel the necessary investments to sustain this growth.

International securities offer the potential for investment plan committees and the portfolio managers they select to enhance returns and reduce portfolio risk by achieving greater diversification. At the same time, additional risk may be present when investing in international securities. Table 4–3 presents data on the return and risks for two groups of international stocks and, for comparison purposes, the return and risks for U.S. stocks.

The diversification or risk-reducing benefits of investing in international securities arise because the cycles of returns in

TABLE 4-3

International and U.S. Stock Returns and Risk (Percent per Year, Compounded Annually, US$)

Time Period	Index	Return	Risk
1970–1995	EAFE*	9.4	11.60
1970–1995	S&P 500	11.9	16.60
1989–1995	Emerging markets	9.4	13.10
1989–1995	Small stocks	14.5	20.00

*EAFE; Europe, Australia, and the Far East.

Source: © Computed using data from, *Stocks, Bonds, Bills, and Inflation, 1996 Yearbook,*™ Ibbottson Associates, Chicago (annually updates work by Roger G. Ibbotson and Rex Sinquefield). Used with permission. All rights reserved.

many of these markets are not highly correlated with the cycle of returns in U.S. markets. As explained more completely in Chapter 6, portfolio risk is reduced by including in the portfolio securities whose returns ideally move in the opposite direction or, in the absence of this ideal, securities whose returns move together weakly.

Historically, the returns on foreign equities have not moved closely in tandem with U.S. stocks. Table 4–4 presents data on the correlations of returns among several indexes of U.S. securities and several indexes of international securities. The correlations of returns of international securities returns with those on U.S. securities are, generally, considerably less than the correlations of returns among only U.S. securities.

In light of the relatively low correlation of returns among U.S. and international securities, risk can likely be reduced by including foreign securities in a portfolio. Chart 4–1 presents an efficient frontier, which is a graph representing a set of portfolios that provide the highest return for a given level of risk. The chart is generated for a portfolio of a fixed dollar size by changing the proportions or percentages invested in U.S. securities, as represented by the S&P 500 index, and foreign securities, as represented by the Europe, Australia, and Far East (EAFE) index. As varying percentages are invested in the stocks represented by the S&P 500 and EAFE (in the chart, changes of 10 percentage points) the returns and risks for each of these portfolios are computed for the period from 1975 to 1994.

To clearly see the benefits from international investing, look first at the portfolio that has 100 percent invested in U.S. stocks. Its return was slightly more than 14.5 percent per year, and its risk was marginally greater than 17 percent per year. Compare this portfolio with the returns and risks on portfolios that included increasing percentages of foreign stocks, up to the one with 40 percent invested in U.S. stocks and 60 percent invested abroad. All of these portfolios have higher returns *and* less risk than a portfolio comprised of 100 percent U.S. equities.

TABLE 4-4

Correlations of Returns Among U.S. and International Securities

	S&P 500	R2000	MSEAFE	MSEMF	LBLTGCB	SBWGB
Standard & Poor 500 U.S. Large Cap Equity Index		0.8624	0.4726	0.3782	0.4087	0.0412
Russell 2000 U.S. Small Cap Equity Index	0.8624		0.4226	0.4825	0.2601	0.1718
Morgan Stanley EAFE International Equity Index	0.4726	0.4226		0.3899	0.2575	0.5504
Morgan Stanley Emerging Market (Free) Equity Index	0.3782	0.4825	0.3899		0.0574	0.0101
Lehman Brothers Long-term U.S. Government/Corporate Index	0.4087	0.2601	0.2575	0.0574		0.2867
Salomon Brothers Non-U.S. World Government Bond Index	0.0412	0.1718	0.5504	0.0101	0.2867	

	Inception
Standard & Poor 500 U.S. Large Cap Equity Index	12/25
Russell 2000 U.S. Small Cap Equity Index	12/78
Morgan Stanley EAFE International Equity Index	12/69
Morgan Stanley Emerging Market (Free) Equity Index	12/87
Lehman Brothers Long-Term U.S. Government/Corporate Index	12/72
Salomon Brothers Non-U.S. World Government Bond Index	12/84

Correlation coefficients calculated using monthly returns. Time periods based on index inception. Example: MSEAFE returns begin 12/69, and R000 begins 12/78. Therefore, correlation between the two was calculated utilizing monthly returns for the time period 12/78 through 12/95.

Source: Smith Barney Inc.

CHART 4-1

Allocations to U.S. Equities and International Equities
20-Year Period Ending December 31, 1994

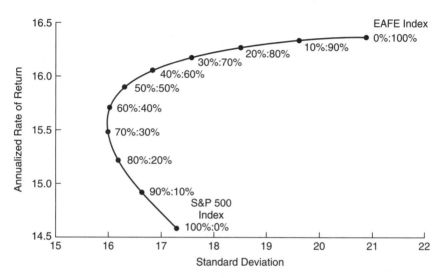

There are several alternative means of investing in foreign securities. American Depository Receipts (ADRs) are claims to shares
of foreign stocks. These claims are listed and traded on U.S. stock
exchanges. Investors can also purchase securities directly in the financial markets of other countries. Stock exchanges exist in more
than 60 countries, from Jamaica to New Zealand, and new exchanges are being formed at a rapid pace. The rules, regulations,
and operations of foreign stock exchanges, however, may be significantly different than those of U.S. exchanges.

In addition to the avenues just outlined, there is a growing
number and variety of mutual funds for international investing.
There are funds that invest in the securities of a single country,
called *country funds,* as well as funds that invest in a particular re-
gion of the world, such as Latin America. Funds also exist that
mimic the returns and risk on global market indexes such as the
EAFE or the Morgan Stanley Capital International Index.

International investors face a number of new risks not confronted when they invest in U.S. markets. They face *economic* or *market risk* specific to the country or countries in which they have invested. This is the risk that an unexpected change in country-specific economic conditions can adversely affect market returns. Relatedly, they may also face *political risk* owing to unanticipated changes in governments and government policies, which could result in such things as the nationalization of an industry, or other political changes that adversely alter the investment climate. Financial markets in emerging market economies, moreover, may not be highly capitalized or extremely liquid. Additionally, requirements regarding public company disclosure and reporting of relevant financial and business information may be less stringent in overseas markets.

International investors also confront *exchange rate* or *currency risk*. This is the risk that the total return from international investing will be different than that expected because of unforeseen changes in the exchange rate between the U.S. dollar and the foreign currency in which the investments were made. That is, the dollar return from an international investment depends on two factors: the returns produced on the investment, which are denominated in the foreign currency in which they were made, and any exchange rate changes between the U.S. dollar and the foreign currency.

Should the U.S. dollar appreciate in value relative to the foreign currency, then each unit of the foreign currency can be exchanged for fewer dollars. The total return on the investment will decline as a consequence. In contrast, should the dollar decline in value relative to the foreign currency, then the total return on the foreign investment will be greater as a result.

In a highly informative book, Jeremy Siegel presents estimates of the incremental risk to international investing associated with exchange rate changes.[3] His data cover the period from 1970 through 1992. He estimates that for a collection or index of countries, exchange rate risk increases overall risk by about 3.30 percentage points, or by approximately 16 percent.

Portfolio managers frequently hedge the exchange rate risk in the portfolios they manage. The purpose of the hedge is to lock in returns denominated in dollars. Portfolio managers generally use one of the derivative contracts previously discussed, particularly foreign exchange rate forward contracts, to hedge foreign exchange rate risk.

COMMODITIES AND COLLECTIBLES

Commodities and so-called collectibles are the final investment class that investment committees might consider as permissible investment vehicles. *Commodities* refers to a range of physical assets such as precious metals (gold, silver, etc.), base metals (copper, aluminium, etc.), and energy-related products (crude oil, natural gas, etc.). *Collectibles* include art, antiques, memorabilia, and the like. These assets can be purchased directly on spot markets or, in the case of many commodities on futures markets, as well as indirectly via the purchase of the financial assets of companies that produce, process, and distribute them.

The motivation for considering commodities and collectibles as potential investment vehicles is that their return/risk characteristics might improve overall portforlio performance. Improved portfolio performance may be achieved if commodities and collectibles enhance portfolio diversification while providing the necessary liquidity to buy or sell them at reasonable transaction costs. The lack of liquidity can be particularly troublesome in the case of collectibles. Continuous trading may not be present for certain types of collectibles, and the markets in which buying and selling occur might have small numbers of either buyers or sellers. Information on market conditions may also be difficult to obtain, and fees and commissions to brokers and dealers, as well as storage and insurance costs, might be high.

Information on the prospective diversification benefits from investing in commodities can be seen from an index of commodity futures prices developed by J.P. Morgan and Company. The J.P.

TABLE 4–5

Historical Correlations of Returns

Index	Return (%)
U.S. Consumer Price Index	+ 41
U.S. Industrial Production Index	+35
30-Year U.S. Treasury Bond Index	−51
J.P. Morgan U.S. Bond Index	−36
S&P 500	−41
Unexpected U.S. Producer Price Index	+74
IFC Emerging Market Stock Index (1985)	−17

Source: J.P. Morgan and Company

Morgan Commodity Index (JPMCI) is a total return index composed of an optimized weighting of industrial commodities (energy and base and precious metals) futures prices. The JPMCI represents diversified, liquid, investible commodities traded on organized futures exchanges. Table 4–5 presents the correlation of returns on the JPMCI with a variety of economic and financial market indicators based on quarterly data for 1984 through 1994.

The data in the table suggest that, for the period depicted, commodities have provided returns that are positively correlated with inflation and inflation surprises and negatively correlated with returns on financial assets.

S U M M A R Y

Investments such as convertible securities, warrants, derivative contracts, international securities, real estate, and commodities may provide the investment committee with opportunities to enhance returns and improve risk management. Investment committees need an understanding of the basic features of these alternative investments to determine how well such investments can assist the fund to meet its return objectives. As markets for the given types of investment vehicles become even more liquid and efficient, greater consideration of them when determining permissible investments is warranted.

REFERENCES

1. Ross, Westerfield, and Jaffe provide an excellent discussion of the reasons companies issue securities with attached warrants and convertible features. For more detail, see Ross, Stephen A.; and Randolph W. Westerfield; and Jeffrey Jaffe. *Corporate Finance,* 4th ed. Burr Ridge, IL: Richard D. Irwin, 1996, pp. 606–25.
2. For a fuller treatment of the tax status of REITs, see Haight, G.T. and D.A. Ford. *REITs* (Chicago: Probus Publishing, 1987).
3. Siegel, Jeremy J., *Stocks for the Long Run: A Guide to Selecting Markets for Long-Term Growth.* (Burr Ridge, IL: Richard D. Irwin, 1994), p. 124.

CHAPTER 5

Return Measures

INTRODUCTION

Traditionally, individuals responsible for monitoring investment performance have faced difficulties in accurately measuring the returns achieved by funds and in evaluating the performance of the fund's manager. These difficulties were even more bothersome when the performance results of one fund manager were compared with those of other managers. Often the performance measures of the fund managers and the comparison groups were based on divergent calculation methodologies, which prevented meaningful comparisons.

Eventually, investment professionals adopted the dollar-weighted rate of return or, as it is often referred to, the internal rate of return as a uniform measure of investment performance. While the movement toward uniformity was indeed welcome, this measure had significant weaknesses. The actual performance results were distorted when the fund experienced inflows (contributions) and/or outflows (withdrawals) at any time during the measurement period. In these instances, investment performance was systematically overstated or understated, depending on the nature of the flows (i.e., inflows or outflows), and dynamics of the underlying markets.

DOLLAR-WEIGHTED RATE OF RETURN

One of the most commonly used methods for determining a portfolio's performance results is the *dollar-weighted rate of return,* which calculates the percentage increase or decrease in the market value of a portfolio for a given measurement period. This return measure simply calculates the percentage of increase or decrease that the fund has experienced over a given investment horizon. This dollar-weighted rate of return (DWRR) is calculated as follows:

$$DWRR = \frac{(MV_1 - MV_0)}{MV_0}$$

DWRR = Dollar Weighted Rate of Return

MV_1 = the market value of the fund at the end of the measurement period

MV_0 = the market value of the fund at the beginning of the measurement period

The calculation of return using this formula is straightforward. Assume that at the beginning of an investment period, a fund had a market value of $1,000,000. At the end of that same investment period, the market value of the fund was $1,210,000. The dollar-weighted rate of return (i) would be calculated as follows:

$$i = \frac{(\$1,210,000 - \$1,000,000)}{\$1,000,000}$$

$$= \frac{\$210,000}{\$1,000,000}$$

$$= 21\%$$

The dollar-weighted rate of return would be 21 percent. This rate of return appears to be a proper indicator of performance. In fact, the fund's assets increased from the initial value of $1,000,000 to $1,210,000, or by 21 percent over the measurement period. Thus, in this instance the dollar-weighted rate of return correctly reflected the fund's performance.

The dollar-weighted rate of return can also be calculated as the *internal rate of return* that equates the present value of the portfolio at the end of the period to its value at the beginning of the period. In terms of notation,

$$MV_0 = MV_1 / (1 + DWRR)^1$$

This manner of using the dollar-weighted rate of return also provides an estimate of the average return on a portfolio over longer time periods by taking the beginning value of the portfolio, adding to this the present value of expenditures for new securities, and equating this total to the present value of proceeds from the sale of securities plus the present value of any dividends or interest received.

Impact of Cash Withdrawals on Return

The dollar-weighted rate of return measure, while simple to calculate, is not a suitable method for calculating performance in most cases. This is especially true when the amount of funds available for investing changes during the measurement period. For funds that either disburse monies or receive cash contributions, the dollar-weighted rate of return will produce misleading results. To illustrate the impact that withdrawals have on investment returns using the dollar-weighted rate of return, consider two index funds, both fully invested in the S&P 500 at the beginning of an investment period. Assume that the funds remain fully invested in the S&P 500 throughout the period. However, Fund B is required to disburse $50,000 midway through the measurement period. Table 5–1 presents key data for both funds.

Using the information from Table 5–1, the dollar-weighted rate of return can be calculated for both funds:

For Fund A,

$$i = \frac{(\$1,210,000 - \$1,000,000)}{\$1,000,000}$$

TABLE 5-1

Comparison of Investment Performance Dollar-Weighted Rate of Return Measure, Cash Withdrawal Scenario

Date	S&P 500	Fund A Market Value (No Withdrawal)	Fund B Market Value Prior to Withdrawal	Market Value After Withdrawal
1/1	500	$1,000,000	$1,000,000	
7/1	550	1,100,000	1,100,000	1,050,000*
12/31	605	1,210,000		1,155,000

*Reflects $50,000 withdrawal on July 1 from Fund B.

$$= \frac{\$210,000}{\$1,000,000}$$

$$= 21\%$$

For Fund B,

$$i = \frac{(\$1,155,000 - \$1,000,000)}{\$1,000,000}$$

$$= \frac{\$155,000}{\$1,000,000}$$

$$= 11.5\%$$

Since both fund managers pursued the identical investment strategy (i.e., invested in the S&P 500), their investment performance results should be the same. Yet, using the dollar-weighted rate of return method, Fund A's performance was 21 percent, while Fund B's was 11.5 percent. This difference in returns is due to the cash withdrawal from Fund B. This withdrawal was not within the control of the fund manager, and, therefore, his performance results should be not influenced by it.

Impact of Cash Contributions on Return

Table 5–2 reports the investment performance of the two funds, this time assuming Fund B receives contributions of $50,000 midway through the measurement period. Table 5–2 presents key data for both funds.

Fund A's performance, as measured by the dollar-weighted rate of return, does not change. The calculation of Fund B's return is as follows:

$$i = \frac{(\$1,265,000 - \$1,000,000)}{\$1,000,000}$$

$$= \frac{\$265,000}{\$1,000,000}$$

$$= 26.5\%$$

Fund B's $50,000 cash contribution results in a 26.5 percent return using the dollar-weighted rate of return formula. Again, the managers of Fund A and B followed identical investment strategies. However, Fund B's $50,000 cash contribution makes its manager's performance appear to be superior to that of Fund A's manager.

TABLE 5–2

Comparison of Investment Performance Dollar-Weighted Rate of Return Measure, Cash Contribution Scenario

		Fund A	Fund B	
Date	S&P 500	Market Value (No Contribution)	Market Value Prior to Contribution	Market Value After Contribution
1/1	500	$1,000,000	$1,000,000	$1,000,000
7/1	550	1,100,000	1,100,000	1,150,000*
12/31	605	1,210,000		1,265,000

*Reflects $50,000 cash contribution on July 1 from Fund B.

Obviously, in circumstances where funds were either added or withdrawn from the portfolio, the dollar-weighted rate of return provides misleading information because the dollar-weighted rate of return is directly affected by the size and timing of these contributions and withdrawals. Since money managers cannot control these adjustments, their performance must be based on a measure that is unaffected by cash contributions and withdrawals.

UNIT RATE OF RETURN

The *unit rate of return* is the standard method employed to evaluate the performance of money managers. This performance measure considers explicitly the impact that the timing of contributions and withdrawals has on investment performance. Thus, it allows for a fair evaluation of a fund manager's performance free from the distortions associated with the use of the dollar-weighted rate of return method.

This approach requires that dollar-weighted returns are calculated prior to any cash contribution or withdrawal. The geometric average of all the dollar-weighted returns calculated during the evaluation period is the unit rate of return. Each time a cash contribution and/or withdrawal occurs, the market value of the fund is increased or decreased by the amount of the cash inflow or outflow. The new market value is then used as the base from which the next return is measured. This process is repeated whenever additional contributions and/or withdrawals occur throughout the remaining evaluation period. The measure of calculation is as follows:

$$\text{Unit Rate of Return} = \left[\frac{MV_1}{MV_0} \times \frac{MV_2}{MV_1 + C_1} \right] - 1$$

where

MV_0 = market value of fund at the end of period 0

MV_1 = market value of fund at the end of period 1, immediately prior to any cash inflow or outflow

MV_2 = market value of fund at the end of period 2

C_1 = cash inflow or outflow in period 1

The calculation of the unit rate of return (i) can be illustrated using the earlier example for Funds A and B. For Fund A, the return would be

$$i = \left[\frac{\$1,100,000}{\$1,000,000} \times \frac{\$1,210,000}{\$1,100,000} \right] - 1$$

$$= [1.10 \times 1.1] - 1$$

$$= 1.21 - 1$$

$$= 21\%$$

The return for Fund A, using the unit rate of return, is 21 percent. Fund B calculations can first be illustrated by assuming that the fund experienced a \$50,000 cash withdrawal (Table 5–1):

$$i = \left[\frac{\$1,100,000}{\$1,000,000} \times \frac{\$1,155,000}{\$1,050,000} \right] - 1$$

$$= [1.1 \times 1.1] - 1$$

$$= 1.21 - 1$$

$$= 21\%$$

Using the unit return measure, the return for Fund A (21 percent) is identical to the return for Fund B (21 percent), even though Fund B experienced a \$50,000 withdrawal during the measurement period.

Next, the unit rate of return for Fund B can be calculated under the assumption that a \$50,000 contribution (Table 5–2) is made during the measurement period. The return for Fund B is

$$i = \left[\frac{\$1,100,000}{\$1,000,000} \times \frac{\$1,265,000}{\$1,050,000} \right] - 1$$

$$= [1.1 \times 1.1] - 1$$

$$= 1.21 - 1$$

$$= 21\%$$

ANNUALIZED RATES OF RETURN

Financial experts seldom base their recommendations on short-term investment performance. Rather, performance may be evaluated over substantially longer periods of time because of different investment styles. It is often advised that performance be tracked over an entire market cycle, permitting for portfolio evaluation over varying market climates. Investment professionals recommend that performance measured over time periods of one year or longer be annualized. Providing this information requires that short-term performance measures be annualized or restated as average annual rates of return. This is accomplished by calculating the geometric average of a series of returns.

To illustrate, consider the quarterly investment returns of Fund C, which are presented in Table 5–3. These returns could be either dollar-weighted or unit rates of return.

To annualize quarterly returns, they must first be converted into returns relative. This is accomplished by adding 1.00 to the quarterly percentage return. For example, the first quarter (Q1) return of 3.5 percent would have a return relative of 1.035 (1.00 + 0.0350 = 1.0350). The quarterly and returns relative are reported in Table 5–4.

Fund C's annualized return for 1996 is found by calculating the geometric average of the quarterly return relatives (1.035 × 1.027

TABLE 5–3

Fund C Quarterly Returns

Quarter	Return (%)
Q1	3.5
Q2	2.7
Q3	1.3
Q4	0.3

TABLE 5–4

Fund C Returns Relative, 1996

Quarter	Return (%)	Return Relative
Q1	3.5	1.035
Q2	2.7	1.027
Q3	1.3	1.013
Q4	0.3	1.003

$\times 1.013 \times 1.003 = 1.07999$), producing 7.999 percent. Thus, $1,000 invested in Fund C at the beginning of the year would be worth $1,079.99 by the end of the year.

This process is also used to develop average annualized returns for longer periods. For example, the average annualized returns for a two-year period can be found by multiplying the eight quarterly returns relative. A five-year return would be found by multiplying the 20 quarterly returns relative during that period. Exhibit 5–1 presents an example of the use of the unit and dollar-weighted return measures.

ARITHMETIC AND GEOMETRIC RETURN AVERAGES

The *geometric mean* is commonly used when estimating investment performance in terms of growth rates. Using the *arithmetic mean*, a more commonly understood measure, would be inappropriate. To see why, consider the investment performance of Fund D as presented in Table 5–5.

As the data in Table 5–5 indicate, an initial investment of $100,000 invested in Fund D increases to $200,000 in one year (a 100 percent increase). The $200,000 grew to $1,000,000 in the second year (a 400 percent increase). Using the arithmetic mean, the first year growth rate of 100 percent is added to the second year growth

TABLE 5–5

Fund D Market Values

Year	Market Value	Growth Rate (%)
0	$100,000	–
1	200,000	100
2	1,000,000	400

rate of 400 percent. The sum of these is then divided by 2, yielding an arithmetic mean annual growth rate of 250 percent per year.

Table 5–6 reports the results of using the arithmetic mean as an estimate of investment growth rate. As the table shows, the growth rate of 250 percent computed previously is applied to the initial investment of $100,000. At the end of one year, the initial investment grows to $350,000 [$100,000(1 + 2.50)]. Applying the same growth rate to the $350,000 in the fund at the beginning of year two results in an estimate of $1,225,000, [$350,000(1 + 2.50)] at the end of the investment period. Thus, the arithmetic mean provides an estimated value of the portfolio at the end of year two, which is $225,000 greater than the actual value as reported in Table 5–5. The arithmetic mean's estimate overstates the actual value by 22.5 percent.

Next, the estimated growth rate is calculated using the geometric mean. Under this method, one plus the first year's growth rate (100 percent) is multiplied by one plus the second year's growth rate (400 percent). Then, the square root of the product (10) provides a 3.1623 geometric growth rate.

Table 5–7 applies the geometric mean growth rate to the $100,000 initial investment. As before, the growth rate of 3.1623 is applied to the initial investment of $100,000. This yields $316,230 ($100,000 × 3.1623) at the end of the first year. Applying this growth rate to the $316,230 available at the beginning of year two results in an estimated ending portfolio value of $1,000,014 ($316,230 ×

TABLE 5–6

Arithmetic Mean Growth Calculation

Year	Beginning Value	Growth Rate Perecnt	Ending Value
1	$100,000	250	$350,000
2	$350,000	250	$1,225,000

TABLE 5–7

Geometric Mean Growth Calculation

Year	Beginning Value	Growth Rate Perecnt	Ending Value
1	$100,000	3.1623	$316,230
2	$316,2320	3.1623	$1,000,014

3.1623). The slight difference ($14) is due to the rounding of the geometric growth rate.

This illustration demonstrates the superiority of the geometric mean as compared with the arithmetic mean when estimating the average growth rate of an investment portfolio. It is for this reason that the geometric mean is the preferred method for analyzing investment performance.

TOTAL RETURN AND ITS COMPONENTS

The discussion of rates of return relates to the change in the portfolio's value over measured periods of time. This process involves comparing the fund's market value at the end of a specified period with its market value at the beginning of the same period. The percentage of increase or decrease represents the fund's total return. Return performance evaluation is then based on this measure.

Although performance measured in this manner is useful, decomposing the total return measure into its current income and capital gain (loss) components can provide valuable insight into how the total return is achieved. This is especially helpful in evaluating portfolios that have different goals. For example, a fund with an income objective would need to pay careful attention to the current yield component of the total return measure. On the other hand, the capital appreciation component of total return would be of particular interest to evaluators of growth-oriented portfolios.

The breakdown of total return into its components is as follows:

$$\text{Total return} = \frac{\text{Capital gain (loss)}}{\text{Beginning market value}} + \frac{\text{Income}}{\text{Beginning market value}}$$

The capital gain (loss) component is measured by calculating the percentage gain or loss in the fund's principal, that is, the percentage increase (decrease) in the market value of its assets. The income component is found by dividing the sum of dividends and interest income by the beginning market value of the fund.

Table 5–8 presents the total return and their components for two funds, E and F, each having an initial value of $10,000,000. Total returns are stated in terms of percentages and dollars. Fund E is an income-oriented portfolio, and fund F is a growth-oriented portfolio. As the table indicates, Fund E's total return equals 10 percent, which primarily consists of income (7.5 percent) with the additional return of 2.5 percent due to the increase in the fund assets market value. Thus, Fund E has an income equaling $750,000 to distribute to its investors.

In contrast, the total return of Fund F is comprised mainly of capital gains or increases in the market value of its assets (9.5 percent) and, to a much lesser extent, the income component (2.5 percent). While fund F's total return is greater than fund E, its income component is only $250,000 or one-third of that available to investors in the income-oriented fund. While the total returns of each

TABLE 5–8

Total Return Components

Portfolio	Total Return	Capital Gain (Loss)	Income
In percentages:			
Fund E	10%	2.5%	7.5%
Fund F	12%	9.5%	2.5%
In dollars:			
Fund E	$1,000,000	$250,000	$750,000
Fund F	$1,200,000	$950,000	$250,000

type of fund will vary based on market conditions, growth-oriented funds are designed to provide less current income to their investors than are income-oriented funds.

Tax Considerations

Investment returns will also be affected by the tax status of the investor. When evaluating the investment performance of a qualified retirement plan, such as a 401(k) plan, the income earned is tax deferred. In these instances, performance is measured without adjusting the returns. However, for portfolios that are taxable, the evaluator needs to convert the return measures to their after-tax equivalents. The evaluator must explicitly consider the investor's federal, state, and local tax rate for each income category when calculating the after-tax return on the portfolio.

In terms of federal taxes, individual tax rates associated with investment activity will depend on whether the investor has income and/or capital gains or losses. Interest and dividend income are taxed at the individual investor's tax rate. At present (1996) these tax rates are 15 percent, 28 percent, 31 percent, 36 percent, and 39.6 percent depending on the amount of taxable income and the filing status of the sponsor.

Capital gains are subject to a maximum tax rate of 28 percent. Short-term capital losses (less than one year) are fully deductible. Long-term capital losses can be used to offset long-term capital gains. In addition, individual taxpayers are allowed to write off an additional $3,000 per year in long-term capital losses. Besides federal income tax, the evaluator must also consider where the sponsor resides and any state or local tax requirements associated with investment income.

Table 5–9 illustrates the adjustments required to convert the investment returns for Fund E in Table 5–8 to after-tax returns. Assume that the investor is in the 31 percent tax bracket. As shown in the table, the capital gain portion of total return (i.e., 2.50 percent) would be taxed at the current maximum rate of 28 percent. The after-tax rate of return would be 1.80 percent, or the pretax capital gain times one minus 28 percent. That is, the after-tax rate of return, r_T, is equal to the before-tax rate of return, r, times 1 minus the tax rate, T:

$$r_T = r(1 - T)$$

Additionally, the income portion of the total return (i.e., 7.50 percent) would be subject to the investor's marginal tax rate of 31 percent. This would result in an after-tax return of 5.175 percent for the income portion of the total return. Thus, the after-tax return on the portfolio would be 6.975 percent.

Nominal versus Real Rates of Return

Investors are not only concerned with the dollar returns on their portfolios but, more importantly, with the purchasing power of their portfolio returns as well. Investors are aware of the effects of inflation on the purchasing power of their wealth and desire information on investment performance relative to inflation when judging investment results and making investment decisions. It is

TABLE 5-9

Total Return, After-Tax Rate of Return

Fund E	Before-Tax Return (%)	Marginal Tax Rate (%)	After-Tax Return (%)
Capital gain	2.50	28	1.800
Income	7.50	31	5.175
	10.00		6.975

therefore important to distinguish between current-dollar nominal returns and inflation-adjusted, so-called real returns.

As an example, consider a sponsor who invests $25,000 today and expects a current-dollar nominal return averaging 12 percent per year for 20 years—the historic average return on large capitalization equities. At the end of 20 years, $25,000 would grow, in dollar terms, to about $241,158. Suppose also that the inflation rate averages 3.25 percent per year for the 20 years—its historic average.

The purchasing power of the $241,158 would only be about $127,800, some 47 percent less than the sponsor planned to have. In other words, because of inflation every dollar in 20 years would only have a purchasing power of roughly 53 cents! The sponsor would need about $1.90 in 20 years to buy what one $1.00 would purchase today.

The example clearly illustrates the importance of adjusting nominal, dollar-based returns for inflation to arrive at a real rate of return. The exact relationship between real and nominal returns is given by the following equation:

$$r = \frac{1+R}{1+P} - 1$$

where

r = real rate of return

R = nominal rate of return

P = percentage change in the price level

The exact relationship can be rearranged to

$$r = \frac{R-P}{1+P}$$

and is often approximated as

$$r = R - P$$

In terms of our example, the sponsor's nominal return of 12 percent per year with an inflation rate of 3.25 percent annually yields a real return of

$$8.47\% = \frac{12\% - 3.25\%}{(1 + 3.25\%)}$$

Dividend Reinvestment

The growth rate of a portfolio is not only a function of its investment success but also whether income earned on the fund's assets is either reinvested or disbursed. Therefore, funds that require that part or all of their income be distributed will experience a lower growth rate than if this constraint were not present. Consider the total return of Fund E in Table 5–10, which illustrates the total return and its capital gain and income components.

Assume that Fund E has a policy requiring that all of its income be distributed each year. While the total return for the year is

TABLE 5–10

Total Return Components

	Total return	=	Capital gain (loss)	+	Income
Fund E	10%	=	2.5%	+	7.5%

10 percent, the fund's growth rate will only be 2.5 percent. If the fund is charged with distributing 5 percent of its total return, then the fund will grow at 5 percent. The 5 percent growth rate is found by adding the 2.5 percent capital gain to the 2.5 percent of income retained (i.e., 7.5 percent minus 2.5 percent) by the fund. Thus, the growth rate of the fund is directly affected by its income distribution requirements.

As this example demonstrates, dividends or interest reinvestment assumptions play a significant role in the calculation of returns. Therefore, it is necessary, when comparing performance among managers, that income reinvestment be treated in a consistent manner.

In addition to the size of cash distributions, the timing of the distributions also influences growth measurements. Funds vary in the timing of distribution requirements. For example, distribution may be made on either a monthly, quarterly, or annual basis. These timing differences may alter the performance slightly. Therefore, this aspect of dividend/interest reinvestment should not be overlooked.

COMPOUND GROWTH

The impact of compound growth and the decision to reinvest income can have a profound impact on the value of a portfolio over a period of time. Compound growth occurs when income (dividends, interest, capital gains) earned on the initial investment, and then income earned on the subsequent value of the fund, is allowed to accumulate by remaining in the fund. This effect can be demonstrated by viewing the performance of the S&P 500 over a period of 20 years.

Chart 5–1 reports the value of $1.00 invested in the S&P 500 over a period of 20 years beginning January 1, 1975. As the chart illustrates, a dollar invested at that time would have grown to $6.63 by the end of 1994, assuming that dividends were distributed. If dividends were reinvested, the growth of the portfolio would have been even more dramatic. In this instance, the same dollar invested

CHART 5-1

S&P 500 Stock Index
Study of Total Returns

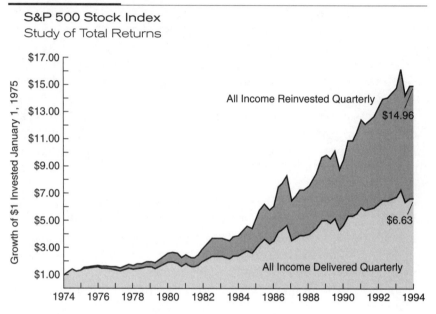

would be worth $14.96 at the end of this 20-year period. This represents an increase of almost 15 times the original investment, or more than twice the amount that would have resulted if dividends were distributed. Thus, the reinvestment of income is the key to achieving growth.

Gross versus Net of Fees

The issue of how to treat management fees when reporting investment performance is of particular interest to individuals responsible for evaluating fund managers. Some investment advisors report performance net of fees, while others provide investment performance figures without adjusting for fees. This gross-of-fee approach is the preferred way to evaluate investment performance since it is free from distortions resulting from varying fee schedules.

TABLE 5-11

Comparison of Money Managers Investment
Performance (Gross Fees versus Net Fees)

	Fund G (%)	Fund H (%)
Return (gross)	14.2	13.9
Fees	0.9	0.4
Return (net)	13.1	13.5

Consider the performance results and fees charged by the two money managers presented in Table 5–11. Fund Manager G's investment performance during the measurement period was 14.1 percent compared with 13.9 percent for the manager of Fund H. Over the measurement period, Fund G earned a higher return. However, if the comparison is made on a net fee basis, Fund Manager H's lower fees result in a return of 13.5 percent as compared with 13.1 percent for Fund G, in spite of the fact that Fund G earned a higher return as measured by investment performance. Obviously, it is also important for evaluators to consider the cost of investment portfolio management services. Currently, the investment community recommends that portfolio managers present returns on a gross-of-fee basis. Portfolio evaluators may request performance figures on both a gross and net-of-fee basis.

SUMMARY

The success of a portfolio is ultimately determined by the rate of return that it has achieved over a specified period of time, given an acceptable risk level. This rate of return is compared with a predetermined index and/or "goal" to determine if the portfolio has earned an acceptable return. The actual target set must be consistent with the investment and risk objectives of the portfolio as spelled out in the investment policy statement. For example, if the

EXHIBIT 5-1

TIME AND DOLLAR-WEIGHTED RETURNS
Sample Account

	Month	Quarter	Year to Date	One Year	Three Years	Five Years	Since 01-31-90
Total Portfolio							
Time-weighted return	1.2	3.0	6.2	22.7	13.7	10.3	12.1
Dollar-weighted return	1.2	3.0	6.3	21.3	13.4	10.5	11.7
Balanced index	1.3	2.8	5.9	25.4	14.4	12.7	12.9
Consumer price index	0.5	1.3	1.9	2.9	2.8	2.9	3.3
Equity Segment							
Time-weighted return	1.5	3.7	7.4	31.6	17.6	12.5	15.0
Dollar-weighted return	1.5	3.7	7.4	32.1	17.4	12.8	14.5
S&P 500	1.5	3.4	7.0	30.0	17.1	14.9	14.9
Dow Jones Industrials	−0.1	3.8	9.6	31.8	20.6	17.2	16.4
Fixed Segment							
Time-weighted return	−0.4	−2.2	−0.4	9.3	6.7	7.3	8.7
Dollar-weighted return	−0.4	−2.2	−0.4	10.6	6.2	7.2	9.0
ML 1–5 Yr Govt/Corp	−0.1	−1.1	−0.2	7.4	4.9	7.0	7.8
LB Interim Govt/Corp	−0.4	−2.0	−1.2	7.8	5.1	7.6	8.2
Cash Segment							
Time-weighted return	0.5	1.8	2.4	6.4	4.7	4.6	5.7
Dollar-weighted return	0.5	1.8	2.4	5.4	4.8	4.6	5.4
Donoghue Mny Mkt	0.4	1.2	1.6	5.3	4.2	4.1	4.8
U.S. Treasury bills	0.4	1.2	1.5	4.9	4.0	3.9	4.5

Total Portfolio

The fiscal year for this policy ends in December.
Rates of return for periods greater than one year are annualized.
The balanced index for the total portfolio segment is composed of S&P 500. ML 1–5 Govt/Corp, and Donoghue Mny Mkt.
S&P 500 represents the S&P 500 Composite Index.
ML 1–5 Yr Govt/Corp represents the Merrill Lynch 1–5 Year Government/Corporate index.
LB Int Govt/Corp represents the Lehman Brothers Intermediate Government/Corporate index.
Donoghue Mny Mkt represents the IBC Donoghue Money Market index.

Source: First Virginia Bank.

investment objectives require the portfolio to assume a specified risk level, then an index or required return that reflects that level of risk must be used.

In addition to the appropriate level of return, the portfolio measurement period must be established. A portfolio's performance is typically measured on a monthly, quarterly, or annual basis. Over the long term, it is useful to measure performance over a given market cycle. Measuring return over an entire market cycle is important when comparing portfolios with differing investment approaches. Evaluation of investment performance over a full market cycle provides vital information on the portfolio's sensitivity to varying market conditions. Furthermore, it affords investment managers an opportunity to focus on the long-term rather than being overly preoccupied with short-term results. To be sure, the choice of investment target returns and measurement periods are important. It is equally important that the appropriate return measure be used.

CHAPTER 6

Return/Risk Measurement

INTRODUCTION

In the preceding chapter, a number of measures of investment return were presented as criteria to aid in the evaluation of investment performance. To be sure, investment evaluators are concerned about the returns generated by funds. However, judging investment performance solely on the basis of return measures is incomplete and will likely result in poor decisions. Risk must also be considered when evaluating portfolio performance.

Risk is the probability or likelihood that the actual investment performance will be different from the desired or expected investment performance—the greater this likelihood, the higher the risks. Risk aversion typifies most investors. In other words, risk is undesirable, and, as a consequence, most investors must be compensated for assuming higher risks with the expectations of higher returns. Given two portfolios with identical returns, the portfolio with lower risk is more desirable. Likewise, at a given level of risk, the portfolio with the higher return is preferred. Thus, portfolio performance must be evaluated on a return/risk basis. In this chapter, the return/risk measures typically used to evaluate portfolio performance results are presented and discussed.

RETURN RELATIVE

In the last chapter, the return relative was developed to measure investment performance over specific time periods. Table 6–1 presents quarterly returns, return relatives, and cumulative return relatives for both the S&P 500 and Fund I for a 20-quarter period. Recall from Chapter 5 that the return relative is simply the quarterly return plus one. As shown in the table, the S&P 500's return relative for the first period is 0.97 (i.e., −0.030 + 1.00). The cumulative return relative, or geometric mean as we discussed in Chapter 5, is found by linking (i.e., multiplying) the individual return relatives. For period 2, the cumulative return relative for the S&P 500 is 1.0309, or 0.970×1.0628.

Using the information contained in this table, the annualized return for the entire 20 quarters (or five years) for the S&P 500 and Fund I can be found using the formula for the geometric mean presented in Chapter 5. The five-year average annualized return for the S&P 500 is 1.0865 [$1.5143^{(.2)}$], or 8.65 percent, while the five-year average annualized return for Fund I is 1.1236 [$1.7907^{(.2)}$], or 12.36 percent. An investment in the S&P 500 would have provided an average annualized return of 8.65 percent, whereas an investment in Fund I would have generated a significantly higher average return of 12.36 percent over this same time period. Thus, on the basis of return, the investment results of Fund I were superior to the S&P 500 over this five-year period.

STANDARD DEVIATION

While Fund I is more attractive from a return standpoint, how attractive is it from a risk perspective? As shown in the table, the S&P's quarterly returns ranged from a low of −13.72 percent to a high of 14.49 percent. Fund I's lowest quarterly return was −16 percent, while its highest quarterly return was 15.6 percent. Thus, the range of quarterly returns for Fund I appear to be greater than that for the S&P 500.

TABLE 6–1

S&P 500 and Fund I Return Relatives

Period	S&P 500			Fund I		
	Quarterly Return	Return Relative	Cumulative Return Relative	Quarterly Return	Return Relative	Cumulative Return Relative
1	−0.0300	0.9700		−0.0302	0.9698	
2	0.0628	1.0628	1.0309	0.0750	1.0750	1.0425
3	−0.1372	0.8628	0.8895	−0.1500	0.8500	0.8862
4	0.0891	1.0891	0.9687	0.0950	1.0950	0.9703
5	0.1449	1.1449	1.1091	0.1500	1.1500	1.1158
6	−0.0019	0.9981	1.1069	−0.0001	0.9999	1.1158
7	0.0535	1.0535	1.1662	0.0750	1.0750	1.1995
8	0.0831	1.0831	1.2631	0.1050	1.1050	1.3254
9	−0.0254	0.9746	1.2310	−0.0260	0.9740	1.2909
10	0.0194	1.0194	1.2549	0.0310	1.0310	1.3309
11	0.0308	1.0308	1.2936	0.0440	1.0440	1.3895
12	0.0508	1.0508	1.3593	0.0580	1.0580	1.4701
13	0.0427	1.0427	1.4173	0.0550	1.0550	1.5510
14	0.0052	1.0052	1.4247	0.0350	1.0350	1.6053
15	0.0255	1.0255	1.4610	−0.0050	0.9950	1.5972
16	0.0230	1.0230	1.4946	0.0560	1.0560	1.6867
17	0.0986	1.0986	1.6420	0.1560	1.1560	1.9498
18	−0.1206	0.8794	1.4440	−0.1600	0.8400	1.6378
19	0.0490	1.0490	1.5147	0.1100	1.1100	1.8180
20	−0.0003	0.9997	1.5143	−0.0150	0.9850	1.7907

Rather than visually estimating the range or variability of returns, a more accurate method of measuring risk, called the *standard deviation,* is generally used. The standard deviation provides a
more precise measure of the volatility of actual quarterly returns
relative to the average quarterly return. The resulting statistic provides the evaluator with a numeric estimate of risk.

TABLE 6-2

S&P 500 Standard Deviation

(1) Quarter	(2) Actual Return	(3) Average Return	(4) Difference (2) – (3)	(5) Squared Difference
1	−0.0300	0.0232	−0.0532	0.0028
2	0.0628	0.0232	0.0397	0.0016
3	−0.1372	0.0232	−0.1604	0.0257
4	0.0891	0.0232	0.0660	0.0043
5	0.1449	0.0232	0.1218	0.0148
6	−0.0019	0.0232	−0.0250	0.0006
7	0.0535	0.0232	0.0304	0.0009
8	0.0831	0.0232	0.0600	0.0036
9	−0.0254	0.0232	−0.0485	0.0024
10	0.0194	0.0232	−0.0037	0.0000
11	0.0308	0.0232	0.0077	0.0001
12	0.0508	0.0232	0.0277	0.0008
13	0.0427	0.0232	0.0196	0.0004
14	0.0052	0.0232	−0.0179	0.0003
15	0.0255	0.0232	0.0024	0.0000
16	0.0230	0.0232	−0.0001	0.0000
17	0.0986	0.0232	0.0755	0.0057
18	−0.1206	0.0232	−0.1438	0.0207
19	0.0490	0.0232	0.0259	0.0007
20	−0.0003	0.0232	−0.0235	0.0005
			Sum =	0.0860

Table 6–2 demonstrates this technique using the S&P 500 quarterly data from Table 6–1. Columns 1 and 2 represent the period and quarterly returns obtained in the period, respectively. Column 3 is the average quarterly return over the five-year period. Column 4, labeled Difference, is found by subtracting column 3 from column 2. Finally, column 5 represents the squared difference.

When using annualized returns, it is customary to present standard deviations on an annualized basis. The formula for annualized standard deviation is as follows:

$$\sigma = \left\{ \left[\frac{(\sum x_i - \mu)^2}{n} \right] * 4 \right\}^{(.5)} \tag{6-1}$$

where

  σ = annualized standard deviation
  x_i = quarterly returns
  μ = average quarterly returns
  n = number of quarters

Using this formula and the data from Table 6–2, the S&P 500's annualized standard deviation is also obtained:

$$\sigma = \left\{ \left[\frac{(0.08600)}{20} \right] * 4 \right\}^{(.5)}$$

$$\sigma = 13.11\%$$

Fund I's standard deviation calculations are presented in Table 6–3. As before, columns 1, 2, and 3 represent the period, quarterly return, and average quarterly return, respectively. Columns 4 and 5 represent the difference and squared differences, respectively. Using Equation 6–1 and the data from Table 6–3, Fund I's annualized standard deviation is found as follows:

$$\sigma = \left\{ \left[\frac{0.1163}{20} \right] * 4 \right\}^{(.5)}$$

$$\sigma = 15.25\%$$

A comparison of the annualized standard deviations reveals that the S&P 500 has less risk than that of Fund I. The annualized

TABLE 6-3

Fund I Standard Deviation

(1) Quarter	(2) Actual Return	(3) Average Return	(4) Difference (2) – (3)	(5) Squared Difference
1	–0.0302	0.0259	–0.0561	0.0031
2	0.0750	0.0259	0.0491	0.0024
3	–0.1500	0.0259	–0.1759	0.0309
4	0.0950	0.0259	0.0691	0.0048
5	0.1500	0.0259	0.1241	0.0154
6	–0.0001	0.0259	–0.0260	0.0007
7	0.0750	0.0259	0.0491	0.0024
8	0.1050	0.0259	0.0791	0.0063
9	–0.0260	0.0259	–0.0519	0.0027
10	0.0310	0.0259	0.0051	0.0000
11	0.0440	0.0259	0.0181	0.0003
12	0.0580	0.0259	0.0321	0.0010
13	0.0550	0.0259	0.0291	0.0008
14	0.0350	0.0259	0.0091	0.0001
15	–0.0050	0.0259	–0.0309	0.0010
16	0.0560	0.0259	0.0301	0.0009
17	0.1560	0.0259	–0.0103	0.0001
18	–0.1600	0.0259	–0.1859	0.0346
19	0.1100	0.0259	0.0841	0.0071
20	–0.0150	0.0259	–0.0409	0.0017
			Sum =	0.1163

standard deviation of the S&P 500 is 13.11 percent, while it is 15.25 percent for Fund I. Therefore, on this basis, Fund I exposes its investors to more risk than the S&P 500.

Table 6–4 summarizes the return/risk characteristics of the S&P 500 and Fund I. The S&P 500 provided investors with both a lower return and lower risk than those who invested in Fund I.

TABLE 6–4

S&P 500 versus Fund I Return/Risk Profile

	S&P 500 (%)	Fund I (%)
5-year annualized return	8.65	12.36
Standard deviation	13.11	15.25

PORTFOLIO RISK MEASURE

Standard deviation provides an accurate assessment of the risk for individual securities. Risk measures for portfolios of securities also use variance and its square root, the standard deviation. However, the computation of a portfolio's risk is more complicated than that for individual securities. This added complication provides the key to efficiently reducing risk via diversification.

Consider a portfolio of only two securities, stock 1 and stock 2. The actual return on this portfolio will depend on the returns obtained by each stock and the weights of each stock (i.e., the percentage of the portfolio represented by each stock in the portfolio) as given by Equation 6–2:

$$R_p = w_1{}^*r_1 + w_2{}^*r_2 \qquad (6-2)$$

where

R_p = the portfolio's rate of return

w_1 = the percent of the portfolio invested in stock 1

w_2 = the percent of the portfolio invested in stock 2

r_1 = the return on stock 1

r_2 = the return on stock 2

The variance of this portfolio is depicted in Equation 6–3. Note that since we are, for now, using variance, which is the square of the standard deviation, as our measure of portfolio risk that the W's and S's in equation 6-3 are squared.

$$\sigma^2 = w_1^2 * \sigma_1^2 + w_2^2 * \sigma_2^2 + 2w_1w_2\,\text{Cov}\,(r_1, r_2) \qquad (6\text{--}3)$$

where

σ^2 = portfolio variance

σ_1^2 = variance of stock 1

σ_2^2 = variance of stock 2

w_1 = the percent of the portfolio invested in stock 1

w_2 = the percent of the portfolio invested in stock 2

Cov (r_1, r_2) = the covariance of returns between stocks 1 and 2

Equation 6–3 tells us that a portfolio's risk is determined by three items: (a) the risk associated with each individual security as measured by its variance, (b) the percent of the portfolio invested in each security as measured by its weight, and (c) the weighted covariance of the security's return. The covariance is the most critical of the three determinants. Covariance provides a measure of the degree to which returns on the two securities move together, that is, co-vary. Covariance measures the interaction of security returns. In our hypothetical two-stock portfolio there will be two covariances: the covariance of the return of stock 1 with stock 2 and the covariance of the return of stock 2 with stock 1. While the numerical values of these covariances will be the same, both covariances are employed in the measurement of portfolio variance. This is the reason the third term on the right side of Equation 6–3 starts with 2. Hence, portfolio risk is comprised of the risk associated with each separate security plus twice the interaction of the security's returns as measured by their covariance.

To comprehend how important the covariances are in determining the risk of a portfolio of securities, consider an equity portfolio of 30 stocks. The risk of this portfolio will be determined by the following:

1. The weight assigned to each stock, of which there are 30.

2. The risk or variance of each stock, of which there are 30.

3. The covariance of the returns on each pair of stocks, of which there are $N(N-1)/2$. In our portfolio of 30 stocks, there would be 435 covariances.

We can therefore conclude that it is the interactions of the returns on the securities in a portfolio, that is, the covariances, that have the greatest influence on the portfolio's risk. This fundamental principle can be applied to reducing a portfolio's risk.

One practical shortcoming of using covariance as a measure of the interactions of security returns is that, in theory, the numerical values of covariance are unbounded; that is, they can assume any values. As an alternative, the correlation coefficient of the security returns is used. The relationship between the covariance and correlation coefficient is given by Equation 6–4:

$$\rho_{1,2} = \frac{\mathrm{Cov}\,(r_1, r_2)}{\sigma_1 \cdot \sigma_2} \qquad (6.4)$$

where

$\rho_{1,2}$ = the correlation coefficient of the returns on securities 1 and 2

$\mathrm{Cov}\,(r_1, r_2)$ = The covariance of the returns on securities 1 and 2

σ_1, σ_2 = The standard deviations of the returns on securities 1 and 2

Correlation coefficients assume values from a minimum of –1 to a maximum of +1. A correlation coefficient between the return on securities 1 and 2 of +0.5 would tell us two things. First, the positive sign indicates that the returns on securities 1 and 2 move in the same direction. When the return on security 1 is rising (falling), the return on security 2 is also rising (falling). Second, the magnitude of the correlation coefficient reveals the degree to which the securities' returns move. In our example of a correlation coefficient of +0.5, this would indicate that for every percentage point change in the return on security 1, the return on security 2 changes by one-half (0.5) of a percentage point.

The formula for portfolio risk can now be modified by substituting the expression for correlation coefficient for that of the covariance to obtain Equation 6–5:

$$\sigma_p^2 = w_1^{2} {}^* \sigma_1^2 + w_2^{2} {}^* \sigma_2^2 + 2w_1 w_2 \sigma_1 \sigma_2 \, \rho_{1,2} \qquad (6\text{–}5)$$

Formula 6–5 for portfolio risk can now be used to illustrate how the adroit selection of securities with different correlation coefficients can alter the riskiness of a portfolio. We will use the following numerical example:

$w_1 = 0.50$; 50 percent of the portfolio is invested in security 1

$w_2 = 0.50$; 50 percent of the portfolio is invested in security 2

$\sigma_1 = 0.20$; security 1 has a risk measured by standard deviation of 20 percent

$\sigma_2 = 0.30$; security 2 has a risk measured by standard deviation of 30 percent

$\rho_{1,2} = +1, 0, -1$; three cases for the correlation coefficient of returns on securities 1 and 2 will be presented.

Case 1: Perfect Positive Correlation between the Returns on Securities 1 and 2, $\rho = +1$

$\sigma_p^2 = (0.5)^2(0.2)^2 + (0.5)^2(0.3)^2 + (2)(0.5)(0.5)(0.2)(0.3)(1)$

$\sigma_p^2 = 0.0625$

$\sigma_p = 0.25$ or 25 percent

Case 2: No Correlation between the Returns on Securities 1 and 2, $r = 0$

$\sigma_p^2 = (0.5)^2(0.2)^2 + (0.5)^2(0.3)^2 + (2)(0.5)(0.5)(0.2)(0.3)(0)$

$\sigma_p^2 = 0.0325$

$\sigma_p = 0.18$ or 18 percent.

Case 3: Perfect Negative Correlation between the Returns on Securities 1 and 2, $\rho = -1$

$\sigma_p{}^2 = (0.5)^2(0.2)^2 + (0.5)^2(0.3)^2 + (2)(0.5)(0.5)(0.2)(0.3)(-1)$

$\sigma_p{}^2 = 0.0025$

$\sigma_p = 0.05$ or 5 percent

Table 6–5 clearly reveals how including securities in a portfolio with the lower correlation coefficients reduces portfolio risk. In case 1, where the returns on securities 1 and 2 were perfectly positively correlated, the portfolio risk was 25 percent. If the securities selected for the portfolio had been chosen so that their returns were completely uncorrelated (case 2), portfolio risk would have fallen to 18 percent or by about 28 percent. In case 3 where the returns on the securities had a hypothetical correlation of –1 (perfectly negative correlation), portfolio risk would be only 5 percent, a situation where the portfolio would have shown 80 percent less risk than in case 1.

The lesson should be abundantly clear. To reduce portfolio risk, include securities whose correlation of returns is as low (ideally, negative) as possible.

Professional investment managers seeking to reduce the risk of their sponsor's portfolios spend considerable effort identifying the correlation coefficients of individual securities or asset classes of securities. Table 6–6 provides a matrix of correlation coefficients for a number of asset groups. Such tables are used to choose assets to include in a portfolio so as to minimize its risk.

TABLE 6–5

Summary

Case	Correlation Coefficient	Portfolio Risk (%)
1	+1	25
2	0	18
3	–1	5

TABLE 6-6

Correlations of Historical Annual Returns

Series	Large Company Stocks	Small Company Stocks	Long-Term Corporate Bonds	Long-Term Government Bonds	U.S. Treasury Bills	Inflation
Large company stocks	1.00					
Small company stocks	0.81	1.00				
Long-term corporate bonds	0.26	0.11	1.00			
Long-term government bonds	0.19	0.03	0.94	1.00		
U.S. Treasury bills	−0.04	−0.09	0.22	0.24	1.00	
Inflation	−0.02	0.04	−0.15	−0.14	0.41	1.00

Source: © Computed using data from *Stocks, Bonds, Bills and Inflation, 1996 Yearbook,*™ Ibbotson Associates, Chicago (annually updates work by Roger G. Ibbotson and Rex Sinquefield). Used with permission. All rights reserved.

SCATTER DIAGRAM

The preceding return/risk relationships are often compared with other indexes and/or portfolios using a scatter diagram. Chart 6–1 plots the return/risk characteristics of the S&P 500 and Fund I as well as other hypothetical funds (making up the universe) on a scatter diagram. The vertical axis represents the annualized rate of return, while the horizontal axis measures risk (standard deviation). The scatter diagram is divided into four quadrants, with the origin representing the median annualized rate of return and risk measures. Data points for both the S&P 500 (8.65 percent, 13.11 percent) and Fund I (12.36 percent, 15.25 percent) are plotted on the scatter diagram.

The actual points plotted will lie in one of the four quadrants. Portfolios lying in the northwest quadrant are the most desirable since they provide the investor with returns greater than the median level and risks lower than the median fund reporting. In

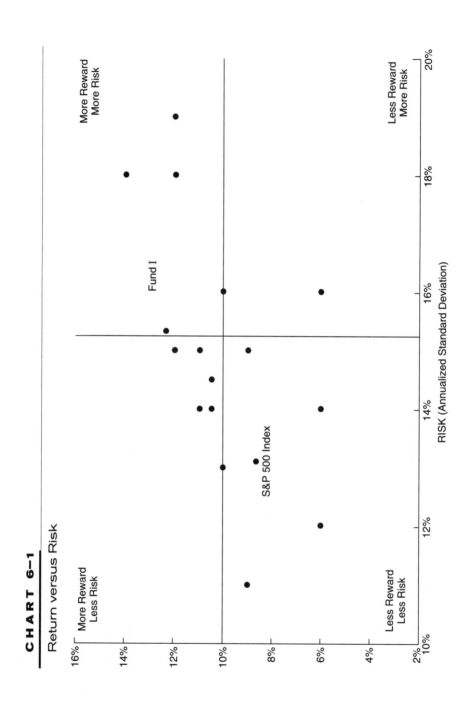

CHART 6-1

Return versus Risk

contrast, portfolios residing in the southeast quadrant are the least desirable since these funds provide both lower returns and higher risks than the median portfolios.

COEFFICIENT OF VARIATION

The coefficient of variation (COV) provides a direct comparison between a fund's return and risk characteristics. The coefficient of variation is simply the fund's standard deviation divided by its return (arithmetic). This ratio allows the analyst to normalize risk relative to return. The higher the ratio, the greater the risk in proportion to return. Table 6–7 presents the coefficients for the S&P 500 and Fund I. As shown in the table, the coefficient of variation is 2.823 for the S&P 500 and 2.946 for Fund I. These data mean that for every 1 percentage point of return earned in the S&P 500, 2.823 percentage points of risk were assumed; while to obtain 1 percentage point of return on Fund I, 2.946 percentage points of risk were taken. The coefficient of variation suggests that Fund I is less attractive because more risk is taken per percentage point of return.

REGRESSION ANALYSIS

The investment performance of a particular portfolio is often compared with the performance of the overall market as represented by an index such as those presented in Chapter 2. Portfolio managers frequently compare their portfolio's return and risk attributes

TABLE 6–7

S&P 500 versus Fund I Coefficients of Variation

	S&P 500	Fund I
Quarterly return	2.32%	2.59%
Standard deviation	6.55%	7.63%
Coefficient of variation	2.823	2.946

with those associated with a relevant market index, which allows inferences to be drawn regarding the performance of a fund relative to the overall market itself. The evaluator can compare the investment performance of the fund relative to the risk being taken by the fund's managers.

Regression analysis is a valuable tool used by investment professionals in the evaluation of portfolio performance. The fundamental idea is to statistically fit a straight line or curve through an array of data such that the sum of the squared errors, the difference between the predicted and actual values of the data, is minimized. The basic regression equation is:

$$Y_t = \alpha + \beta \cdot X + e_t \qquad (6\text{--}6)$$

where

Y_t = portfolio return in time period t
X = index return in time period t
α = regression intercept
β = regression slope
e = residual term

Equation 6–6 also provides an estimate of beta, which measures the sensitivity of the portfolio's return to variations in the market return. Thus, it measures the relative riskiness or volatility of the portfolio to the index. A portfolio with a beta equal to 1 suggests that the volatility of the portfolio is equal to that of the index, while a beta greater than 1 would indicate that the portfolio possesses more volatility than the market. Conversely, a beta less than 1 indicates that the portfolio's volatility is less than that of the market. The formula for beta is as follows:

$$\beta = [N(\Sigma \, x_i \, y_i) - (\Sigma x_i)(\Sigma y_i)] \, / \, [N(\Sigma x_i^2) - (\Sigma x_i)^2] \qquad (6\text{--}7)$$

where

β = portfolio's beta
N = number of observations
x_i = measured return of index at time I
y_i = measured return of portfolio at time I

The regression's intercept, alpha, measures the excess of the portfolio's return to that of the index. Alpha can be viewed as providing a measure of the portfolio's return when the return on the market index is zero. Alpha, or the Jensen Index (JI) as it is commonly referred to, is an indicator of management's contribution to investment performance. A positive alpha indicates that the portfolio achieved a return superior to that of the index on a risk-adjusted basis. Conversely, a negative alpha would indicate that the investment manager underperformed the market on a risk-adjusted basis. The formula for obtaining alpha (α) is as follows:

$$\alpha = [(\Sigma y_i - (\beta \Sigma x_i)] / N \qquad (6\text{--}8)$$

The coefficient of determination, R^2, measures the degree to which the variability of the portfolio's returns is associated with the variability of the index. The formula for R^2 is as follows:

$$R^2 = \frac{[N(\Sigma x_i y_i) - (\Sigma x_i)(\Sigma y_i)]}{[N(\Sigma x_i)^2 - (\Sigma x_i)^{2(.5)}][N(\Sigma y_i)^2 - (\Sigma y_i)^{2(.5)}]} \qquad (6\text{--}9)$$

This measure indicates the degree of diversification achieved by the portfolio and can assume a value from 0 to 1. For example, an R^2 of 0.0 would indicate that none of the portfolio's variability is explained by the variability of the index. An R^2 of 0.9 would indicate that 90 percent of the variability in the portfolio's return is explained by the index. A portfolio with an R^2 of 1.0 is considered to be a fully diversified portfolio in that the only source of portfolio risk is the risk associated with the market index itself.

The residual terms, e_t, represent the difference between the actual return earned on the portfolio for a particular time period and the return predicted by the regression equation for that specific period. The residual term therefore represents so-called forecast errors. These residuals also offer insight into the value of the regression equation. Ideally these forecast errors are distributed such that episodes where actual returns on the fund are greater than the forecasted returns are canceled or offset by episodes where the opposite occurs. In short, the average forecast error is ideally zero. Moreover, ideally these forecast errors should have unchanging variability. In cases where these conditions fail to hold, the investment evaluator should look to other evaluation criteria because the presence of alpha and beta suggests that those statistics are likely to be highly misleading.

PORTFOLIO SIZE AND DIVERSIFICATION LEVELS

Total risk or the amount of variability in a fund's return consists of systematic and unsystematic risk. *Systematic risk* refers to risk attributed to changes in the market index, while *unsystematic or unique risk* is that which is specific to an individual security's return. In effect, the R^2 measure provides information concerning the amount of portfolio variability, which is explained by the market index. This portion of the variability in return is referred to as systematic risk. If the regression equation indicates that the R^2 is 0.9, then 90 percent of total variability is related to the market, and the other 10 percent is unrelated or unsystematic.

Studies have shown that by increasing the number of securities in a portfolio, the level of unsystematic risk decreases. Chart 6–2 illustrates this relationship. In fact, the dropoff in risk is great-

CHART 6–2

Portfolio Size and Risk

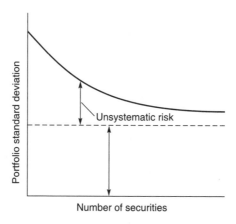

Number of securities

est in the early stages of securities additions. Furthermore, as more securities are added, the overall portfolio risk will decline at a decreasing rate. In theory, by adding additional securities, the total portfolio risk could decrease to the point where only systematic risk remains. At this point, the portfolio's R^2 will be 1.00.

REGRESSION ANALYSIS OF FUND I

Table 6–8 presents the calculations required to estimate Fund I's alpha, beta, and R^2. The estimated equation is:

% Return on Fund I_t = .51% + 1.2015 [% return S&P 500_t] + e_t

TABLE 6–8

Quarterly Returns of S&P 500 versus Fund I

Quarter	Return (x_i) (%)	Return (y_i) (%)	x^2	y^2	$x*y$
1	−3.00	−3.02	0.0009	0.0009	0.0009
2	6.28	7.50	0.0039	0.0056	0.0047
3	−13.72	−15.00	0.0188	0.0225	0.0206
4	8.91	9.50	0.0079	0.0090	0.0085
5	14.49	15.00	0.0210	0.0225	0.0217
6	−0.19	−0.01	0.0000	0.0000	0.0000
7	5.35	7.50	0.0029	0.0056	0.0040
8	8.31	10.50	0.0069	0.0110	0.0087
9	−2.54	−2.60	0.0006	0.0007	0.0007
10	1.94	3.10	0.0004	0.0010	0.0006
11	3.08	4.40	0.0009	0.0019	0.0014
12	5.08	5.80	0.0026	0.0034	0.0029
13	4.27	5.50	0.0018	0.0030	0.0023
14	0.52	3.50	0.0000	0.0012	0.0002
15	2.55	−0.50	0.0007	0.0000	−0.0001
16	2.30	5.60	0.0005	0.0031	0.0013
17	9.86	15.60	0.0097	0.0243	0.0154
18	−12.06	−16.00	0.0145	0.0256	0.0193
19	4.90	11.00	0.0024	0.0121	0.0054
20	−0.03	−1.50	0.0000	0.0002	0.0000

Using the quarterly returns, Fund I's alpha is estimated to be 0.512 percent on a quarterly basis or 2.05 percent annualized. Thus, Fund I's stock selection provides an annual return of about 2 percent that is independent of the return on the S&P 500. Likewise, Fund I's beta is estimated to be 1.2015. This indicates that the fund has greater risk, about 20 percent, than the market as a whole. Finally, Fund I's R^2 is 0.936. This indicates that more than 93 percent of the variability in Fund I's returns is explained by the market, with the remaining variability of return due to the firm specific factors.

Chart 6–3 presents the market characteristic line for Fund I. The results of the preceding regression analysis suggest that the fund has performed well on a risk-adjusted basis. The fund can be characterized as being well diversified and having more volatility than the market as a whole.

CHART 6–3

Regression Equation Line

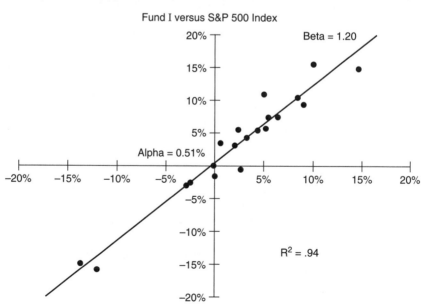

Fund I versus S&P 500 Index

ADDITIONAL PERFORMANCE MEASURES

In addition to the performance evaluation techniques illustrated earlier, there are three additional measures that are frequently used. The first measure, the Sharpe index, is a measure of the fund's reward to variability. The Sharpe index (SI) measure is defined as follows:

$$SI = \frac{R_j - R_f}{sd_j} \qquad (6\text{--}10)$$

where

   R_j = the average return of portfolio j
   R_f = the risk free rate of return using T-bills
   sd_j = the standard deviation of returns of portfolio j

Note that the numerator of the Sharpe index (i.e., $R_j - R_f$) measures the so-called excess return of a fund, while the denominator measures the fund's overall variability. In essence, the numerator provides the evaluator with a measure of the additional return or "premium" earned by taking on risk, while the denominator reports the level of risk taken during the measurement period. The higher the Sharpe index, the greater return premium per unit of risk.

Another performance measure, the Treynor ratio, is similar to the Sharpe index except that it compares the fund's excess return with the fund's market risk, as measured by its beta. The formula is as follows:

$$TR = \frac{(R_j - R_f)}{\beta_j} \qquad (6\text{--}11)$$

   where β_j = portfolio j's beta

Thus, the Treynor ratio relates the trade-off between the additional return earned (i.e., above the risk-free rate) and the fund's exposure to market risk. The higher the ratio, the greater the benefit from the trade-off. Each of these measures provides a basis for evaluating performance on a risk-adjusted basis and can be useful in the eval-uation process.

Still another performance measure is the appraisal ratio. This measure is the ratio of the portfolio's alpha to the nonmarket or unique risk of the portfolio. Recall that a portfolio's alpha measures the average return over and above that predicted by the market re-turn, given the portfolio's beta. The unsystematic risk is risk that, in principle, can be eliminated via diversification. Hence, the ap-praisal ratio indicates abnormal return per unit of diversifiable risk. The appraisal ratio formula is as follows:

$$AP = \frac{\alpha_p}{\sigma_{(e)}} \qquad (6\text{--}12)$$

where

AP = appraisal ratio
α_p = alpha of the portfolio
$\sigma_{(e)}$ = diversifiable risk

SUMMARY

Investment performance must be evaluated on the basis of not only the returns but on the level of risk taken to achieve these returns as well. Along these lines, there are several tools available to properly gauge performance on a return/risk basis. These measures include the fund's standard deviation and its alpha, beta, and coefficient of determination. Additional measures, such as the Sharpe index, Treynor ratio, and the appraisal ratio, can assist in evaluating port-folio performance. These and other similar measures allow a man-ager to view a fund's performance results in the context of the risk associated with the fund. As such, they are important evaluation tools and should be relied upon as a part of the normal evaluation process.

CHAPTER 7

Portfolio Performance Overview

INTRODUCTION

A periodic review of performance results is necessary to determine the extent to which portfolio managers have met the investment objectives of the fund. This requires the evaluator to compare the actual investment results with predetermined established benchmarks. These benchmarks, or performance requirements, will generally be stated in terms of achieving returns relative to an index or selected universe as stipulated in the investment policy statement. The role of the evaluator is to measure fund performance against these criteria. Furthermore, the evaluator must understand the underlying factors affecting performance results.

A portfolio's investment performance over a given period of time will be the result of two important decisions made on the part of its management. First, the manager has to decide within the constraints of the portfolio's policy guidelines the appropriate allocation of assets among equities, fixed income, and cash equivalents. Second, the manager is responsible for the securities selected within each category. In evaluating the manager's investment performance, both of these factors must be considered.

In this chapter we focus on evaluating overall portfolio performance and the manager's asset allocation decisions. The chapter

concludes with an examination of the cash and equivalent component of the portfolio. Chapters 8 and 9 examine the performance of
the equity and fixed-income components, respectively.

PERFORMANCE RESULTS

To illustrate the methods used to evaluate the performance of a
given fund, a hypothetical balanced portfolio, Fund XYZ, will be
used. Table 7–1 reports the quarterly performance results for this
fund from the first quarter of 1991 to the second quarter of 1996.
Column 1 indicates the quarter, while columns 2, 3, and 4 report
the investment returns for the fund's equity, fixed-income, and
cash and equivalent components, respectively. Finally, column 5
represents the total quarterly return for the fund.

Typically, the investment policy statement allows professional
managers to decide how assets are allocated among equities, fixed-
income securities, and cash and equivalents. Specifically, as discussed in Chapter 2, the policy statement specifies acceptable
ranges for each asset component. For illustration purposes, we assume that the portfolio is allocated over the measurement period as
follows: 60 percent equities, 30 percent fixed-income securities, and
10 percent cash and equivalents. These weights are assumed for
Fund XYZ and for computing the composite index.

Over time, the relative performance of the components will
alter the investment mix. For example, if equities in any given period
outperform the other components, then their market value and,
therefore, relative weight, increase. Managers monitor this shift and
rebalance the portfolio, when necessary, to ensure that the actual
asset mix is within the guidelines of the investment policy statement.

In our illustration, we will "rebalance" the portfolios each
quarter to maintain the initial 60 percent equities, 30 percent fixed-
income securities, and 10 percent cash and equivalents relationship. Later, an analysis of the manager's asset allocation and
securities selection decisions will be conducted.

The total fund returns are derived by multiplying the individual index returns by their corresponding weights. These weights are the same as for Fund XYZ. For example, the total composite index return for the second quarter of 1996 is found as follows:

$$(4.4825\%)(0.6) + (0.4702\%)(0.3) + (1.2754\%)(0.1) = 2.9581\%$$

COMPOSITE INDEX

The results presented in Table 7–1 must be compared with the investment objectives. Two performance benchmarks are used to determine whether the fund's investments results are satisfactory. First, the fund's results are compared with a composite index that consists of equity, fixed-income, and cash and equivalent indexes. Each component index must be carefully chosen to ensure that it meets the objectives of the fund. For illustration purposes, the S&P 500 is used for the equity component, while the Lehman Brothers Government/Corporate Index is used as a benchmark for the fixed-income portion of the portfolio. Finally, the Lehman Brothers Three-Month Treasury Bill index is used to evaluate the fund's cash and equivalent component.

The quarterly returns for these three indexes over our five-year period are presented in Table 7–2. Column 1 represents the investment quarter. Columns 2, 3, and 4 report the investment returns of the equity, fixed-income, and cash indexes, respectively. Column 5 represents the composite index.

UNIVERSE COMPARISON

In addition to the use of a composite index, investment performance can be evaluated relative to other funds with similar investment objectives and constraints. These other portfolios are referred to as the investment universe. Many investment consulting organizations maintain databases on various types of universes. These include the Frank Russell Company, SEI, and Wilshire Associates, to

TABLE 7–1

Fund XYZ Quarterly Returns
(Percentages)

Quarter		Equities	Fixed Income	Cash	Total Fund*
1991	Q1	14.3974	2.3700	1.6010	9.5095
	Q2	−0.4511	1.7101	1.4692	0.3893
	Q3	6.5298	5.2316	1.4006	5.6274
	Q4	7.7894	5.6400	1.1954	6.4852
1992	Q1	−1.4591	−0.9879	1.0091	−1.0709
	Q2	2.3912	4.9399	0.9379	3.0105
	Q3	4.0100	5.0001	0.8359	3.9896
	Q4	4.5598	0.9519	0.7432	3.0958
1993	Q1	4.1609	4.7921	0.7801	4.0122
	Q2	1.0300	3.1102	0.7432	1.6254
	Q3	2.9579	3.0500	0.7692	2.7667
	Q4	3.1310	−0.9725	0.7781	1.6647
1994	Q1	−3.1794	−3.0453	0.7986	−2.7414
	Q2	0.3219	−1.1459	0.9500	−0.0556
	Q3	5.1790	5.1542	1.1413	4.7678
	Q4	1.8945	3.5420	1.7965	2.3790
1995	Q1	10.4572	4.5200	1.3487	7.7652
	Q2	9.7943	6.1908	1.1981	7.8536
	Q3	7.9784	1.7893	1.4387	5.4677
	Q4	6.2190	4.6856	1.4109	5.2782
1996	Q1	5.2864	−1.9870	1.2698	2.7027
	Q2	4.6329	0.5109	1.3287	3.0659

*Portfolio weights: equity (60%), fixed income (30%), cash (10%)

name a few. Frank Russell's 35 balanced account universe will be employed to illustrate the use of this methodology.

The comparison of investment results is often depicted graphically to give a better picture of the range of performance among the universe participants. Chart 7–1 illustrates this approach in bar

TABLE 7–2

Composite Indexes Quarterly Returns (Percentages)

Quarter		S&P 500	Lehman Brothers Government/ Corporate	Three-Month Treasury	Composite*
1991	Q1	14.5267	2.6953	1.6692	9.6916
	Q2	-0.2287	1.5111	1.4772	0.4638
	Q3	5.3480	5.7516	1.4267	5.0769
	Q4	8.3846	5.3364	1.3056	6.7622
1992	Q1	-2.5256	-1.5007	1.0235	-1.8632
	Q2	1.9012	4.0503	0.9933	2.4551
	Q3	3.1523	4.8861	0.9027	3.4475
	Q4	5.0349	0.0789	0.7720	3.1218
1993	Q1	4.3670	4.6499	0.7720	4.0924
	Q2	0.4869	3.0010	0.7418	1.2669
	Q3	2.5838	3.3077	0.7720	2.6198
	Q4	2.3185	-0.2921	0.7720	1.3807
1994	Q1	-3.7922	-3.1313	0.7820	-3.1365
	Q2	0.4209	-1.2435	0.9027	-0.0303
	Q3	4.8898	0.4950	1.0738	3.1898
	Q4	-0.0157	0.3679	1.2451	0.2254
1995	Q1	9.7366	4.9827	1.4166	7.4784
	Q2	9.5467	6.4890	1.4772	7.8225
	Q3	7.9462	1.9137	1.4267	5.4845
	Q4	6.0207	4.6587	1.3662	5.1467
1996	Q1	5.3676	-2.3395	1.2855	2.6472
	Q2	4.4825	0.4702	1.2754	2.9581

*Composite index weights: equity (60%), fixed income (30%), cash (10%)

chart form. Performance results are reported for one-, two-, three-, four-, and five-year periods. For each period examined, the range of returns is illustrated by the use of a bar.

Consider the rate of return data presented in year 1. As the bar indicates, the highest portfolio return was 27.825 percent,

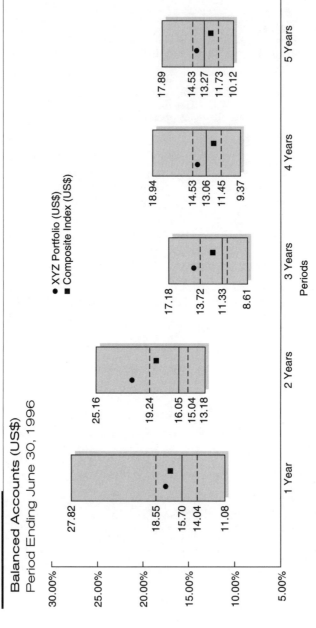

CHART 7-1

Balanced Accounts (US$)
Period Ending June 30, 1996

● XYZ Portfolio (US$)
■ Composite Index (US$)

1 Year: 27.82, 18.55, 15.70, 14.04, 11.08

2 Years: 25.16, 19.24, 16.05, 15.04, 13.18

3 Years: 17.18, 13.72, 11.33, 8.61

4 Years: 18.94, 14.53, 13.06, 11.45, 9.37

5 Years: 17.89, 14.53, 13.27, 11.73, 10.12

Periods

30.00%
25.00%
20.00%
15.00%
10.00%
5.00%

Source: © Frank Russell Company

while the lowest return during this period was 11.08 percent. The 25th percentile, median, and 75th percentile returns are 18.55 percent, 15.70 percent, and 14.04 percent, respectively. During this period, Fund XYZ's return is 17.53 percent (circle), while the composite index's return is 17.22 percent (square). Thus, for the one-year period Fund XYZ outperformed the composite index in terms of return. In addition, it ranks within the second quartile of all funds comprising the selected universe. Fund XYZ outperforms the composite index for all periods measured. Furthermore, it ranks in the top quartile during two out of five measurement periods. Fund XYZ falls within the second quartile during all three remaining measurement periods.

RETURN/RISK ANALYSIS

While the comparison of a fund's return with other funds and indexes serves as an indication of its overall performance, it is also important to compare the degree of risk taken relative to other funds in achieving a given return. Evaluating Fund XYZ's performance relative to the other funds involves the quantification of its risk. A common measure of risk, the *standard deviation*, which we discussed in Chapter 6, compares the quarterly returns with the average returns over the period selected. The resulting measure indicates the riskiness of the fund relative to its return.

Table 7–3 reports the return/risk characteristics of Fund XYZ and the composite index for the five-year period ending June 30, 1996. As the table reveals, Fund XYZ's return exceeds that of the composite index, while its standard deviation is lower than the composite index. A common method of comparing return/risk measures, the *coefficient of variation* (the ratio of standard deviation to average return), can be used to evaluate performance when the return measures differ. A comparison of the coefficients of variation indicates that the composite index is more risky than Fund XYZ. Thus, the fund provides investors with a higher return than the composite while exposing them to lower risk.

TABLE 7-3

Return Risk Profile Index Fund
Five-Year Measures

Performance Measure	Fund XYZ	Composite Index
Annualized return	14.09%	12.41%
Annualized standard deviation	5.33%	5.63%
Coefficient of variation	0.378	0.454

Evaluating a fund's performance over time can be accomplished by comparing its return and risk with those of other funds with the same objectives. A common technique utilized to compare a fund's return/risk measure with those of a universe is to graphically segment funds into quadrants. Chart 7–2 illustrates this technique, again using balanced accounts as the fund's universe. The composite is also plotted in this chart. Annualized rates of return are represented along the vertical axis, while annualized standard deviations are represented along the horizontal axis. The return/risk performance of each fund is then plotted on the chart. The chart is divided into four quadrants. The return and risk of the median funds within the universe are used to delineate these quadrants. Quadrant I represents funds with high return and high risk attributes. Funds found in Quadrant II represent low return/high risk, while funds in Quadrant III are labeled as having low return/low risk. Finally, funds located in Quadrant IV represent high return/low risk portfolios. Ideally, fund managers strive to have their funds located in the "northwest" or in Quadrant IV.

As indicated by the circle in Chart 7–2, Fund XYZ is located in Quadrant IV, while the composite index is located in Quadrant III. Thus, Fund XYZ compares favorably on a return/risk basis. Specifically, it provides investors with a return higher than the median fund while simultaneously exposing investors to lower risk than

CHART 7-2

Balanced Accounts (US$)
Five-Year Period Ending June 30, 1996

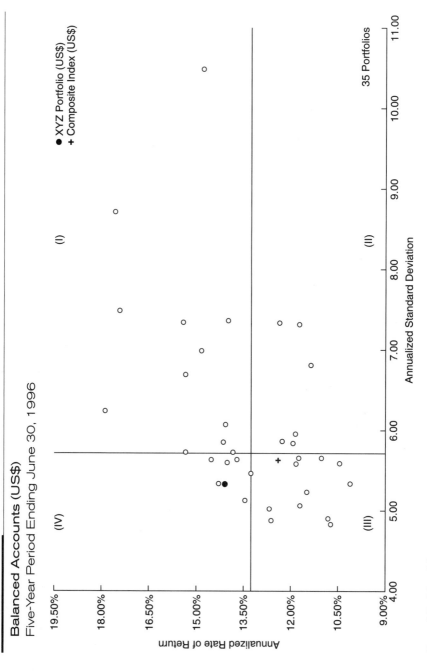

● XYZ Portfolio (US$)
+ Composite Index (US$)

35 Portfolios

Annualized Standard Deviation

Annualized Rate of Return

Source: © Frank Russell Company

157

the median firm in the universe. Investment in the composite index during this same measurement period would have resulted in both lower risk and lower return than the median of the funds represented in this universe.

EVALUATING THE ASSET ALLOCATION DECISION

Total portfolio performance will be affected by both the manager's asset allocation decision and the performance of the securities within each asset category. It is useful to separate the impact of the asset allocation and security selection decisions on performance results. The evaluator should examine the effect of asset allocation and security selection on a quarter by quarter basis. This technique is demonstrated by using the most recent quarterly returns for both Fund XYZ and the composite index (Tables 7–1 and 7–2). Assume that Table 7–4 represents the asset allocation parameters of Fund XYZ. According to these guidelines, the managers of Fund XYZ are permitted to invest up to 15 percent of its assets in cash and equivalents, between 30 and 75 percent in equities, and between 15 and 45 percent in fixed-income securities.

Table 7–5 reports the actual asset allocation as well as the actual returns for each of the components. During the second quarter, 60 percent of its assets was invested in equities, 30 percent

TABLE 7–4

Fund XYZ Asset Allocation Range

Investment Type	Range (%)
Cash and equivalents	0–15
Equity securities	30–75
Fixed income securities	15–45

TABLE 7-5

Fund XYZ (2nd Quarter 1996) Actual Fund Performance

(1) Asset Category	(2) Actual Allocation Percentage (%)	(3) Actual Quarterly Return (%)	(4) Weighted Return (%)
Equities	60	4.6329	2.77974
Fixed income	30	0.5109	0.15327
Cash and equivalents	10	1.3287	0.13287
	100	Actual Portfolio Total Return	3.06588

was in fixed-income securities, and the remaining 10 percent was in cash equivalents. Column 1 in the table represents the asset type, column 2 reports the actual asset allocation weights used by the investment manager, and column 3 lists the second quarter return for each asset type. Finally, column 4, which is the weighted return, is found by multiplying the asset allocation percentage in column 2 by the individual component's return in column 3. Fund XYZ's quarterly return for the second quarter 1996 was 3.0659%.

As the table reveals, during the second quarter, equity securities provide the highest return (4.63 percent) followed by cash and equivalents (1.3287 percent), while fixed-income securities yielded the lowest return (0.5109 percent) during this period. This type of decomposition allows for an examination of the various asset categories' effect on investment performance (i.e., 3.0659 percent).

The information in Table 7-5 can be used to assess the effects of alternative asset allocation decisions on the portfolio's return. What if the portfolio manager had invested the portfolio's funds in different percentages than the 60 percent equities, 30 percent fixed-income, and 10 percent cash equivalents that he actually used? What if he had used the 60 percent, 30 percent, 10 percent asset

TABLE 7-6

Fund XYZ (2nd Quarter 1996) Portfolio Return Assuming
Optimal Asset Allocation

Asset Category	Allocation Percentage (%)	Quarterly Return (%)	Weighted Return (%)
Equities	75	4.6329	3.474675
Fixed income	10	0.5109	0.051090
Cash and equivalents	15	1.3287	0.199305
	100		3.725070

allocation but, instead, had purchased different securities? The answers to these questions are provided in Table 7–6 and Table 7–8.

Obviously, had the investment manager been 100 percent invested in equity securities during this period, total portfolio return would have been 4.63 percent rather than 3.07 percent. However, the portfolio manager was not free to invest 100 percent of the portfolio in common stock, but was limited according to the investment guidelines. Instead, a maximum of 75 percent was allowed to be invested in equities. The next highest performance component for the period was cash and equivalents. The maximum allowable invested in this component was 15 percent. The remaining 10 percent of the portfolio's assets could have been invested in fixed-income securities, the lowest performing component. Therefore, it is more appropriate to evaluate performance given the constraints placed upon the investment manager. Given the investment result for the second quarter of 1996 and the asset allocation guidelines reported in Table 7–4, the "optimal" weighting would have been as follows:

Equities	75%
Fixed income	10
Cash and equivalents	15
	100%

The maximum returns possible, given the asset allocation constraint and securities selected within each investment category, are presented in Table 7–6. As the table reports, a total return of 3.725 percent would have been obtained if Fund XYZ's asset allocation had been 75 percent equities, 10 percent fixed income, and 15 percent cash and equivalents, while holding the identical securities within each category.

The portfolio's total return during this period would have increased by more than 21.5 percent (i.e., 3.725 percent versus 3.066 percent) if the fund manager's allocation decision mirrored the optimal weighting. It should be pointed out that this strategy would have also exposed the fund to more risk since equities are regarded as riskier than fixed-income securities and cash equivalents. Nevertheless, this approach illustrates the impact of asset allocation on investment returns.

Table 7–7 reveals what the portfolio's return would have been if the asset allocation percentages were not allowed to change from those actually used, but if the portfolio manager had selected different securities within each asset class. This assumes that the portfolio manager bought, in essence, the three market indexes. The table reveals that, given the fund's asset allocation, the fund's overall security selection fared well compared with the composite index.

TABLE 7–7

Index Fund Asset Selection Analysis

Asset Category	Allocation Percentage (%)	Quarterly Return (%)	Weighted Return (%)
Equities	60	4.4825	2.6895
Fixed income	30	0.4702	0.1410
Cash and equivalents	10	1.2754	0.1275
	100		2.9580

In Table 7–7, column 2 presents the actual asset allocation percentages of Fund XYZ for the second quarter of 1996, while column 3 presents the actual quarterly returns of the market indexes for the same time period from Table 7–2. The weighted returns in column 4 are the products of columns 2 and 3.

The portfolio's total return during this period would have decreased by about 3.52 percent (i.e., 2.958 percent versus 3.0659 percent) based on security selection. A closer look reveals that for the most recent quarter, the fund's equity performance (4.63 percent) was better than the S&P 500 (4.48 percent), while its fixed-income performance (0.511 percent) exceeded the Lehman Brothers Government/Corporate Index (0.470 percent). Ultimately, the fund's cash and equivalent component (1.329 percent) fared better than the index's Three-Month Treasury Index (1.275 percent).

Finally, the impact of the asset as well as security selection decisions are examined in Table 7–8. The data in this table show the portfolio's total return assuming

1. The ideal or best asset allocation percentages developed in Table 7–6 and
2. The quarterly returns achieved from the market indexes as reported in Table 7–7.

It should not be a surprise that a higher equity allocation would have resulted in higher performance figures. While the

TABLE 7–8

Index Fund Evaluation—Asset Allocation and Selection

Asset Category	Allocation Percentage (%)	Quarterly Return (%)	Weighted Return (%)
Equities	75	4.4825	3.36187
Fixed income	10	0.4702	0.04702
Cash and equivalents	15	1.2754	0.19131
	100		3.60020

TABLE 7-9

Fund XYZ Range of Possible Returns 2nd
Quarter 1996

Investment Choices	(%)
Actual Fund Return (Table 7–5)	3.0659
Return if Optimal Asset Allocation Had Been Made (Table 7–6)	3.7251
Return if Optimal Security Selection Had Been Made (Table 7–7)	2.9580
Return if Both Optimal Asset Allocation and Security Selection Had Been Made (Table 7–8)	3.6002

quarterly return is higher than Fund XYZ's actual return, it is still lower than the return that XYZ could have earned if it employed similar weights. As the preceding analysis reveals, the choice of asset mix plays an important role in achieving investment results. In fact, the asset allocation decision often impacts performance more than the selection of individual securities.

Table 7–9 summarizes the range of returns under the various investment choices cited previously. Column 1 represents alternative securities selection and asset allocation choices available to the money managers, while column 2 reports the quarterly return associated with each choice. As the table reports, the highest quarterly return (3.7251 percent) would have been achieved if the investment manager had selected the optimal asset allocation percentages.

This analysis provides insight into the performance of Fund XYZ. The impact of the investment manager's asset allocation decision as well as the security selection decision can be evaluated relative to assumed asset allocations and investments in appropriate indexes. In the preceding example, the investment manager invested less in equities than permitted (i.e., 60 percent versus 75 percent). The reallocation of assets weights led to an improvement of return as highlighted in Table 7–6. In fact, this scenario generated the highest returns. Clearly, this is due to the superior performance of Fund XYZ's equity component.

PORTFOLIO DECOMPOSITION ANALYSIS

The professional manager's decision regarding the portfolio's asset allocation as well as the selection of securities within these components determine the fund's relative performance. As Table 7–5 reported, the return on Fund XYZ was 3.066 percent during the second quarter of 1996. This return was due to the favorable performance of the fund's securities relative to the individual benchmark indexes. At the same time, the allocation of assets was suboptimal. As Table 7–8 recounts, the benchmark portfolio's return was 3.6002 percent. Recall that this return is based on a combination of the individual indexes' returns (i.e., S&P 500 total return index, Lehman Brothers Government/Corporate Index, and Three-Month Treasury Index) and the optimal weights (i.e., 75 percent equities, 15 percent cash and equivalents, and 10 percent fixed-incomes securities). The difference between Fund XYZ's actual performance results and that of the benchmark portfolio is as follows:

Composite index return	3.600%
Fund XYZ return	–3.066
Deviation	0.534%

Thus, Fund XYZ's returns were 0.534 percent below the benchmark.

The relative impact of the manager's asset allocation and security selection decisions can be separated to identify the source of this deviation. Table 7–10 reports the percentage deviation caused by the suboptimal asset allocation decision. Column 1 represents the asset class, while columns 2 and 3 are the fund and composite

TABLE 7-10

Asset Allocation Deviation (Second Quarter 1996)

Asset Type	Portfolio Weight	Composite Weight	Weight Difference	Return Difference	Asset Allocation Contribution
Equity	0.60	0.75	−0.15	0.00882	−0.00132
Fixed income	0.30	0.10	0.20	−0.03130	−0.00626
Cash and equivalents	0.10	0.15	−0.05	−0.02325	0.00116
					−0.00642

weights, respectively. Column 4 represents the difference between the portfolio weights (column 2) and composite index weights (column 3). Column 5 is found by subtracting the aggregate benchmark return (3.6002 percent) from each of the fund's component returns (in the case of equities, 4.6329 percent minus 3.6002 percent, or 0.8823 percent). The same procedure is used for the fixed-income and cash and equivalent return difference measures. Column 6 represents the asset allocation deviation and is found by multiplying columns 4 and 5.

As the table reports, the manager's asset allocation decision alone resulted in a 0.642 percent return decrease from the benchmark. However, the total deviation between the fund and benchmark index was only 0.534 percent. Thus, the manager's security selection had to reduce the overall deviation by 0.108 percent.

This positive deviation can be isolated using Table 7–11. Column 1 presents the asset type, while columns 2 and 3 report the fund and the benchmark returns, respectively. Column 4 represents the difference between the portfolio's component returns (column 2) and the benchmark's component returns (column 3). Column 5 depicts Fund XYZ's asset mix percentages. Finally, column 6 reports the influence of Fund XYZ's components due to the security selection contributor.

TABLE 7-11

Security Selection Deviation (Second Quarter 1996)

Asset Class	Portfolio Return	Benchmark Return	Difference	Fund Weights	Selection Contribution
Equity	0.0463	0.0448	0.0015	0.60	0.00090
Fixed income	0.0051	0.0047	0.0004	0.30	0.00012
Cash and equivalents	0.0133	0.0128	0.0005	0.10	0.00005
					0.00108

As the table indicates, the manager's security selection had a positive impact on the fund's investment performance. The results of Tables 7–9 and 7–10 are summarized as follows:

Asset allocation difference	−0.642%
Security selection difference	+0.108
Deviation of return	−0.534%

Thus, the fund's subpar performance return (i.e., −0.534 percent) was a result of a suboptimal asset allocation decision (−0.642 percent). The manager's security selection decision actually achieved results superior (0.108 percent) to that of the benchmark. The preceding approach can be employed by the investment committee to isolate the relative impact of the manager's asset allocation and security selection investment decisions on investment performance.

EVALUATION OF CASH AND EQUIVALENT COMPONENT

The next step in the evaluation of investment results is to examine the performance characteristics of the individual components. In this section, we begin this process by evaluating the cash and equivalent component of the portfolio. An in-depth evaluation of the equities and fixed-income components will be conducted in Chapters 8 and 9, respectively.

Cash is evaluated in the same manner as the other two components. Specifically, a comparison index and universe are selected based on the investment guidelines contained in the policy statement. For illustration purposes, the Salomon Brothers Three-Month Treasury Bill Index is used to index the data, while the Short-Term Investment Funds (STIF) and Cash Accounts are used as the universe. These data are presented in Chart 7–3.

The circles contained in the bar chart represent the annualized rate of return for the fund's cash and equivalent component, while the square represents the Salomon Brothers Three-Month Treasury Bill Index's return during each period. Again, the top of each bar represents the highest return for a given fund within the investment universe, while the bottom of the bar reflects the lowest return of a fund within the universe. The 25th percentile, median, and 75th percentile are represented by horizontal lines drawn across the bar chart. Supporting data are contained at the bottom of the chart for each period measured.

As the chart indicates, the cash and equivalent component performs poorly in all comparisons. In fact, its return is less than the minimum STIF and cash account's returns for the one-, two-, four-, and five-year measurement periods. However, the cash and equivalent return component outperforms the Treasury Bill Index's in every period. In terms of return, the cash and equivalent component falls short of the performance goals.

Chart 7–4 reports the performance results incorporating risk into the analysis. The scatter diagram presented in this chart is very revealing. Although the five-year annualized return is low, so is the risk. Again, the cash component's return/risk position is indicated by a circle and is located in the southeast quadrant. This indicates that it achieves a lower return and a higher risk than the median portfolios. Using a return/risk criterion, the

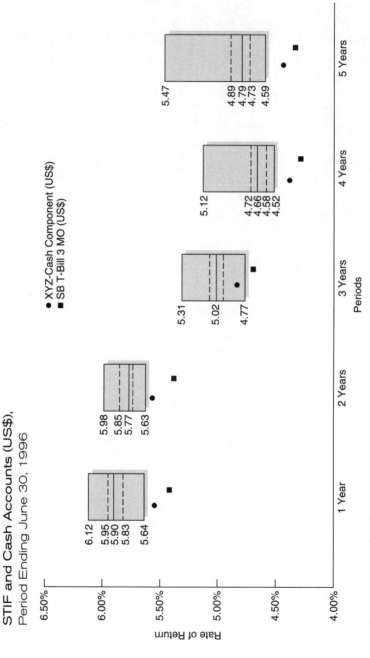

CHART 7-3

STIF and Cash Accounts (US$),
Period Ending June 30, 1996

● XYZ-Cash Component (US$)
■ SB T-Bill 3 MO (US$)

Rate of Return

6.50%
6.00%
5.50%
5.00%
4.50%
4.00%

1 Year
6.12
5.95
5.90
5.83
5.64

2 Years
5.98
5.85
5.77
5.63

3 Years
5.31
5.02
4.77

4 Years
5.12
4.72
4.66
4.58
4.52

5 Years
5.47
4.89
4.79
4.73
4.59

Periods

Source: © Frank Russell Company

168

CHART 7-4

STIF and Cash Accounts (US$),
Five-Year Period Ending June 30, 1996

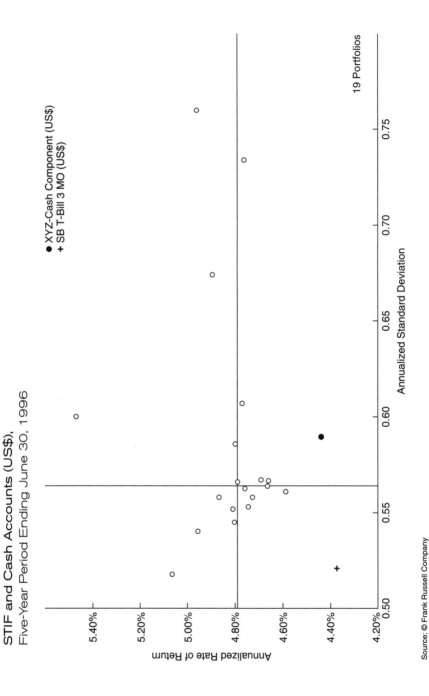

● XYZ-Cash Component (US$)
+ SB T-Bill 3 MO (US$)

Annualized Standard Deviation

Annualized Rate of Return

19 Portfolios

Source: © Frank Russell Company

169

cash component has a slightly higher return and higher risk than the index.

Table 7–12 presents the summary statistics corresponding to Chart 7–4. The universe consists of 19 portfolios. The maximum five-year annualized return and standard deviation are 5.47 percent and 0.76 percent, respectively. In addition, the median return is 4.79 percent, while the median standard deviation is 0.56 percent. The 25th and 75th percentile are also reported in the table. Fund XYZ's cash and equivalent component has a return of 4.45 percent and a standard deviation of 0.59 percent. Thus, in terms of its return/risk characteristics, the cash portion of the portfolio is below the universe's minimum range. Finally, the cash and equivalent component generates a slightly greater return than the index, but it also incurs greater risk.

The component analysis illustrated earlier suggests that both the equity and fixed-income portions of Fund XYZ perform well. This is true when examining performance results using both the return measures and return/risk measures. In both instances, these

TABLE 7–12

Return/Risk Analysis, Cash and Equivalent Component
Five-year Annualized Measures, 19 Portfolios

	Return (%)	Standard Deviation (%)
Maximum	5.47	0.76
25th percentile	4.89	0.60
Median	4.79	0.56
75th percentile	4.73	0.55
Minimum	4.59	0.52
Cash component	4.45	0.59
S&P 500	4.37	0.52

Source: Frank Russell Company

components fared well when compared with selected indexes and universes. In contrast, the cash and equivalent component's performance results are poor when compared with the returns achieved by the universe and index. After taking into account the return/risk characteristics of this component, investment performance still leaves something to be desired.

SUMMARY

The evaluation of portfolio performance must be based on specific, measurable criteria. Performance can be measured against an index or an investment universe. In selecting an index (or indexes), the evaluator must be careful that the measure selected matches the desired characteristics of the fund to be evaluated. Even so, the evaluator must recognize that indexes do not reflect the transaction costs and fees that are reflected in managed investment accounts.

Given this problem, evaluators should also use investment universes as a means of comparison. These universes, or groupings of funds with desired characteristics, provide a better means of comparison. These benchmarks can be used to evaluate overall portfolio performance and/or their components. Regardless of the comparison method, performance should be evaluated on the basis of return and risk.

As part of the evaluation process, the fund's performance relative to security selection and asset allocation should be examined. The effect of each decision on overall performance provides the evaluator with proper insight as to the origins of the fund's investment performance, which aids in the identification of factors influencing the success of the fund.

CHAPTER 8

Equity Performance Evaluation

INTRODUCTION

In the preceding chapter, performance results of Fund XYZ were evaluated. In addition to examining the fund's overall return, the effect of the fund manager's asset allocation decision was examined. The chapter concluded with an evaluation of the cash and equivalent component of the fund. In this chapter, equity performance characteristics are examined in more depth. Chapter 9 focuses on the evaluation of fixed-income portfolios.

There are several ways to evaluate the equity portion of a portfolio and that of a fund comprised primarily of equity securities. For example, the equity results can be compared with an index possessing similar characteristics. In this instance, managers might be required to achieve investment results consistently better than the selected index. In addition, performance results can be evaluated in terms of an investment universe. Here, portfolio managers might be expected to achieve a ranking within the top quartile of the universe.

In addition, insights into the performance of the fund may be obtained by employing a *sector approach*. This approach allows the investment policy committee to identify the causes for differences in returns between the performance of the fund's equity component and the comparison index. This technique separates the return deviations into sector and selection categories.

Greater insight into the return/risk characteristics of a portfolio can be achieved by examining the market characteristics of the
equity portfolio. Specifically, the alpha, beta, and R² can be calculated to evaluate performance results. Additionally, other performance measures such as the Sharpe index, Jenson index, Treynor
ratio, and Appraisal ratio, which were discussed in Chapter 6, can
be used to further the evaluation process.

Another approach, *attribution analysis*, can be helpful. Different
investment styles are marked by unique financial characteristics.
For example, an income-oriented portfolio and a growth-oriented
portfolio would be expected to have different attributes. Specifically, capitalization, price/earnings ratios, earning growth rates,
dividend yields, betas, and other financial characteristics of these
equity portfolios should differ significantly. Attribution analysis allows the investment committee to compare the characteristics of
their fund with those of funds with similar objectives.

EQUITY PERFORMANCE CRITERIA

Typically, the equity component of a portfolio is compared with an
index and/or universe as provided in the investment policy statement. The investment committee selects the appropriate benchmarks based on the portfolio's objectives, risk tolerances, and any
other characteristics that are unique to the fund. The S&P 500 Index
and Frank Russell's Equity Accounts universe will be used to illustrate this technique.

Table 8–1 reports the quarterly return of the S&P 500, Fund
XYZ, and the Three-Month Treasury Bill Index from the first quarter of 1991 through the second quarter of 1996. Column one lists the
period, while columns 2, 3, and four report the corresponding
quarterly returns of the S&P 500, Fund XYZ, and 3-month Treasury
Bill. This data will be used to illustrate the techniques available for
equity performance evaluation.

Chart 8–1 compares the performance of Fund XYZ's equity
component with the S&P 500 and more than 200 portfolios consti-
tuting an investment universe. These bar charts display the one-,

TABLE 8-1

Quarterly Returns (Percentages)

Period	S&P 500 Index	Fund XYZ	Three-Month Treasury Bill
1991 Q1	14.5267	14.3974	1.6692
Q2	–0.2287	–0.4511	1.4772
Q3	5.3480	6.5298	1.4267
Q4	8.3846	7.7894	1.3056
1992 Q1	–2.5256	–1.4591	1.0235
Q2	1.9012	2.3912	0.9933
Q3	3.1523	4.0100	0.9027
Q4	1.9012	4.5598	0.7720
1993 Q1	5.0349	4.1609	0.7720
Q2	4.3670	1.0300	0.7418
Q3	0.4869	2.9579	0.7720
Q4	2.5838	3.1310	0.7720
1994 Q1	2.3185	–3.1794	0.7820
Q2	–3.7922	0.3219	0.9027
Q3	0.4209	5.1790	1.0738
Q4	4.8898	1.8945	1.2451
1995 Q1	9.7366	10.4572	1.4166
Q2	9.5467	9.7984	1.4772
Q3	7.9462	7.9784	1.4267
Q4	6.0207	6.2190	1.3662
1996 Q1	5.3676	5.2864	1.2855
Q2	4.4825	4.6325	1.2754

two-, three-, four-, and five-year annualized rates of return for Fund XYZ and the S&P 500. The squares contained in the bar chart represent the annualized rate of return for the fund's equity component, while the circles indicate the S&P 500 return for each period. The top of each bar represents the highest return for a given portfolio within the universe, while the bottom of the chart reflects the lowest return of a portfolio within the investment universe. In

CHART 8-1

Equity Accounts (US$)
Period Ending June 30, 1996

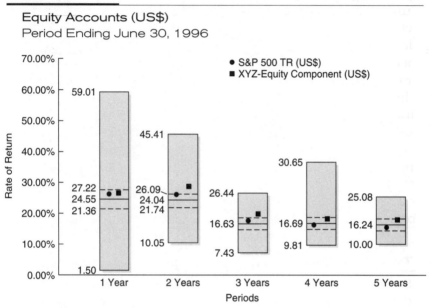

Source: © Frank Russell Company

addition, the horizontal lines contained in the bar chart represent the 25th percentile, median, and 75th percentile ranking within the universe.

As this chart reveals, the equity component's return ranks within the first quartile for both the two- and three-year periods. For the one-, four-, and five-year periods, its return is above the median. For all periods measured, Fund XYZ's equity component provides investors with a higher return than the S&P 500.

SECTOR ANALYSIS

Performance is evaluated based on the investment results of the individual sectors as well as the concentration of funds within a given sector. Under this approach, the return and percentage invested in each sector of the S&P 500 are compared with the sector return and percentage invested in each sector by the fund. The impact of investing within a particular sector can also provide valuable information to the evaluator. This approach is generally used when comparing the performance of a fund with an overall index. For example, using the S&P 500, securities are classified according to industry sectors. These sectors would include consumer nondurables, consumer durables, materials and services, capital goods, technology, energy, transportation, utilities, and finance.

Table 8–2 lists the returns and percentage weights of each sector comprising the S&P 500 and Fund XYZ. Column 1 lists the nine sectors just described. Columns 2 and 3 report the returns and weights for each sector found in the S&P 500, respectively. Columns 4 and 5 report the returns and weights comprising Fund XYZ, respectively.

TABLE 8–2

S&P 500 and Fund XYZ Summary Data
(Second Quarter 1996)

	S&P 500		Fund XYZ	
Sector	Return (%)	Weight (%)	Return (%)	Weight (%)
Consumer nondurables	7.01	33.1	7.150	29.8
Consumer durables	−1.05	2.7	−3.120	3.1
Materials and services	−3.00	8.4	−3.039	3.0
Capital goods	6.20	5.3	6.950	3.8
Technology	7.10	14.3	8.150	15.4
Energy	5.20	9.5	5.300	10.2
Transportation	1.21	1.6	1.140	11.0
Utilities	3.30	11.6	3.350	11.9
Finance	1.50	13.5	.900	11.8

Total Return S&P 500 = 4.4852%
Total Return Fund XYZ = 4.6328%

During the second quarter of 1996, Fund XYZ achieved a return of 4.6325 percent, while the S&P 500 registered a return of 4.4825 percent (Table 8–1). Thus, for the period Fund XYZ's return exceeded that of the S&P 500 by 0.1500 percent. Obviously, the professional manager's superior performance results relative to the S&P 500 Index can be attributed to better security selection within the sectors and/or to investing a greater percentage of the fund's assets in sectors that achieved higher returns.

Sector analysis can assist the investment committee in determining the sources of the 0.150 percent incremental return earned by the fund. The relative impact of security selection and sector weighting can be separated to identify the causes of this variance.

Table 8–3 shows the methodology used to isolate the effect of security selection within each sector. Again, column 1 represents the individual sectors. Column 2 reports the sector weights of Fund XYZ. Columns 3 and 4 report the sector returns of Fund XYZ and the S&P 500, respectively. Finally, column 5 measures the relative secu-

TABLE 8–3

Contribution by Stock Selection

(1) Sector	(2) Fund XYZ Weights (%)	(3) Fund XYZ Rate of Return (%)	(4) S&P 500 Rate of Return (%)	(5) Stock Selection* (%)
Consumer nondurables	.298	7.15	7.01	0.000417
Consumer Durables	.031	−3.12	−1.05	−0.000642
Materials and Services	.030	−3.04	−3.00	−0.000012
Capital Goods	.038	6.95	6.20	0.000285
Technology	.154	8.15	7.10	0.001617
Energy	.102	5.30	5.20	0.000102
Transportation	.110	1.14	1.21	−0.000077
Utilities	.119	3.35	3.30	0.000060
Finance	.118	0.90	1.50	−0.000708
Security contributor				.001042

Column 5 equals Col. 2 (Col. 3 − Col. 4)/100

rity's contribution within each sector and is computed by multiplying column 2 by the difference between columns 3 and 4 divided by 100. The sum of column five represents the percentage difference (0.150 percent) in return due to security selection. As the table reveals, 0.1042 percent of the difference (0.15 percent) between the S&P 500 Index and Fund XYZ's return was due to security selection. The next step is to identify the difference between the index and fund return which was the result of the manager's sector selection.

Table 8–4 calculates the percentage deviation caused by overweighting well-performing sectors while underweighting poorly performing sectors in Fund XYZ (relative to the S&P 500.) This table shows the methodology used to isolate the impact of management's decision concerning sector investment. Column 1 represents the individual sectors. Columns 2 and 3 report the sector weights of Fund XYZ and the S&P 500 Index, respectively. Column 4 displays the S&P 500 rate of return for each sector. Finally,

TABLE 8–4

Contribution by Sector Weighting

(1) Sectors	(2) Fund XYZ Weights (%)	(3) S&P 500 Weights (%)	(4) S&P 500 Rate of Return (%)	(5) Sector Difference* (%)
Consumer nondurables	.2980	.3310	7.01	−0.000834
Consumer durables	.0310	.0270	−1.05	−0.000221
Materials and services	.0300	.0840	−3.00	0.004041
Capital goods	.0380	.0530	6.20	−0.000258
Technology	.1540	.1430	7.10	0.000288
Energy	.1020	.0950	5.20	0.000050
Transportation	.1100	.0160	1.21	−0.003076
Utilities	.1190	.1160	3.30	−0.000035
Finance	.1180	.1350	1.50	0.000507
Sector contributor				0.000461

*Column 5 equals (Col.2 – Col. 3) × (Col. 4 – 4.483%)/100

column 5 measures the individual sector's contribution to the return variance, and is computed by first subtracting the S&P 500
Indexes' weights from Fund XYZ's weights. Next, the S&P 500
Indexes return (4.483%) is subtracted from the S & P 500's individual sector returns. Finally, these two amounts are multiplied together, and the product is divided by 100. The sum of column five
represents the percentage point difference in return due to sector
selection. Thus, the manager's sector weighting decision resulted
in an additional 0.0461 percent return above the S&P 500 Index.

Thus, the results of Table 8–3 and 8–4 are summarized as follows:

$$
\begin{array}{lcccc}
\text{Difference in Return} & = & \dfrac{\text{Return on}}{\text{Fund XYZ}} & - & \dfrac{\text{Return on}}{\text{S\&P 500}} \\[2ex]
.1500 & = & 4.6325 & - & 4.4825 \\[2ex]
\dfrac{\text{Difference due to}}{\text{security selection}} & = & .1042 & & \\[2ex]
\dfrac{\text{Difference due to}}{\text{sector allocation}} & = & \underline{.0461} & & \\[2ex]
\text{Total difference in returns} & & .1503 & &
\end{array}
$$

RETURN/RISK COMPARISON

In the preceding analysis, Fund XYZ was evaluated on the basis of
investment return. While this is indeed important, performance
should not only be based on return but also on the level of risk
taken in achieving the return. Therefore, the performance of Fund
XYZ will now be evaluated on the basis of return/risk characteristics. Chart 8–2 presents a scatter diagram containing the return and
standard deviation for the equity component, the S&P 500, and 229
portfolios, which comprise the investment universe. As the chart
indicates, the equity portion of Fund XYZ (circle) lies in the northwest quadrant, indicating a higher return and a lower risk than the
median portfolios. In contrast, the S&P 500 (represented by the
plus sign) has both a lower return and a lower risk than the median

CHART 8-2

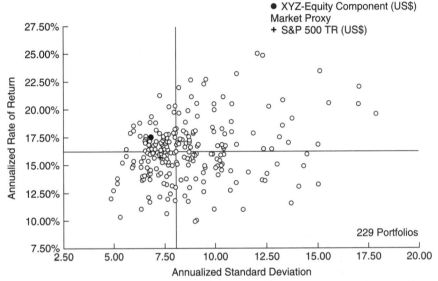

Equity Accounts (US$)
Period Ending June 30, 1996

● XYZ-Equity Component (US$)
Market Proxy
+ S&P 500 TR (US$)

Annualized Rate of Return

229 Portfolios

Annualized Standard Deviation

Source: © Frank Russell Company

portfolio. Thus, on a return/risk basis, Fund XYZ's equity component is performing well.

Key data underlying Chart 8–2 appear in Table 8–5. As the table reports, the selected investment universe consists of 229 portfolios. The portfolio with the highest return had a five-year annualized return of 25.08 percent and an annualized standard deviation of 17.85 percent. The portfolio with the median return and standard deviation was 16.24 percent and 8.08 percent, respectively. The 25th and 75th percentile portfolios are also reported in this table. During this period, Fund XYZ's equity component had a return of 17.56 percent and a standard deviation of 6.82 percent. This compares favorably with the S&P 500's return and standard deviation of 15.73 percent and 7.24 percent, respectively.

TABLE 8–5

Return/Risk Analysis, Equity Accounts (229
Portfolios)
Five-Year Annualized Measures

	Return (%)	Standard Deviation (%)
Maximum	25.08	17.85
25th percentile	17.70	9.93
Median	16.24	8.08
75th percentile	14.83	7.22
Minimum	10.00	4.83
Equity component	17.56	6.82
S&P 500	15.73	7.24

Source: Frank Russell Company

MARKET CHARACTERISTICS

Investment committee members should have a thorough understanding of the return/risk characteristics of equity portfolios. As
discussed in Chapter 6, there are various measures that provide insight into the relationship between a fund and the overall market.
Chart 8–3 provides visual evidence of the relationship between
Fund XYZ and the S&P 500 Index from January 1, 1994, through
June 30, 1996. This chart depicts the quarterly returns of Fund XYZ
and the S&P 500 over this period of time. It is noteworthy to view
the apparent high correlation of their returns over this period.

This relationship can be quantified through the use of regression analysis. Here, the investment performance of Fund XYZ
is compared with that of the market (S&P 500). The resulting risk-
adjusted return measures are used in the regression equation as
follows:

$$Y_t = \alpha + \beta \cdot X + e_t$$

CHART 8–3

Equity Accounts (US$)
Period Ending June 30, 1996

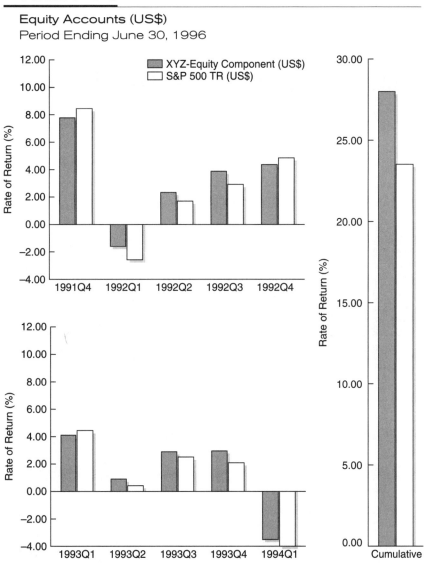

Source: © Frank Russell Company

where

Y_t = portfolio return in time period t
X = index return in time period t
α = regression intercept
β = regression slope
e = residual term

Table 8–6 provides summary statistics for the regression equation.

As the table reveals, Fund XYZ's alpha is estimated to be 0.52 percent (quarterly basis), which represents the return attributable to security selection. Recall from Chapter 6 that the *alpha* (or *Jensen index*) is an indicator of the professional manager's contribution to investment performance. Thus, in this case, professional management was able to achieve a superior return relative to the S&P 500 Index.

TABLE 8–6

MPT Statistics, Fund XYZ Equity Component (US $)
January 1, 1991, through June 30, 1996, 22 Periods

Annualized statistics (%)	
Rate of return	18.62
Standard deviation	8.05
Quarterly statistics (%)	
Maximum return	14.40
Minimum return	−3.18
Average return	4.44
Standard deviation	4.03
Variance	16.22
Regression statistics	
Alpha	0.52
Beta	0.94
R^2	0.98
Correlation	0.99
Standard error	0.56

Source: Frank Russell Company

A portfolio's *beta* is a measure of systematic or market-related risk. For the measurement period, Fund XYZ's beta was estimated to be 0.94. Thus, a 10 percent change in the return of the market would be expected to produce a 9.4 percent change in the return for Fund XYZ. Thus, the fund possesses less systematic risk than the market as a whole.

Finally, the Fund XYZ's R^2 is 0.98. This coefficient of determination suggests that almost all (i.e., 98 percent) of the variability in the fund's return is explained by the market return. In this instance, Fund XYZ performed well on a risk-adjusted basis. This fund is characterized as being well diversified and having less volatility than the S&P 500. The market characteristic line for Fund XYZ using risk-adjusted rates of return and the S&P 500 as the market proxy is presented in Chart 8–4.

CHART 8–4

Risk versus Return Analysis Using Risk-Adjusted Returns
XYZ Portfolio versus S&P 500 Index

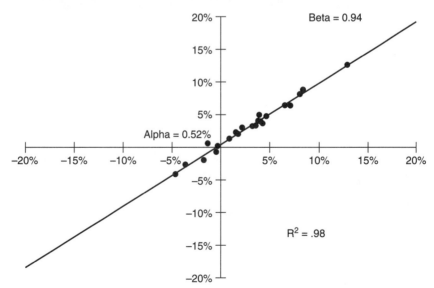

ADDITIONAL PERFORMANCE MEASURES

Several other measures of portfolio risk have been developed. Among them are the Sharpe index, Treynor's ratio, and the Appraisal ratio. Each of these methods attempts to view return in the context of risk.

The *Sharpe index* compares the excess return of a portfolio with its risk. Excess return is defined as the portfolio return in excess of the riskless rate of return. Recall that the numerator of the Sharpe index (i.e., $R_j - R_f$) measures the so-called excess return of the portfolio, while the denominator measures the fund's overall risk or variability. In essence, the numerator provides the evaluator with a measure of the additional return or "premium" earned by taking on risk, while the denominator reports the level of risk taken during the measurement period. The higher the Sharpe index, the greater return premium per unit of risk. Thus, this excess return to variability measure captures the tradeoff between additional return and its associated risk. The Sharpe index (SI) measure is defined as follows:

$$SI = \frac{(R_j - R_f)}{sd_j}$$

where

R_j = the average return of portfolio j

R_f = the risk free rate of return using Treasury bills

sd_j = the standard deviation of returns of portfolio j

For the XYZ portfolio, the Sharpe index (January 1, 1991, to June 30, 1996. using quarterly data) is as follows:

$$SI_{xyz} = \frac{(0.1862 - 0.0454)}{0.0805}$$

$$= \frac{0.1408}{0.0805}$$

$$= 1.749$$

During the same measurement period, the Sharpe index for the S&P 500 is as follows:

$$SI_{S\&P500} = \frac{(0.1700 - 0.0454)}{0.0844}$$

$$= \frac{0.1246}{0.0805}$$

$$= 1.476$$

A comparison of Fund XYZ and the S&P 500 Index's Sharpe measure suggests that the Fund XYZ provides investors with a greater return premium per unit of risk. For every unit of risk, Fund XYZ investors receive 1.749 units of return, while holders of the S&P 500 receive only 1.476 units of return for every unit of risk. Thus, according to the Sharpe index, investors are getting a higher return premium from Fund XYZ than if they had invested in the S&P 500.

The *Treynor ratio* is similar to the Sharpe index except that it compares the fund's excess return with the fund's market risk, as measured by its beta. In essence, the Treynor ratio measures the trade-off between the additional return earned (i.e., above the risk-free rate) and the portfolio's exposure to market risk. The higher the ratio, the greater the reward from the trade-off. Thus, the numerator in the equation is the same as the Sharpe index. However, instead of using total variability, the Treynor ratio divides excess return by the portfolio's beta. The formula is as follows:

$$TR = \frac{(R_j - R_f)}{\beta_j}$$

where

R_j = the average return of portfolio j
R_f = the risk free rate of return using T-bills
β_j = portfolio j's beta

Earlier, Fund XYZ's beta was estimated to be 0.94. Thus, for Fund XYZ the Treynor ratio would be as follows:

$$TR_{xyz} = \frac{(0.1862 - 0.0454)}{0.94}$$

$$= \frac{14.08}{0.94}$$

$$= 0.1498$$

Likewise, the Treynor ratio for the S&P 500 over this same time period is found using the same formula. However, since the beta of the S&P 500 is 1.00, the Treynor ratio for this index would simply equal the numerator of the equation:

$$TR_{S\&P\ 500} = \frac{(0.1700 - 0.0454)}{1.00}$$

$$= \frac{0.1246}{1.00}$$

$$= 0.1246$$

Again, Fund XYZ offers greater reward for the risk taken (this time, market risk), than the S&P 500. Therefore, it affords the investor a greater trade-off between the additional return earned and the portfolio's exposure to market risk than the market index.

Recall from Chapter 6 that the Appraisal ratio divides the portfolio's alpha by the portfolio's unsytematic or diversifiable risk. The portfolio's alpha measures the average return over that predicted by the market return, given the portfolio's beta. The unsystematic risk is the risk that, in principle, can be eliminated via diversification. Hence, the Appraisal ratio indicates an abnormal return per unit of diversifiable risk.

The Appraisal ratio formula is as follows:

$$AP = \frac{\alpha_p}{\sigma_{(e)}}$$

TABLE 8-7

Return/Risk Analysis, Selected Measures

Portfolio	Sharpe Index Coefficient	Treynor Ratio	Appraisal Ratio
Fund XYZ	1.749	0.1498	0.93
S&P 500	1.476	0.1246	N/A

where

α_p = alpha of the portfolio

$\sigma_{(e)}$ = diversifiable risk of the portfolio

For Fund XYZ, the Appraisal ratio is

$$AP_{xyz} = \frac{0.52}{0.56}$$
$$= 0.93$$

Table 8–7 displays the Sharpe index, Treynor ratio, and the Appraisal ratio for Fund XYZ and the S&P 500. As shown in the table, Fund XYZ outperforms the S&P 500 using both the Sharpe index and the Treynor measure. Since the S&P 500 index does not contain unsystematic risk, the appraisal ratio cannot be computed.

ATTRIBUTE ANALYSIS

Investment managers employ different approaches to managing a portfolio. These include value, growth, income, and a number of other styles. Each of these approaches should be reflected in the choice of securities held within a given portfolio. *Attribute analysis* compares the investment characteristics of a fund with those in its investment universe. The fund profile provides a great deal of information concerning the makeup of the fund.

The usefulness of attribute analysis is that it provides the evaluator with a comparison of the characteristics of the portfolio developed by the investment manager relative to the characteristics of portfolios developed by other managers with supposedly similar styles. Suppose the investment committee has chosen an investment manager in order to generate current income for a portion of the fund's equity portfolio. Each of the portfolios that the investment manager develops should have a high market capitalization and dividend yield because these are general characteristics of income portfolios. Similarly, the portfolios should exhibit relatively low price/earnings ratios and betas, and moderate returns on net worth and the three-year earnings growth rate. A more useful comparison, however, is based on an examination of the attribution of the investment manager's income portfolio when compared with portfolios developed by a universe of income managers.

Charts 8–5 through 8–10 compare Fund XYZ's market data with a selected universe. Specifically, the charts compare the fund's market capitalization, price/earnings ratio, dividend yields, beta,

CHART 8–5

Equity Portfolio Comparison—Market Capitalization (Billions of Dollars)

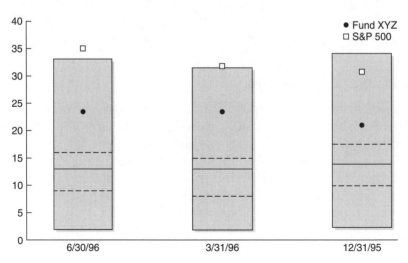

return on net worth and three-year earnings growth rates, respectively, with the investment universe via the use of bar charts.

The information in Chart 8–5 reveals that Fund XYZ's investment manager assembled a portfolio whose market capitalization was high and rising and, at the end of June 1996, was in the top quartile of all portfolios managed by income managers.

Chart 8–6 reveals that the portfolio managers selected stocks with an aggregate price/earnings ratio either below or at the median of the distribution of P/E ratios among income managers. Relatedly, the dividend yields on Fund XYZ (Chart 8–7) were on the high end of all comparable income portfolios. The portfolio also contained stocks whose aggregate risk as measured by portfolio beta (Chart 8–8) was below the midpoint of all similar portfolios. Furthermore, Fund XYZ built a portfolio whose return on equity (Chart 8–9) was above the median. Finally, the portfolio's earnings

CHART 8–6

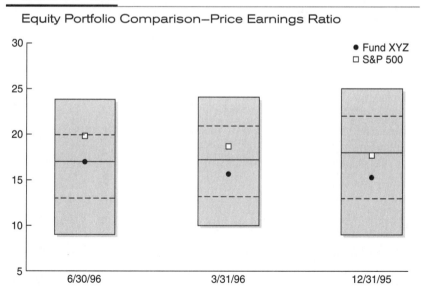

Equity Portfolio Comparison–Price Earnings Ratio

CHART 8-7

Equity Portfolio Comparison—Dividend Yield

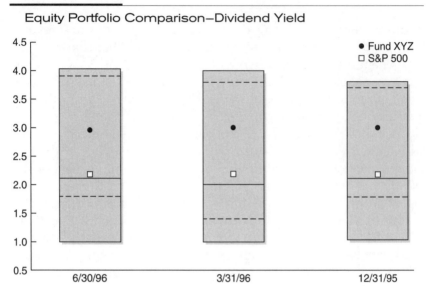

CHART 8-8

Equity Portfolio Comparison—Beta

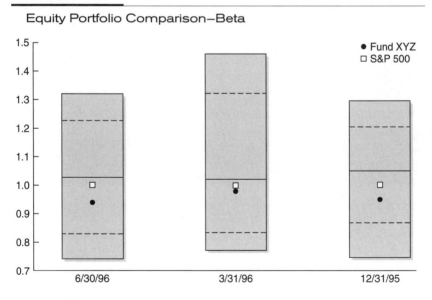

CHART 8-9

Equity Portfolio Comparison—Return on Equity (%)

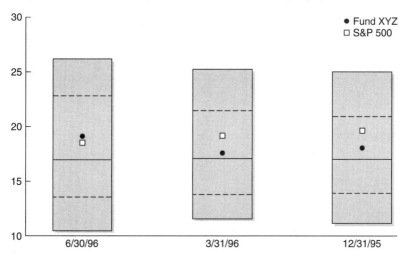

CHART 8-10

Equity Portfolio Comparison—Three-Year Earnings Growth Rate (%)

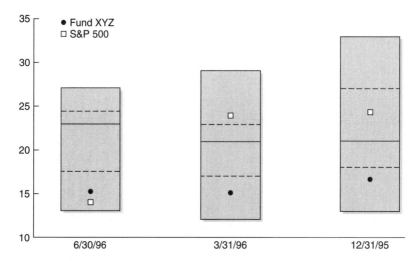

growth rate (Chart 8–10) ranked in the lowest quartile of all portfolios compiled by investment managers.

Having compared the attributes of the income equity portfolio developed by the investment manager of Fund XYZ with those of his peers, we could conclude that the manager's actions are, in fact, designed to produce current income without high risk. The investment manager of Fund XYZ is acting in accordance with the objectives established by the investment sponsors.

SUMMARY

There are several approaches that the investment committee can undertake in the evaluation of equity performance. The starting point in such an analysis is to identify benchmarks by which to compare the investment results of the portfolio. It is important to select a benchmark that reflects the goals and objectives of the portfolio under evaluation. In addition to the selection of an appropriate index, investment universes are available for comparison purposes.

Using these benchmarks, portfolio performance can be examined on both a return basis and a risk-adjusted return basis. In addition to overall performance, portfolios can be evaluated using a sector approach, where the investment manager is judged not only on security selection but also on sector selection. More sophisticated techniques, such as modern portfolio theory, use tools such as regression analysis to measure investment performance against the market. The resulting data provide useful information such as market risk, the degree of diversification, and excess returns achieved through security selection.

Finally, financial and market characteristics of firms with similar goals and objectives can be compared through attribution analysis. Here such traits as capitalization, price/earnings ratio, dividend yield, earnings growth rate, return on net worth, and beta can be evaluated to gain a better understanding of the fund's financial and market attributes compared with peer group portfolios.

CHAPTER 9

Fixed-Income
Performance Evaluation

INTRODUCTION

The objectives in evaluating a fund's fixed-income portfolio are to determine if the portfolio developed by the fund's manager, and its components, are in compliance with the dictates of the investment policy statement and to ascertain the portfolio's sources of return and risk. This last objective, in particular, will help the investment committee determine if the fund's manager has enhanced the fund's value beyond what could be obtained from a passive, indexed strategy.

As we discussed in Chapter 2, a well-designed investment policy statement should specify the return and risk characteristics desired for the overall portfolio. With regard to a fund's fixed-income component, characteristics pertaining to the issuers of fixed-income securities, acceptable overall and individual risks, and the maturity distribution also need to be specified.

ISSUERS OF FIXED-INCOME SECURITIES

Issuers of fixed-income securities include the U.S. Treasury, agencies of the federal government, domestic and foreign corporations, and state and local (municipal) governments. Each of these original issuers offer fixed-income securities with a seemingly ever-growing and widening array of features.

The pace of innovations has been extremely rapid in the financial sector for about the last 25 years, and the pace of change arguably is accelerating. Many of these innovations have occurred in the markets for fixed-income securities. For example, the market for mortgage-backed fixed-income securities was virtually nonexistent in the early 1970s. Today it represents more than 20 percent of the U.S. bond market.

The surge in the variety and complexity of fixed-income instruments being offered by issuers provides opportunities for investment committees and the managers they select (and oversee) to enhance yields. However, the greater complexity of such investment vehicles also poses potential problems if committee members do not understand their general properties and if the manager(s) do not comprehend the return and risk properties in significant detail. Taking advantage of the yield-enhancing opportunities associated with more complex fixed-income instruments while mitigating their risk is no easy feat.

The investment committee must determine—and specify in the investment policy statement—the types of fixed-income instruments (by issuer) that are permissible for the manager to purchase. Additionally, the committee might consider placing constraints on the specific types of securities, by type of issuer, the fund manager can purchase. The limits of these constraints will depend on the committee's understanding of the properties of various fixed-income securities and the committee's confidence and trust in the knowledge and ability of the fund manager(s).

QUALITY OF FIXED-INCOME SECURITIES

The investment committee must also determine and specify in the investment policy statement the quality or risk characteristics that are desired for the fixed-income portion of the fund. While an apparently straightforward task, this exercise can quickly become a daunting and perplexing one. The leading authority on fixed-income markets, Frank J. Fabozzi, discusses 12 separate types of risks that may be associated with investing in fixed-income instruments.[1] Although a detailed discussion of these risks is beyond the scope of this book, a brief description of each risk type is given in Table 9–1. Moreover, a more thorough description of the two most important types of risks associated with fixed-income instruments, credit and interest rate risk, is presented in the following sections.

TABLE 9–1

Types of Risk Associated with Fixed-Income Securities

Risk Type	Description
Call risk	Risk that issuer will retire bond before maturity, thereby exposing investor to reinvestment risk.
Default risk	Likelihood that issuer will not make interest or principal payments at contractually scheduled times.
Event risk	Risk that sudden, unexpected event will impair ability of issuer to make interest and principal payments at contractually scheduled times.
Exchange rate risk	Risk that bonds denominated in a foreign currency will depreciate relative to the dollar, reducing the dollar yield to the investor.
Inflation risk	Risk that inflation will erode the expected purchasing power of the interest and principal payments.
Interest rate risk	Risk that unanticipated increases in market interest rates will reduce the market value of bonds.
Liquidity risk	Risk that the costs of liquidating bonds will significantly reduce return.
Reinvestment risk	Risk that reinvestment of bond proceeds will produce lower returns because of declines in market rates of interest.
Risk risk	Risk that outcome of a bond investment strategy cannot be determined in advance.
Tax risk	Risk that tax rate reductions or repeal of tax-exempt status will lower returns on municipal bonds.
Volatility risk	Risk that the option value components of a bond with an embedded option will decline due to lower interest rate volatility.
Yield curve risk	Risk of nonparallel changes in the term structure of interest rates that produce lower returns on a bond portfolio.

Credit Risk

As mentioned earlier, credit risk refers to the likelihood or probability that a bond's issuer will not make interest payments and principal repayment according to the contractually scheduled timetable. All bonds are subject to default risk, although in practice U. S. Treasury securities are priced so as to be devoid of such risk. Hence, credit or default risk is applicable only to corporate, municipal, and international bonds.

There are two primary methods for measuring the credit risk of either a single bond or a bond portfolio. The first method is to compare the yields on such bonds with U.S. Treasury bonds of similar maturities. Chart 9–1 presents such information. Two points are worth noting. First, as the quality of the issue declines, the yield spread between it and comparable-maturity Treasury securities increases. This clearly indicates that investors require incremental

CHART 9–1

Interest Rate Spreads

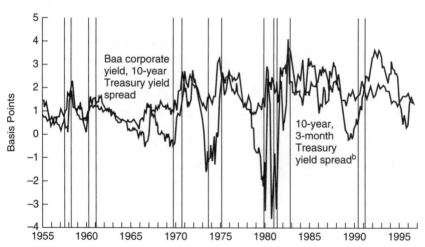

a. All instruments are constant-maturity series.

b. Three-month instrument is quoted from the secondary market on a yield basis: 10-year instrument is a constant-maturity series.

Note: Scale is in hundreds of basis points (i.e. each hash point is 1 percent). Shaded areas indicate recessions.

Sources: Federal Reserve Bank of Cleveland, *Economic Trends* (October 1996).

compensation in the form of higher yields as the credit risk on the bond increases.

The second point worth noting is that yield spreads vary with the stage of the business cycle. Yield spreads generally narrow during economic expansion and widen during economic downturns. Default risk generally decreases in the midst of an economic expansion as corporate cash flows and earnings and state and local government tax revenues increase. In contrast, default risk and associated spreads increase in periods of economic contraction as municipal tax receipts, corporate cash flows, and earnings diminish.

Although an analysis of yield spreads can provide useful insights about bond credit risk, other factors may also influence these spreads. The majority of corporate bonds contain call provisions, for example, so that the yield spread between a corporate bond and a similar-maturity Treasury bond will be affected by call risk and volatility risk as well as credit risk. Consequently, yield spreads may not accurately reflect default risk.

A more serious drawback to the traditional analysis of yield spreads occurs when bonds with identical maturities have different cash flow characteristics. This occurs when, for example, coupon rates of interest on corporate bonds differ from those on identical-maturity Treasury securities. A simple comparison of yield spreads may not accurately illuminate credit risk because it would fail to take into consideration the term structure of interest rates.

The proper way to measure credit quality spreads of non-Treasury bonds to Treasury bonds of the same maturity, in the case where the coupon rates on the bonds differ, is via their cash flow properties. Each expected cash flow from the corporate bond must be determined and then discounted using the theoretical spot rate on Treasury securities for the cash flow's maturity.[2] The sum of these cash flows is then compared with the bond's actual price, and the implied yield difference reflects the default risk on the bond.

The second, and more frequently employed, method of evaluating bond credit risk is to rely on credit ratings provided by companies. Four well-known companies undertake detailed and frequent credit analysis of a reasonably sizable number of corporate bond issues and provide their credit analysis to customers on a regular basis. These four companies are Standard and Poor's Corporation, Moody's Investor Services, Fitch Investor Services, and Duff and Phelps Credit Rating Company. Table 9–2 provides a summary of the credit grading system used by each of these companies.

TABLE 9–2

Corporate Bond Ratings

S&P	Moody's	Fitch	D&P	Comments
Investment Grade				
AAA	Aaa	AAA	AAA	Highest credit worthiness
AA+	Aa1	AA+	AA+	Very high quality
AA	Aa2	AA	AA	
AA–	Aa3	AA–	AA–	
A+	A1	A+	A+	
A	A2	A	A	High medium quality
A–	A3	A–	A–	
BBB+	Baa1	BBB+	BBB+	
BBB	Baa2	BBB	BBB	Lower medium quality
BBB–	Baa3	BBB–	BBB–	
Noninvestment Grade				
BB+	Ba1	BB+		
BB	Ba2	BB		Low quality
BB–	Ba3	BB–		
B+	B1	B+		Speculative
B	B2	B		
B–	B3	B–		Highly speculative
High Yield or in Default				
CCC+				
CCC	Caa	CCC	CCC	High risk
CCC–				
CC	Ca	CC		Extremely speculative
C	C	C		
CI				
		DDD		In default
		DD	DD	
D		D		

Interest Rate Risk

Bond values change in the opposite direction of changes in market rates of interest. As market rates of interest increase (decrease) the market values of fixed-income securities decrease (increase). The fundamental reason for the inverse or negative relationship between bond values and interest rates is described here.

Think of the market value of a bond as the current or present value of the discounted cash flows received by the bondholder. These cash flows are comprised of the coupon payments, usually received semiannually, and the principal repayment, made at maturity, on the bond. The current or present value of the future cash flows is obtained by discounting them at the relevant market rate of interest. As market rates of interest rise or fall, then these higher or lower market rates of interest are used to discount the bond's future cash flows. The use of higher market rates of interest will generate a lower present value to the future cash flow stream from the bond, while the use of lower market rates of interest will produce a higher present value to the future cash flow streams from the bond.

Equation 9–1 expresses mathematically the formula for the price of an option-free coupon bond:

$$P = \sum_{i-1}^{n} = \frac{C_1}{(1+r)^1} + \frac{C_2}{(1+r)^2} + \ldots + \frac{C_n}{(1+r)^n} + \frac{M}{(1+r)^n} \qquad (9\text{--}1)$$

where

    P = market value of the bond
    C = semiannual coupon interest payment
    r = one-half the relevant market rate of interest
    n = number of semiannual payments
    M = maturity value of the bond

As can be seen in Equation 9–1, the cash flow stream on a bond is represented by C and M, while r represents the market rate of interest. Holding the cash flow stream constant, a higher (lower) value for r—that is, higher (lower) market rates of interest—will result in a lower (higher) market value or price for the bond.

An alternative, more intuitive explanation for the inverse relationship between bond prices and interest rates can also be provided. Consider an investor who is purchasing a bond that will be first issued on day 1. The coupon rate of interest the issuer must pay on the bond, for a given maturity, must be the current market rate of interest inclusive of the bond's risk characteristics. Otherwise, the bond would not be sold on day 1 for its par or maturity value.

Now, suppose that one day after purchasing the bond, on day 2, our investor decides to sell it. How much can our investor receive for the one-day-old bond? If interest rates have fallen from day 1 to day 2, then newly issued bonds on day 2 will carry the lower coupon rate of interest, reflecting the decline in the market rate of interest. Our investor is trying to sell a bond that provides higher coupon payments than newly issued ones. As a consequence, there will be a greater demand for our investor's older bond as buyers of bonds prefer, other things equal, bonds with higher than lower coupon payments. The price of the 'older' bond will rise as a result. The opposite scenario would unfold in the event market rates of interest had risen.

Now that we have established the inverse relationship between changes in bond values and interest rate changes, the critical issue is how to measure the sensitivity of an individual bond's price as well as that of a portfolio of bonds to changes in interest rates. Two properties of a bond, its maturity and its coupon rate of interest, affect its price sensitivity. The longer the term to maturity of a bond, other things equal, the greater its price sensitivity. The lower the coupon rate of interest on a bond, other things being equal, the greater its price sensitivity to interest rate changes.

To illustrate the first of these properties, consider two bonds that are identical in all respects except their maturities. Suppose that both bonds are issued at a par value of $1,000 and possess coupon rates of interest of 5 percent. For simplicity, assume that coupon payments are made annually. The bonds differ only in that one bond matures in one year, while the second is an infinitely lived bond known as a consol.

TABLE 9–3

Dollar versus Percentage Price Changes

CouponRate (%)	Maturity	Initial Price	New Price	$ Price Change	% Price Change
5.00	1 year	$1,000	$995.26	$–4.74	–0.47
5.00	Consol	1,000	909.09	–9.10	–9.10
5.00	1 year	1,000	995.26	–4.74	–0.47
10.00	1 year	1,047.62	1,042.65	–4.97	–0.47

Table 9–3 illustrates the dollar and percentage price change in the two bonds resulting from a 10 percent increase in interest rates. That is, interest rates rise by 50 basis points, or one-half percentage point, from 5.00 percent to 5.50 percent. The dollar value of the one-year maturity bond declines by $4.74, or by less than one-half of 1 percent. In contrast, the market value of the much longer maturity consol falls by almost $91 or approximately 9.10 percent.

The second property of a bond affecting its price volalitily, the coupon rate of interest, is depicted in the bottom part of Table 9–3. The two bonds in this example have the same one-year maturities and are both priced to yield 5 percent. They differ only in that the first bond has a 5.00 percent coupon rate of interest, while the coupon rate on the second bond is 10 percent.

Again, suppose interest rates rise by 10 percent so that the relevant discount rate is 5.50 percent. The market value of the 5.00 percent coupon bond declines by $4.74, while the market value of the bond with the 10.00 percent coupon drops by $4.97. In percentage terms, the lower coupon bond falls by slightly more than the higher coupon bond.

DURATION

The price sensitivity of a bond to small changes in interest rates can be approximated by the bond's duration. *Duration* refers to the weighted average time to maturity of a bond, where the weights are the time periods before the present value of a respective cash flow is received. Cash flows whose present values are to be received sooner receive lower weights than those associated with more distant cash flows. The formula for a bond's duration is given as follows:

$$\text{Duration} = \frac{\sum_{i=1}^{t} \frac{T \times C}{(1+r)^t} + \frac{n \times M}{(1+r)^n}}{\sum_{i=1}^{n} \frac{C}{(1+r)^t} + \frac{M}{(1+r)^n}}$$

where

    C = semiannual coupon interest payment

    r = one-half the relevant market interest rate of interest

    n = number of years to maturity

    t = number of semiannual coupon payments

    M = principal value of the bond

    T = period in which cash flow is received

The denominator in the duration formula is the market value of the bond. The numerator, which at first glance appears similar to the denominator, weights the present value of each cash flow, $C/(1+r)^t$, by the time period in which it is to be received; Table 9–4 shows the calculation of the duration of a five-year maturity bond. Again, for simplicity we assume annual coupon payments.

    Using the data from Table 9–3, duration is calculated as follows:

$$\text{Duration} = \frac{\$4,549.031}{\$1,000.00} = 4.549$$

    The duration measure calculated here is known as the *Macaulay duration*, named for Frederick Macaulay, who was among the first to use this measure in studying the returns on fixed-income securities. A slight variant to the Macaulay duration is known as *modified duration*. The formula for it is as follows:

TABLE 9–4

Duration for Five-Year Maturity, 5% Coupon Bond at Yield of 5.00%

Period t	Cash Flow	Present Value at 5.00%	t* Present Value
1	$ 50.00	$ 47.619	$ 47.619
2	50.00	45.351	90.702
3	50.00	43.192	129.576
4	50.00	41.096	167.624
5	$1,050.00	822.702	4,113.510
		$1,000.000	$4,549.031

$$\text{Modified duration} = \frac{\text{Macaulay duration}}{1+r}$$

With regard to the preceding example, the modified duration of the bond would be

$$\text{Modified duration} = \frac{\text{Macaulay duration}}{1+r} = \frac{4.549}{1.05} = 4.33$$

Bond durations have the desirable property of being additive. As a result, the duration of an entire bond portfolio can be computed as the weighted average duration of each bond, where the weights are the proportion of the fund in each bond:

$$\text{Bond portfolio duration} = \sum_{i=1}^{n} W_i \times D_i$$

where

n = number of bonds

W_i = percent of the fund's value represented by each bond

D_i = duration of each bond

Once the duration of a bond (or a bond portfolio) has been calculated, then the approximate percentage price change in the bond
can be determined as follows:

$$\% \text{ price change} = \begin{array}{c}(-\text{Modified} \\ \text{duration})\end{array} \times \begin{array}{c}(\text{Change in interest} \\ \text{rate in basis points})\end{array}$$

With regard to the preceding example, suppose interest rates rose
from 5.00 percent to 5.10 percent. The bond price change would be
approximately

$$-0.00433 = (-4.33)(0.001) = -0.433\%$$

The market value of the bond would be expected to decline by
about $4.33. In reality, it would decline by $4.34.

CONVEXITY

Duration provides a reasonably accurate measure of a bond's price
sensitivity as long as interest rate changes are relatively small.
However, when interest rate changes become large, duration becomes less accurate in approximating a bond's price sensitivity because of a property bonds possess known as their convexity.
Convexity refers to the fact that the inverse price-yield relationship
of a bond is not linear but, instead, curvelinear. Hence, as interest
rate changes become larger, relative to the initial yield, duration (a
linear measure of price sensitivity) becomes less accurate.

To provide a more precise measure of a bond's (or portfolio of
bonds) price sensitivity to sizeable interest rate changes, the convexity of the bond is calculated and used in conjunction with the
bond's duration. Convexity can be thought of as the change in the
change in the bond's price given a change in the rate of change of
interest rates. The formula for a bond's convexity is given as follows:

$$\text{Convexity} = \frac{\sum_{i=1}^{t} \dfrac{T(t+1)C}{(1+r)^{t+2}} + \dfrac{N(N+1)M}{(1+r)^{n+2}}}{\sum_{i=1}^{n} \dfrac{C}{(1+r)^{t}} + \dfrac{M}{(1+r)^{n}}}$$

TABLE 9–5

Data for Convexity Example

Period t	Cash Flows	$1/(1+r)^{t+2}$	$t(t+1)CF$	$\dfrac{t(t+1)CF}{1/(1+r)^{t+2}}$
1	$50.00	0.8638	100	$ 86.38
2	50.00	0.8227	300	246.81
3	50.00	0.7835	600	470.10
4	50.00	0.7462	1,000	746.20
5	1,050	0.7107	31,500	22,387.05
				$23,936.53

For the bond is Table 9–5, its convexity can be calculated as follows:

$$\text{Convexity} = \frac{\$23,936.53}{\$1,000.00} = 23.94$$

To illustrate how duration and convexity can be used to approximate a bond's price change, consider our five-year maturity, 5 percent coupon bond whose modified duration is 4.33 and whose convexity is 23.94. Suppose interest rates jump from 5.00 percent to 9.00 percent, a surge of 400 basis points. The approximate percentage change in the price of the bond is as follows:

$$\frac{\%\ \text{price change}}{\text{due to duration}} = (-\text{Duration}) \times (\text{Change in interest rate})$$

$$= -4.33 \times 0.04$$

$$= -0.1732$$

$$\frac{\%\ \text{price change}}{\text{due to convexity}} = .5 \times (\text{Convexity}) \times (\text{Change in interest rates})^2$$

$$= .5 \times 23.94 \times (0.04)^2$$

$$= 0.0192$$

$$\begin{aligned}
\text{Total \% price} &= \text{\% price change} + \text{\% price change} \\
\text{change} &\quad\ \text{due to duration} \quad\ \text{due to convexity} \\
&= -17.32\% + 1.92\% \\
&= -15.40\%
\end{aligned}$$

Hence, our bond would decline in value by roughly $154.00.

An important responsibility of the investment committee is to provide clear guidelines, if not outright limits, to the fund manager on the amount of price risk that should be associated with the fund's fixed-income portfolio. This can be specified in terms of duration. Moreover, the investment committee, in the periodic reports it receives from the fixed-income fund manager(s), should require that information on the portfolio's duration be included.

MATURITY DISTRIBUTION

The third characteristic the investment committee needs to either specify in the investment policy statement or communicate to the fund manager is the desired *maturity distribution* of the fixed-income portfolio. Generally, yields on bonds increase as bonds' maturities increase. Duration, or price sensitivity, does as well. Hence, the investment committee confronts a trade-off between returns and risk. The investment committee must therefore determine a maturity distribution that is consistent with its return objectives and risk tolerance.

RETURN ANALYSIS

A thorough analysis of the return on a fixed-income portfolio answers the following questions: (1) How much of the return was attributed to the actions of the manager? (2) How much of the return was associated with the investment committee's stipulation regarding issuer, credit quality, duration, maturity, etc? (3) How much of the return was attributed to changes in the interest rate environment?

An innovative, commercially available system designed to provide detailed answers to these questions has been developed by Capital Management Sciences. Their Performance Attribution (PART) system decomposes a fixed-income portfolio's return into various categories so that the investment committee and the portfolio managers can more accurately measure the effects of their decisions on the fixed-income portfolio's performance.

Chart 9–2 presents a schematic overview of the PART system. The total return on a fixed-income portfolio is first divided into two broad categories, income return and price return. *Income return* represents the coupon interest earned on the portfolio as well as the amortization of any premium or discount over the time period. The *price return* category reflects that part of total return attributed to changes in the Treasury yield curve, changes in yield spreads on bonds of different issuers, bond-specific price effects, and transactions costs.

As illustrated in Chart 9–2, the "Treasury curve effect/term structure effects" component of the price return is further subdivided. As a result, the investment committee can ascertain the portion of the total return attributable to changes in the level and slope of the Treasury yield curve. The "sector/quality effect" shows the importance of sector allocation decisions made by the fund manager relative to a chosen benchmark. The "selection effect" captures any portion of the price return that may be unique and specific to the bonds in the portfolio. The sum of these categories represents the total return on the fixed-income portfolio. Any discrepancy between the portfolio's actual return and that computed is attributed to transactions costs or a residual item.

Table 9–6 presents an example of the PART system. The total return on a sample portfolio for the period January 31, 1996 to June 28, 1996 is depicted together with the total return on a representative, benchmark index. The total returns are also decomposed or attributed according to the categories discussed above.

As the data in the table reveal, the sample portfolio's total return was a negative 2.23 percent during the period in question

CHART 9–2

Overview of Performance Attribution System

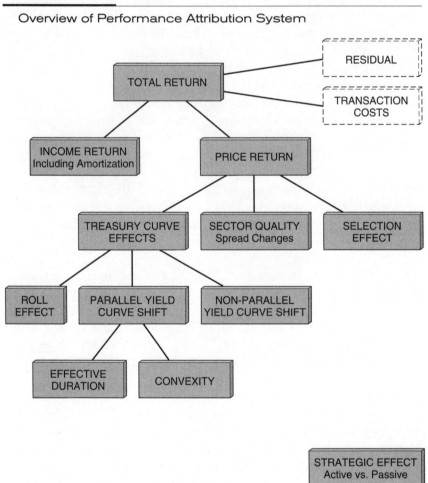

Source: Copyright 1995. Capital Management Sciences.

compared with a total return of approximately negative 1.87 percent on the benchmark index. We can conclude, at least for the period in question, that a passive, indexed strategy would have yielded a better performance (in terms of a smaller loss on the portfolio of about 36 basis points) than the active one pursued by the manager.

TABLE 9-6

Total Return

| | Income Effect | Roll | Term Structure Effects | | | Sector/ Quality | Selection Effect | Transaction Cost | Residual | Total Return |
| | | | Parallel | | | | | | | |
			Effective Duration	Convexity	Nonparallel					
Sample portfolio	2.536	0.12	–3.62	–3.06	–1.00	0.13	–0.234	0.00	–0.109	–2.234
SLAG	2.656	0.08	–4.13	–3.01	–0.91	0.05	0.394	0.00	–0.004	–1.871
Difference	–0.119	0.04	0.52	–0.06	–0.09	0.08	–0.627	0.00	–0.105	–0.364

Source: Capital Management Sciences

The sources of the decline in the sample portfolio's total value—that is, the negative total return—are also presented in Table 9–6 along with those on the benchmark index. The PART system allows us to draw the following conclusions:

1. The primary reasons for the negative total return were (a) rising market rates of interest in conjunction with the interest rate sensitivity of the portfolio, as indicated by the effective duration effect, as well as (b) the manager's strategy for dealing with changes in the slope of the yield curve, as indicated by the nonparallel effect. Combined, these two factors produced a return of negative 4.62 percent.

2. The coupon interest return or income effect partially compensated for these losses, generating a return of 2.54 percent.

3. Relative to a passive strategy, as indicated by the total return components of the benchmark index, the sample portfolio developed by the manager outperformed (did less poorly) in terms of combined interest rate risk effects but underperformed the index in terms of income and selection effects.

AIMR STANDARDS

As in the case with equity portfolios, in recent years the Association for Investment Management and Research (AIMR) has promoted standards in the fixed-income arena for the presentation of information by portfolio managers as well as requirements as to what must be disclosed. These requirements include the following:

- Calculate returns using time-weighted rates of return (as discussed in Chapter 6), on at least a quarterly basis, and geometric linking of returns.
- Include all actual fee-paying, discretionary portfolios in one composite or aggregate measure.
- Deduct all trading costs in calculating returns.

- Disclose whether the performance results are calculated gross or net of management fees.
- Disclose the tax rate assumptions if the results are reported net of taxes.
- Present at least a 10-year performance record. Present results since inception if the firm has been in business less than 10 years.
- Present annual returns for all years.

FIXED-INCOME MANAGEMENT STYLES

Unlike the case with equity portfolio managers, at this time there is not a standardized, widely agreed upon taxonomy of investment styles for portfolio management of fixed-income securities. The absence of an industry standard complicates the evaluation of fixed-income portfolio managers. Plan sponsors should therefore rely on the portfolio strategy they adopt for the fixed-income portion of the fund as well as the constraints they specify for the fixed-income portfolio's issuer, credit quality, duration, and maturity in evaluating fixed-income managers.

Passive Fixed-Income Management

Passive fixed-income managers will pursue either an indexing or an immunization strategy. An *indexing strategy* is one in which the portfolio manager designs a fixed-income portfolio so that its return and risk characteristics replicate those of an appropriately selected fixed-income index. In contrast, an *immunization strategy* is one in which the portfolio manager structures a fixed-income portfolio so that it obtains a predetermined future value, regardless of movements in interest rates.

A fixed-income indexing strategy, in concept, is similar to an equity indexing strategy. A benchmark index, either an existing one as discussed in Chapter 2 or a customized one, is selected for its conformity to the plan's return and risk objectives, and then a fixed-income portfolio is developed to mimic the characteristics of the index. There are several problems in executing a fixed-income indexing strategy that do not exist with an equity indexing strategy.

The first problem is that the broader based, better known fixed-income indexes contain in excess of 4,000 bonds. Some portion of these bonds may be highly illiquid because they are not frequently traded. As a result, it is very difficult to either include these securities in the fund's fixed-income portfolio or to find substitute securities for them. The second practical problem in implementing a fixed-income indexing strategy arises as bonds included in the index mature and are replaced by newly issued ones. The portfolio manager may be required to frequently rebalance the fixed-income portfolio, adding to the transactions costs of implementing this strategy.

In response to the previously mentioned practical problems in implementing a fixed-income indexing strategy, portfolio managers might seek to design a portfolio that closely tracks the targeted index. Stratified sampling approaches to bond indexing are frequently used in this regard.

Under this approach, the benchmark index is decomposed by its characteristics. These might include issuer, duration, credit risk, maturity, etc. Then, one or more bonds from each characteristic grouping or cell is chosen to be included in the fixed-income portfolio so that its performance will closely match that of the index. Table 9–7 illustrates a simplified stratification. Bonds in the benchmark index are decomposed by issuer and credit quality. The percentages of the index represented by each cell are determined as illustrated in Table 9–7. The portfolio manager would then include in the portfolio bonds in each cell in proportion to their representation in the index.

Immunization strategies, in contrast to index ones, are a device for immunizing a fixed-income portfolio from interest rate risk. They are often used when the objective is to provide sufficient funds to pay a future liability or liabilities. The strategy involves selecting assets for the fixed-income portfolio so that the duration

TABLE 9–7

A Hypothetical Stratification of a Fixed-Income Index

| | Issuer | | | |
Credit Quality	Treasury (%)	Agency (%)	Corporate (%)	Municipal (%)
AAA to AA+	16.0	13.0		
AA to AA–			17.0	
A+ to A–				11.4
BBB+ to BBB–			9.6	
BB+ to BB–				
B+ to B–				

of the portfolio's assets is equal to the duration of the portfolio's liabilities. In this way, any decrease (increase) in the portfolio's asset value because of higher (lower) interest rates would be offset by equal decreases (increases) in the portfolio's liability value.

ACTIVE FIXED-INCOME MANAGEMENT

Fixed-income portfolio managers who pursue so-called active styles are attempting to earn a return, adjusted for risk, in excess of that on a predetermined benchmark index. Essentially, managers with active styles operate upon the notion that the existing term structure of interest rates does not completely and accurately reflect what they consider to be temporarily mispriced bonds. In turn, they structure client's portfolios to take advantage of the perceived temporary mispricing. Active bond management styles can be categorized as either *interest rate forecasters* or *sector strategists.*

Interest rate forecasters assume they have a comparative advantage, relative to all other market participants, in correctly anticipating interest rate changes. For example, a fixed-income portfolio manager who anticipates that interest rates will decline by more than that implied by the existing structure of interest rates would lengthen the duration of client's portfolios in order to earn returns in excess of those on a benchmark index. Relatedly, *rate forecasters* will also try to anticipate changes in the slope of the yield curve and structure clients' bond portfolios to earn superior returns from such changes.

Active managers who follow sector strategy styles look for temporarily mispriced bonds across the many sectors of the fixed-income market. These temporary mispricings occur, in their view, because existing interest rate spreads on bonds of different issuers do not accurately reflect relevant risk differentials. For example, a manager might conclude that the appropriately measured spread between corporate and Treasury bonds is too wide, given the manager's outlook for the economy. The manager might then increase the client's holdings of corporate bonds in the expectation that, when the yield spread narrows, the client will earn a return in excess of the benchmark index.

As mentioned earlier, uniform standards for classifying fixed-income manager styles do not currently exist. An illustration of an independent classification system is provided by Wilshire Associates, a prominent firm that provides investment information used to evaluate portfolio managers and provides investment advisory services. The classification system Wilshire has recently introduced is based on the concepts discussed throughout this book and is presented to further illustrate them.

The Wilshire TUCS (Trust Universe Comparison Service) Fixed-Income Portfolio Group starts by grouping fixed-income portfolios according to target index. Grouping portfolios in this way means they all are subject to common interest rate changes during the performance period in question. As a result, ". . . differences within the group are then due to the success of the sector and quality management, duration management relative to the index, selection of individual bonds, and other fixed-income management techniques."[3] Subsequent to this initial grouping, styles of fixed-income managers are based on quantitative assessment of a portfolio relative to three widely used fixed-income indexes: the Lehman Brothers Intermediate, Government/Corporate, and Long-Term Bond Indexes.

The quantitative technique developed by Wilshire Associates employs the fixed-income portfolio's average duration, the variability of its duration, the tracking of its duration relative to the aforementioned indexes, and its average quality. A series of tests, based on the preceding guidelines, is applied to each portfolio. The test results in each portfolio are classified into one of seven management styles: high yield, short-term, intermediate, long-term, matched duration core, interest rate anticipation, and unclassified. The performance of portfolios in each of these styles can then be compared and evaluated against a universe of comparable portfolios.

FIXED-INCOME EVALUATION

The fund's fixed income component can be evaluated in a similar manner. Chart 9–3 presents the one-, two-, three- , four-, and five-year annualized returns of Fund XYZ's fixed-income component with that of the Lehman Brothers Government/Corporate Bond Index using bar charts. The universe selected ranges between 254 and 321 fixed-income accounts. The circles contained in the bar chart represent the annualized rates of return for the fund's fixed-income component, while the squares indicate the Lehman Brothers Government/Corporate Bond Index returns over the same period. As before, the top of each bar represents the highest return for a given portfolio within the universe, while the bottom of the chart reflects the lowest return of a portfolio within the investment universe. Additionally, the horizontal lines contained in the bar chart represent the 25th percentile, median, and 75th percentile. The chart reveals that the fixed-income component ranks in the first quartile for four out of five measurement periods. In contrast, the fixed-income index consistently falls in the second quartile. Thus, for all periods considered, Fund XYZ's returns fare well.

CHART 9-3

Fixed-Income Accounts (US$)
Period Ending June 30, 1996

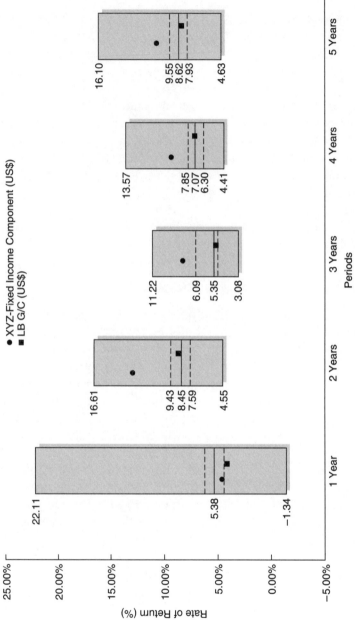

• XYZ-Fixed Income Component (US$)
■ LB G/C (US$)

Rate of Return (%)

25.00%
20.00%
15.00%
10.00%
5.00%
0.00%
−5.00%

Periods

1 Year
22.11
5.38
−1.34

2 Years
16.61
9.43
8.45
7.59
4.55

3 Years
11.22
6.09
5.35
3.08

4 Years
13.57
7.85
7.07
6.30
4.41

5 Years
16.10
9.55
8.62
7.93
4.63

Source: © Frank Russell Company

Chart 9–4 presents a profile of the return/risk characteristics of Fund XYZ's fixed-income component, the Lehman Brothers Government/Corporate Bond Index, and the selected investment universe (fixed-income accounts). Viewing the scatter diagram reveals slightly different results than simply focusing on return. In terms of return/risk, the fixed-income component resides in the northeast quadrant. This indicates that it achieves both a higher return and a higher risk than the median. In contrast, the Lehman Brothers index achieved a slightly lower return than the median, while experiencing more risk. Thus, by all measures, the fixed-income component performs well.

CHART 9–4

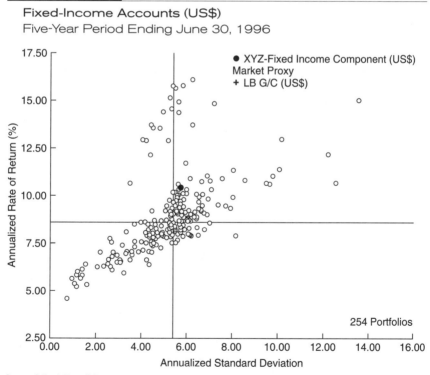

Fixed-Income Accounts (US$)
Five-Year Period Ending June 30, 1996

● XYZ-Fixed Income Component (US$)
Market Proxy
+ LB G/C (US$)

254 Portfolios

Source: © Frank Russell Company

TABLE 9–8

Return/Risk Analysis, Fixed-Income Accounts
Five-Year Annualized Measures, 254 Portfolios

	Return (%)	Standard Deviation (%)
Maximum	16.10	13.46
25th percentile	9.55	5.88
Median	8.62	4.38
75th percentile	7.93	4.38
Minimum	4.63	0.76
Fixed-income component	10.42	5.68
S&P 500	8.48	5.79

Source: Frank Russell Company

Data relating to Chart 9–4 appear in Table 9–8. The table reveals that the selected fixed income universe consists of 254 portfolios. The maximum fixed-income portfolio has a five-year annualized return of 16.10 percent and an annualized standard deviation of 5.38 percent. The median return and standard deviation are 8.62 percent and 5.14 percent, respectively. The 25th and 75th percentile are also reported in this table. During this period, Fund XYZ's fixed-income component has a return of 10.42 percent and a standard deviation of 5.68 percent. During this period, the Lehman Brothers Government/Corporate Bond Index has a return of 8.48 percent and a standard deviation of 5.79 percent.

SUMMARY

Fixed-income securities include those issued by the U.S. Treasury, agencies of the federal government, domestic and foreign corporations, and state and local (municipal) governments. Two of the most important types of risks associated with fixed-income instruments are credit and interest rate risk. Credit risk or default risk deals with the likelihood that the borrower will be able to make timely interest payments and principal repayment. Interest rate risk refers to the risk that bond values will be adversely affected by changes in interest rates.

The evaluation of the fixed-income portfolio should begin with a comparison of its return with that of an appropriate index. The index selected should represent the types of securities that are permitted according to the policy statement. For example, if the policy document specifies that only U. S. government securities are to be purchased, then the index should be one that is comprised of these securities. If, on the other hand, the policy statement provides for investment in corporate or municipal securities, then an index representative of these types of securities should be used.

REFERENCES

1. Fabozzi, Frank J., *Bond Markets, Analysis and Strategies,* 3rd ed. Upper Saddle River, N. J.: Prentice-Hall, Inc., 1996.
2. The theoretical spot rate is the yield to maturity determined by treating each expected cash flow as a zero coupon instrument. See Fabozzi, *Bond Markets, Analysis and Strategies,* 3rd ed. Ch. 5.
3. Wilshire Associates, Incorporated, *Trust Universe Comparison Service,* Fixed Income Manager Style Universe, Second Quarter, 1996.

CHAPTER 10

Mutual Funds as an Investment Vehicle

INTRODUCTION

Mutual funds have exploded in popularity in recent years and have emerged as a useful and important investment vehicle for a growing number of institutional and individual investors. Mutual fund assets surged an astounding $2 trillion in the past 10 years. Total assets of the more than 7000 different mutual funds from which investors can choose approached $2.5 trillion at the end of 1995. At year-end 1993, approximately 40 percent of mutual fund assets were owned by institutional investors, with individual investors holding the remaining 60 percent.

The spiraling growth in the number of separate mutual funds, the range of assets in which they invest, and the total dollar amount of the assets of these investment vehicles has coincided with the generally strong performance of domestic as well as international financial markets in recent years. Mutual funds also offer certain advantages as an investment vehicle, which has undoubtedly contributed to their growth. An understanding of the advantages and potential disadvantages of mutual funds as an investment vehicle can aid investment committees in deciding whether such funds can assist them in achieving the goals of their investment plans.

INVESTMENT COMPANIES

Investment companies operate mutual funds. Investment companies, in turn, are organized and created by so-called management companies. The management company, after creating the investment company, then contracts with it to develop the mutual funds sold by the investment company; the management company then usually serves as the investment adviser to the funds. As the fund's investment adviser, the management company is responsible for the management of the fund's portfolio of securities. In this respect, the management company then employs the services of portfolio managers, securities analysts, securities traders, researchers, and so forth, who are charged with the actual investment of the fund's assets.

Investment companies are financial intermediaries, as are commercial banks, insurance companies, and pension plans. The distinguishing feature of financial intermediaries, as opposed to securities brokers and dealers, is that they create and issue financial claims or liabilities on themselves. When an investor purchases shares in a mutual fund, the fund uses the investor's money to purchase predetermined types of securities (equities, bonds, etc.), generally according to the fund's prospectus and stated investment policy. Ownership of these securities resides with the investment company. The investor receives shares of the mutual fund in which he or she invests. These mutual fund shares are issued by the investment company.

Income earned by the mutual fund from its investments is distributed to shareholders in proportion to the number of shares they own in the fund. Therefore, if the securities owned by the mutual fund appreciate in value, or if the securities owned by the fund are sold at a profit, or if they pay interest or dividends, all the investors in the fund receive a proportionate gain. Investors who invest $1 million in the fund obtain the same percentage rate of return or yield per share as those who invest $10 million.

Investors in mutual funds are also the fund's shareholders. Accordingly, they have the right to vote for and elect the fund's board of directors. The directors are responsible for implementing the fund's investment policies and objectives, appointing officers to manage the fund's operations, and contracting with the management company as well as with the principal underwriters, who may wholesale the fund's shares to securities dealers, the custodian who safeguards the fund's assets, and the transfer agent that performs the shareholder recordkeeping services.

Mutual funds are regulated by the Securities and Exchange Commission, under the auspices of the Securities Acts of 1933 and 1934 and the Investment Company Act of 1940. The first two acts, which are not specific to mutual funds, require (among other things) the registration of fund shares prior to their public sale and the publication of prospecti that provide reasonably detailed information on such things as the fund's investment policies and objectives. In contrast, the Investment Company Act is specific to the mutual fund industry. This act requires that investment companies publically issue statements regarding their investment objectives, and these objectives may not be changed without shareholder approval. In addition, issuance of debt is restricted, outsiders must serve as members of the board of directors, and the fund must be operated for the benefit of the shareholders—not the managers.

FEATURES OF MUTUAL FUNDS

The first important feature of a mutual fund is whether it is an open-end or closed-end fund. *Open-end funds* issue an unlimited number of shares. As investors put additional money into open-end funds, the fund issues additional shares. Similarly, as investors redeem shares they own in an open-end fund, the fund retires the shares. Consequently, the number of shares in the typical open-end mutual fund fluctuates frequently.

Shares in mutual funds are issued and redeemed at their net asset value (NAV), or the value per share of the mutual fund. At the end of each business day, the fund adds up the value of all securities held in its portfolio, subtracts expenses, and divides this amount by the total number of shares outstanding. This simple calculation gives the NAV, which investors can then use to determine the market value of their holdings in the mutual fund.

Closed-end funds, in contrast, make a one-time offering of shares and do not issue or redeem shares at NAV. Instead, shares of closed-end funds are traded and listed on either organized or over-the-counter securities markets, and their price can differ from NAV.[1]

The second important feature of mutual funds is whether they are no-load or load funds. *No-load funds* do not require a fee to purchase the fund, while *load funds* involve sales fees when the fund is initially purchased. Additionally, some funds may require a *back-end load* or fee when the investor redeems all of their shares in the fund or transfers shares to a different fund. And, in some cases, funds may assess a fee to support the distribution and marketing of the fund. These latter fees are called 12b-1 fees, which refers to the Securities and Exchange Commission rule that permits them. Moreover, funds generally assess an annual management fee to pay for the contract services of the investment adviser(s).

The third important feature of mutual funds is their *investment objectives*. The vast majority of mutual funds invest in either stocks, bonds, or short-term money market instruments. But the phenomenal growth of the mutual fund industry has produced a dramatic rise in the number of funds, their investment objectives, and the instruments from which investors can choose. The number of funds has more than doubled—to almost 7,000—since 1986, and the Investment Company Institute (the national association of the mutual fund industry) now has 21 broad categories of investment objectives for mutual funds and 18 separate categories for specialized mutual funds. These investment objectives are listed in Table 10–1. They should be viewed as indicative of the range of investment objectives that mutual funds may pursue rather than an exhaustive or definitive listing.

TABLE 10–1

Mutual Fund Investment Objectives

Basic Funds	Specialty Funds
Aggressive growth	Adjustable rate mortgage
Balanced funds	Asian and Pacific Basin
Corporate bond	Convertible securities
Flexible portfolio funds	Country funds
GNMA funds	Emerging markets
Global bond	Energy stock
Global equity	Environmental securities
Growth funds	European stock
Growth and income	Health and biotechnology
High-yield bond	Index funds
Income—bond	Latin American funds
Income—equity	Natural resources securities
Income—mixed	Small-company growth
International funds	Specific social objectives
National municipal bond	Technology securities
Precious metals funds	U.S. regional securities
State municipal bond	Utilities funds
Taxable money market	
Taxable money market—national	
Taxable money market—state	
U.S. government income	

Source: *1995–1996 Directory of Mutual Funds*. Investment Company Institute.

ADVANTAGES OF MUTUAL FUNDS

Mutual funds may provide a cost advantage to investors in achieving their investment objectives. The lower costs of investing are the primary advantage of mutual funds. Mutual funds may provide a lower cost method of achieving a desired asset allocation and portfolio composition. They may provide a lower cost means of achieving a desired degree of portfolio diversification. Mutual funds may provide a lower cost means of obtaining professional investment management services, and they may provide lower transactions costs in the purchase and sale of securities.

The cost advantages mutual funds may provide arise from economies of scale and scope in the pooling of investor's monies. In theory, investors can, on their own or via professional investment managers, develop an asset allocation strategy, undertake securities research, and execute securities transactions. However, the costs of doing these things could be extremely high—especially for investment committees whose funds are relatively small in dollar size. By pooling the monies of a large number of investors, each of whom might be investing a relatively small dollar amount, mutual funds behave like large investors. As large investors, mutual funds provide their shareholders with the benefits of economies of scale in investing. Because they trade large blocks of securities and allow investors to purchase fractional shares of many different securities, mutual funds may achieve substantial savings in brokerage fees and commissions. The pooling of investors' monies allows mutual fund shareholders to hold shares in a diverse collection of securities, potentially reducing risks. Additionally, the costs of the services of the portfolio managers, securities analysts, traders, etc., employed by most mutual funds are spread over all investors. As a result, the cost of receiving professional investment management services may be reduced.

The cost advantages provided by mutual funds suggest that they might be an especially attractive investment vehicle for investment committees who choose in-house or self-management of their fund's assets. Additionally, mutual funds might provide a cost advantage to committees whose fund's dollar size is relatively small.

SELECTING MUTUAL FUNDS

With about 7,000 separate mutual funds from which to choose, the task of finding the ones most likely to meet the committee's investment objectives has become more complex. The large number of funds from which a committee can select also suggests a higher likelihood of finding funds that best suit the objectives of the committee. Researching mutual funds, in this regard, has replaced the researching of individual securities.

A useful starting point for an investment committee is to match their fund's investment objectives with the listing of investment objectives for mutual funds, such as those provided in Table 10–1. Tax-exempt sponsors, for example, might exclude from their search national and state municipal bond funds, whose interest income is exempt from federal income taxes. Sponsors seeking the benefits of international diversification might focus on global equity funds, international funds, or specialty funds such as the Latin American funds.

Subsequent to identifying mutual funds whose broad investment objectives are consistent with those of the committees, the next step is to collect information on specific mutual funds. This information is available from a number of sources. The Investment Company Institute, for example, publishes an annual directory of mutual funds. This directory, among other things, provides a listing of member funds by their investment objectives. The 1995–1996 directory, as an illustration, contains summary information on more than 400 separate funds classified as having growth and income as their primary investment objective.[2]

The financial press is a second source of mutual fund information. Publications such as *The Wall Street Journal*, *Investors Business Daily*, and *Barron's* provide daily and/or weekly information on funds' net asset value, the change in NAV from the prior business day, and year-to-date total return. *The Wall Street Journal* and *Barron's* provide detailed information on fund performance according to investment objectives on a quarterly and annual basis. Specialty print publications such as *Mutual Fund* magazine and electronic information on mutual funds via the Internet may also be useful to investment committees to indentify specific mutual funds whose investment objectives match those of the investment committee.

Mutual fund research organizations are a third source of information on mutual funds. The information provided by these organizations can be highly valuable in a variety of ways to investment committees. *Morningstar Mutual Funds* and *Lipper Analytic Services* are two prominent and highly respected mutual fund research organizations that provide extensive information on mutual funds.

Once a collection of specific mutual funds has been identified, then the *prospectus*, the *statement of additional information*, and the *annual and semiannual reports* on each of these funds should be obtained and thoroughly reviewed. The Investment Company Act of 1940 requires that this information be made readily available to actual and potential mutual fund shareholders. Information on the fund's investment objectives and strategy, its risk tolerance, the names and professional backgrounds of the fund's portfolio managers, condensed financial statements, fees charged by the fund, and the tax consequences of investing in the fund are provided in the prospectus. The annual and semiannual reports to shareholders provide detailed information of the fund's financial performance.

MUTUAL FUND RISK

The risks associated with investing in mutual funds vary significantly depending on several factors. The stated investment objectives of the fund provide the first indication of its risk. For example, aggressive growth funds are likely to be considerably more risky than balanced funds. The former seek maximum capital gains as their investment objective and, to achieve this goal, may invest in the securities of high-risk companies. Balanced funds, in contrast, place greater emphasis on preservation of principal and may invest in a diversified collection of equity and debt to obtain this objective. Stated investment objectives, however, as previously noted are neither definitive nor restrictive. Health and biotechnology funds, for example, might have the same general investment objectives and risk as technology security funds or small-company growth funds. Because of the closeness of some funds' investment objectives, additional information is necessary to adequately assess fund risk.

A second factor influencing the risk of investing in mutual funds is the operational risk of the fund itself. Mutual funds may purchase as few as 30 securities; some funds hold in excess of 500 separate securities. Some funds may restrict holdings in a particular security to not more than 5 percent of total assets, while other funds may permit as much as 20 percent of the fund's assets to be invested in a specific financial asset. Additionally, some portfolio managers may concentrate a fund's assets in securities whose returns are highly correlated with each other or employ potentially riskier investment techniques such as short sales. While relatively infrequent, there have been occasions when a fund's portfolio managers have radically restructured a fund's portfolio at precisely the wrong time in terms of meeting investment objectives.

Relatedly, expense management of a fund affects its net asset value and, hence, total return and the variability of this return. Inefficient management of the costs of operating a fund could boost its liabilities, reducing net asset value and providing investors with an unexpectedly lower total return.

Monitoring the operational risk associated with a mutual fund can, at times, be challenging. Amy C. Arnott, editor of the *Morningstar Mutual Funds* reports, has written eloquently on these challenges.[3] She notes that while mutual funds are required to report their portfolio compositions on a semiannual basis to shareholders, during the intervening periods it may be difficult for shareholders to determine what kind of securities compose a fund and the changes that might be occurring in it.

As is the case with investing via the purchase of individual securities, diversification can also be applied as a risk reduction technique when investing in mutual funds. That is, mutual funds can be used to implement an asset allocation strategy. The idea is to choose mutual funds whose investment objectives and implied securities composition are such that overall portfolio risk is reduced.

EVALUATING MUTUAL FUND PERFORMANCE

Mutual funds, as we have discussed, are a lower cost method of obtaining professional portfolio management services for many investors. The methods and techniques employed in analyzing and evaluating the performance of portfolio managers, particularly returns-based analysis, have increasingly been adapted to the evaluation of mutual fund performance.

Morningstar, Inc. is a leading provider of information and analysis on mutual fund performance. Morningstar's reports on mutual funds provide an array of information that investment committees can use to evaluate performance.

Morningstar categorizes mutual funds by their stated investment objectives. The 37 separate categories for mutual funds it has developed in this regard are similar to the ones listed earlier but, in Morningstar's view, are better suited to its evaluation methodology. As we discussed earlier, the proliferation of fund categories may be a source of confusion to investment sponsors. Morningstar uses style boxes as an aid in evaluating a fund's performance.

Exhibit 10–1 presents the style boxes Morningstar uses for equity and fixed-income mutual funds. Investment styles for equity funds are classified as either value, growth, or blend, based on criteria developed by Morningstar. These criteria are based on a funds' average price-to-earnings ratio relative to that of the S&P 500 index and the fund's average market-to-book value ratio relative to that of the S&P 500. This type of quantitative measure provides a more precise classification of a fund. Analagous criteria, such as employing maturity and credit quality ratings, are used to categorize a fixed-income fund's quality. The style boxes then

EXHIBIT 10-1

FIDELITY BLUE CHIP GROWTH

Fidelity Blue Chip Growth

Fidelity Blue Chip Growth Fund seeks long-term capital appreciation.

The fund normally invests at least 65% of assets in common stocks issued by blue-chip companies. It defines these as companies with market capitalizations of at least $200 million, if the company's stock is included in the S&P 500 or the Dow Jones Industrial Average, or $1 billion if not included in either index. Management selects companies that it expects to achieve high long-term earnings growth. The fund typically maintains representation in as many market sectors as possible, but may concentrate in the strongest sectors of the market.

Portfolio Manager(s)

John McDowell. Since 4-96

Performance 06-30-96

	1st Qtr	2nd Qtr	3rd Qtr	4th Qtr	Total
1992	−5.35	0.43	4.39	6.99	6.17
1993	4.38	7.93	8.43	1.92	24.50
1994	0.79	0.66	7.75	0.49	9.85
1995	4.97	11.89	9.23	0.06	28.38
1996	1.79	2.91	—	—	—

Trailing	Total Return %	+/− S&P 500	+/− Wil 5000	% Rank All Obj.	Growth of $10,000
3 Mo	2.91	−1.58	−1.50	35 74	10,291
6 Mo	4.74	−5.34	−5.52	46 94	10,474
1 Yr	14.48	−11.50	−11.74	41 90	11,448
3 Yr Avg	17.75	0.54	0.96	8 20	16,324
5 Yr Avg	20.16	4.45	4.08	5 7	25,053
10 Yr Avg	—	—	—	— —	—
15 Yr Avg	—	—	—	— —	—

Most Similar Funds in MMF

Fidelity Contrafund	Strong Fit
Fidelity Growth Company	Fair Fit
Fidelity Magellan	Fair Fit

Tax Analysis

	Tax-Adj Return %	% Pretax Return
3 Yr Avg	14.20	80.0
5 Yr Avg	17.72	87.9
10 Yr Avg	—	—

Potential Capital Gain Exposure: 13% of assets

Risk Analysis

Time Period	Load-Adj Return %	Risk % All	Rank¹ Obj	Mstar Return	Score Risk	Morningstar Risk-Adj Rating
1 Yr	11.05					
3 Yr	16.56	70	42	1.32	0.76	★★★★
5 Yr	19.43	67	25	1.63	0.73	★★★★★
Incept	18.96	—	—	—	—	

Average Historical Rating (67 months): 4.9★s

¹1=low, 100=high

Other Measures

	Standard Index S&P 500	Best Fit Index SPMid400
Standard Deviation	9.90	Alpha	1.8	4.4
Mean	16.93	Beta	0.90	0.89
Sharpe Ratio	1.26	R-Squared	52	67

Portfolio Analysis 01-31-96

Share Chg (07-95) 000	Amount 000	Total Stocks 266 Total Fixed-Income 6	Value $000	% Net Assets
	378,230	US Treasury Bond 6.875%	422,139	5.17
295	5,245	General Motors	276,043	3.38
4,949	4,949	Home Depot	227,636	2.79
128	3,347	Chrysler	193,260	2.37
1,258	4,121	Allstate	179,774	2.20
939	2,228	MGIC Investment	143,674	1.76
	125,830	US Treasury Bond 7.125%	142,601	1.75
1,477	1,481	Philip Morris	137,752	1.69
−775	1,991	Caterpillar	128,196	1.57
1,786	3,222	Deere	120,834	1.48
−310	1,375	Computer Sciences	104,825	1.28
−293	1,355	Digital Equipment	98,090	1.20
866	866	American International Group	83,865	1.03
1,093	1,093	Aetna Life & Casualty	81,414	1.00
524	524	General Re	80,111	0.98
	67,210	US Treasury Bond 7.5%	79,927	0.98
987	987	El duPont de Nemours	75,868	0.93
−993	1,554	Oracle	74,213	0.91
2,222	2,394	Lear Seating	70,922	0.87
3,068	3,068	Fuji Bank	69,610	0.85
582	582	CIGNA	68,992	0.84
996	996	Rohm & Haas	68,987	0.84
187	1,088	Armstrong World Industries	63,920	0.78
1,956	1,956	RJR Nabisco Holdings	63,584	0.78
952	2,364	Manpower	63,538	0.78

Investment Style			Stock Portfolio Avg	Rel S&P 500	Rel Objective
Style Value Blnd Growth		Price/Earnings ratio	23.1	1.01	0.91
		Price/Book Ratio	3.6	0.77	0.75
		5 Yr Earnings Gr%	15.0	0.85	0.64
		Return on Assets %	6.5	0.79	0.69
		Debt % Total Cap	35.9	1.13	1.22
		Foreign%	11.0		
		Med Mkt Cap $mil	8,236	0.40	1.05

(Size: Large / Med / Small)

Special Securities % of assets 01-31-96	
● Private/Illiquid Securities	Trace
○ Structured Notes	0
● Emerging-Markets Secs	1
● Options/Futures/Warrants	Yes

Composition % of assets 04-30-96		Market Cap	
Cash	10.4	Giant	25.3
Stocks	89.6	Large	34.8
Bonds	0.0	Medium	32.6
Other	0.0	Small	6.7
		Micro	0.7

Sector Weightings	% of Stocks	Rel S&P
Utilities	0.3	0.05
Energy	9.4	1.02
Financials	20.7	1.54
Industrial Cyclicals	27.7	1.62
Consumer Durables	13.7	3.65
Consumer Staples	3.7	0.33
Services	7.2	0.67
Retail	5.4	0.90
Health	4.7	0.45
Technology	7.1	0.65

Exhibit 10-1   Concluded

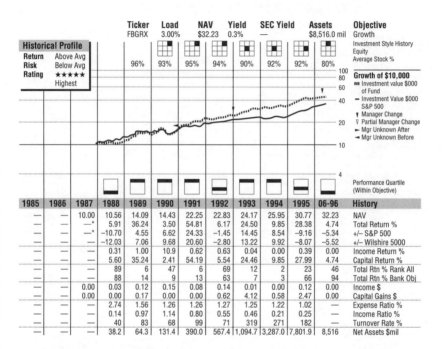

	Ticker	Load	NAV	Yield	SEC Yield	Assets	Objective
	FBGRX	3.00%	$32.23	0.3%	—	$8,516.0 mil	Growth

Historical Profile
Return   Above Avg
Risk   Below Avg
Rating   ★★★★★
         Highest

Investment Style History
Equity
Average Stock %

Average Stock %: 96% 93% 95% 94% 90% 92% 92% 80%

Growth of $10,000
▪▪▪ Investment value $000
    of Fund
— Investment Value $000
    S&P 500
▼ Manager Change
▽ Partial Manager Change
◄ Mgr Unknown After
◄ Mgr Unknown Before

Performance Quartile
(Within Objective)

1985	1986	1987	1988	1989	1990	1991	1992	1993	1994	1995	06-96	History
—	—	10.00	10.56	14.09	14.43	22.25	22.83	24.17	25.95	30.77	32.23	NAV
—	—	—*	5.91	36.24	3.50	54.81	6.17	24.50	9.85	28.38	4.74	Total Return %
—	—	—*	-10.70	4.55	6.62	24.33	-1.45	14.45	8.54	-9.16	-5.34	+/- S&P 500
—	—	—	-12.03	7.06	9.68	20.60	-2.80	13.22	9.92	-8.07	-5.52	+/- Wilshire 5000
—	—	—	0.31	1.00	10.9	0.62	0.63	0.04	0.00	0.39	0.00	Income Return %
—	—	—	5.60	35.24	2.41	54.19	5.54	24.46	9.85	27.99	4.74	Capital Return %
—	—	—	89	6	47	6	69	12	2	23	46	Total Rtn % Rank All
—	—	—	88	14	9	13	63	7	3	66	94	Total Rtn % Bank Obj
—	—	0.00	0.03	0.12	0.15	0.08	0.14	0.01	0.00	0.12	0.00	Income $
—	—	0.00	0.00	0.17	0.00	0.00	0.62	4.12	0.58	2.47	0.00	Capital Gains $
—	—	—	2.74	1.56	1.26	1.26	1.27	1.25	1.22	1.02	—	Expense Ratio %
—	—	—	0.14	0.97	1.14	0.80	0.55	0.46	0.21	0.25	—	Income Ratio %
—	—	—	40	83	68	99	71	319	271	182	—	Turnover Rate %
—	—	—	38.2	64.3	131.4	390.0	567.4	1,094.7	3,287.0	7,801.9	8,516	Net Assets $mil

Analysis by Cebra Graves 07-05-96

Fidelity Blue Chip Growth Fund is returning to its roots.

This fund sprouted from Fidelity's institutional business. Its first manager, Richard O'Rourke, ran it as an extension of his highly defined, institutional, large-cap growth portfolio and it fit snugly into the upper right hand corner of the style box. In 1993, however, Michael Gordon took over management of the fund, and quickly made it a maverick. He redirected the bulk of the fund's assets into small- and mid-cap firms, and threw 19% of the fund overseas.

By doing so, Gordon avoided the malaise that affected many other large-cap growth offerings at the time. Shareholders seemingly forgave the fund for no longer living up to its name, and its powerful returns attracted lots of new money. During the fourth quarter of 1995, however, Gordon's huge technology stake (39% of assets) got punished, and his subsequent retreat into bonds and cash proved equally ill-timed. For the past year, the fund has lagged the S&P 500 by more than seven percentage points.

When Magellan's Jeff Vinik resigned to start his own company, Gordon (who had acted in tandem with many of Vinik's investment decisions) joined him. In the wake of Gordon's departure, Fidelity took the opportunity to return this fund to its original mission. Like O'Rourke, new manager John McDowell also runs institutional money and appreciates the value of consistency. He has fully reinvested the fund in stocks, and has slanted the portfolio toward larger companies and such high-growth sectors as technology and health care.

Such moves radically redefine this fund's character. Investors who bought the fund for Gordon's aggressive, idiosyncratic style will no longer be happy here. Those who bought it for large-cap growth exposure, however, now have the fund they probably wanted.Ex 10.01

Address	82 Devonshire Street		
	Boston, MA 02109		
Telephone	800-544-8888		
Advisor	Fidelity Managment & Research		
Subadavisor	FMR (U.K.)/FMR (Far East)		
Distributor	Fidelity Distributors		
States Available	All		
Report Grade	B+		
Income Distrib	Annually		

Minimum Purchase	$2500	Add: $250	IRA: $500
Min Auto Inv Plan	$2500	Systematic Inv: $100	
Date of Inception	12-31-87		
Expenses & Fees			
Sales Fees	3.00%L		
Management Fee	.3%+52% max./.27% min.(G)+(−).2%P		
Actual Fee	Mgt: 0.69% Dist:—		
Expense Projections	3Yr: $61 5Yr: $85 10Yr: $151		
Annual Brokerage Cost	0.62%		

Source: *Morningstar Mutual Fund Report* July 1996.

provide a representation of a fund's risk, its investment methodology, and the size of the companies (maturity of bonds in the case of a fixed-income fund) in which the fund invests.

Exhibit 10–1 provides a sample of a Morningstar mutual fund report. The style box is in the lower right portion of the exhibit. The style boxes in the upper part of the exhibit indicate changes, if any, in the fund's investment style over time.

The comprehensive nature of the report is obvious from an inspection of the exhibit. Several features, from our perspective, are worth noting. First, the report starts by categorizing the fund's investment objective and briefly summarizing the background of the portfolio manager(s). Absolute and relative performance results are then reported, including those adjusted for taxes. Quantitative risk analysis is also presented, including the standard deviation of the fund's total return, its portfolio beta relative to one or more market benchmarks, the Sharpe ratio discussed in Chapter 6, and Morningstar's own risk assessment. Other information presented includes historical financial data; the composition of the fund by securities, sectors, and market capitalization; and expense and fee information. An analyst's assessment of the fund is also presented.

SUMMARY

Mutual funds might provide a lower cost means of implementing an investment committee's investment strategy than either direct security purchases or the services of a professional portfolio manager. Mutual funds' cost advantages appear to make them especially appealing to committees of relatively small funds or to committees who choose to act as their own investment managers.

Mutual fund performance evaluation has been greatly enhanced by organizations who specialize in providing this service to investors.

REFERENCES

1. As Bodie, Kane, and Marcus report, a satisfactory explanation of the reasons for the divergence of a closed-end fund's share price from its NAV has yet to emerge. See Bodie, Z.; A. Kane; A. J. Marcus. *Investments*. 3rd ed. Burr Ridge, IL: Richard D. Irwin, 1996, p. 107.
2. *1995–1996 Directory of Mutual Funds*. Washington, D.C.: The Investment Company Institute, 1995, pp. 105–23.
3. "Portfolios, Please." *Morningstar Mutual Funds*, July 5, 1996, pp. 51–52.

CHAPTER 11

Searching for an Investment Manager

INTRODUCTION

The investment committee will have to periodically conduct a portfolio manager search. For a newly created portfolio, this process usually begins shortly after the committee drafts the investment policy statement. For funds already in existence, a periodic review of the portfolio's investment performance may trigger discussions among committee members with regard to changing professional managers. Usually, a series of disappointing investment performance results provides the impetus for discussions concerning the wisdom of continuing with the same investment manager. In either event, it is likely that committee members will, at some time, be called upon to engage in a search for a new money manager.

The selection of a portfolio manager is one of the most important responsibilities of those charged with serving on investment committees. The search process itself is a major undertaking and requires a significant commitment of time and energy for those involved. The process requires the design and development of criteria for choosing a new manager, the identification of prospective fund managers, the solicitation of proposals, and the evaluation of submitted proposals. Moreover, after the initial review of proposals, the committee must decide which fund manager(s) to evaluate further. Finally, the committee must select a fund manager(s). This may be the single most important decision made by the committee.

THE SEARCH COMMITTEE

The composition of the search committee can vary. The search process can be conducted by the entire investment committee or by a subcommittee. For larger investment committees, it may be advisable to appoint a subcommittee to conduct the search for an investment manager. Once the search committee completes its charge, it should then make recommendations to the full committee.

The composition of the search committee should be representative of the investment committee. Individuals with prior experience in conducting investment management searches should be included in this committee. The committee's activities will be such that having members with administrative and technical skills is essential. Therefore, personnel possessing these skills should be actively involved in the process.

The role of the chair is critical to the effectiveness of the committee. The chair is required to assign various responsibilities associated with conducting the search. These responsibilities include overseeing the solicitation of proposals, maintaining and condensing the data and other materials provided by candidates, communicating with candidates, scheduling meetings, arranging for reference checks, and presenting the committee's recommendations to the investment committee.

ESTABLISHING GOALS

The process of identifying candidates should begin with the establishment of criteria for investment managers. The manager's job is to operate the fund in a manner consistent with the goals of the fund. The manager is charged with achieving a set of predetermined performance objectives while operating within the constraints specified in the fund's investment policy statement.

Therefore, it is necessary that the candidate's compatibility with the sponsoring organization's philosophy, as well as with the portfolio's goals and objectives, be explicitly considered.

The starting point, then, is to define the type of investment manager whose management philosophy and approach are consistent with the goals of the fund. If the investment goals require a growth-oriented approach to investing, then candidates with expertise in successfully managing growth portfolios should be primarily considered. Likewise, a portfolio with an income-oriented or value-oriented goal should be matched with those candidates who employ these investment approaches. Thus, the search committee must evaluate the compatibility of its goals with the candidates' investment management styles. In short, before the search process is started, the investment committee must carefully identify its needs.

THE NUMBER OF MANAGERS

One of the first decisions that should be made by the search committee is whether to consider more than one investment professional to manage the fund's assets. There are several reasons a committee might consider multiple managers. For example, multiple managers may permit an incrementally higher level of diversification for the fund. In addition to enhanced securities diversification, multiple managers may provide additional diversification in style or investment approach. Along these lines, the committee could choose to hire a value manager, a growth manager, and perhaps a high-tech manager. Regardless of investment approaches, the successful managers should be well disciplined enough to stick to their own techniques. If the objectives of the portfolio change so that new investment approaches are required, the committee should immediately reevaluate the suitability of their current investment manager(s).

Multiple managers may be attractive if the sponsor wants a balanced portfolio. In this instance, the committee selects a manager for its equity portfolio and one for its fixed-income portfolio. Each manager would be responsible for achieving goals suitable for the type of assets he or she controls. Thus, the committee could choose to employ the services of multiple managers for each component of the balanced fund. Many investment professionals recognize that different skills are required to manage equities and fixed-income securities.

Also, there are costs associated with employing multiple fund managers. Extra time and effort will likely be required to monitor and evaluate the performance of additional managers. That is, the cost of evaluating one manager, who is responsible for investing the entire fund, is likely less than that of evaluating several managers, each of whom is responsible for one portion of the fund. Moreover, there is a large and growing body of research literature that is consistent with the view that it is extremely difficult for fund managers to consistently outperform the relevant market index benchmarks, especially on a risk-adjusted basis. Perhaps as a consequence, many fund managers in reality have very similar portfolios in terms of asset allocation and securities held. Recognizing this, the investment committee should take care that, if it intends to use multiple managers, they actually obtain the benefits in terms of incremental diversification and enhanced performance rather than duplication of efforts.

The choice of how many managers to employ may be influenced by the size of the portfolio. Smaller funds may not be suitable for a multimanager approach. The fee structure of fund managers may prohibit multiple managers. Furthermore, asset reallocation between fund managers would be more difficult to coordinate with multiple managers.

When the size of the investment portfolio is small, an attractive alternative may be to adopt a mutual fund strategy. This choice provides even the smallest investment portfolios with diversification and professional management at relatively low cost. In these instances, a two-step approach may be appropriate. First, the investment committee must decide on the asset allocation range, given the requirements of the portfolio. Here, the committee can seek professional assistance. Second, the committee would choose among various mutual funds whose goals and objectives mirror that of the portfolio.

CANDIDATE IDENTIFICATION

After the committee determines the proper investment management style, it must identify a list of potential candidates for proposal solicitation. This requires that the committee identify successful investment managers whose philosophies and management styles match the requirements of the fund. Typically, this involves the identification of investment managers who have achieved attractive performance results based on their stated objectives on a consistent basis.

At this point, the investment committee should focus on several factors to aid in identifying prospective candidates. Attention should be paid to more easily identifiable, quantitative criteria as well as more subjective ones. As we discuss later, the past investment results and fee structures of potential managers should be thoroughly scrutinized. In a world where performance and fees tend to converge over time, however, the choice of one or more managers may ultimately be based on such issues as quality of service, compatibility of investment philosophies, trust, and communications.

Remember that the choice of an investment manager involves, in essence, establishing a business relationship with an entire organization. Engaging the services of a stellar investment strategist may yield only frustration and disappointment if, for example, phone calls to the organization are not returned or if operational inadequacies prevent account statements from being transmitted in a timely, accurate, and informative manner.

While variations in the performance of operating units exist in all organizations, we are of the view that such variations are relatively smaller in good organizations than in poor investment management organizations. Simply put, consistently achieving investment objectives required by sponsors requires consistently strong performance by all operating units of an investment organization. However, in an industry where vestiges of once-heavy regulation still remain, this is not always found.

The growth of the investment management industry has been largely based on strengths in the marketing of investment services and on achieving solid gross returns for clients. Total Quality Management approaches in the investment services industry, as has been the situation in much of the broader services sector, are still relatively new. The investment committee should recognize these features of the industry and, in our view, base its recommendations on a number of quantitative as well as critical qualitative factors.

A variety of organizations provide investment management services, including registered investment advisors, asset management divisions within security broker-dealers, insurance companies, bank trust departments, and some mutual funds. The range of services and the size of such organizations are enormous. The larger investment management organizations obviously provide a full range of investment services and products, encompassing most—if not all—of the components of a well-developed investment process as well as the complete range of investment styles and products. Smaller investment companies, in contrast, may specialize in particular niches of the investment process. Trade-offs might exist between the choice of either a larger or smaller investment company along such dimensions as depth of professional staff, fees, personal attention, and service quality.

One trend in the investment industry that is gaining popularity among both large and small organizations is the use of outside managers to actually invest a fund's monies. The investment committee should be aware of whether the organization they employ is actually investing their funds or, instead, directing others to do so. Proponents of this "managing the managers" approach contend that it allows for greater specialization with attendant gains. Critics, however, argue that it merely adds an additional layer to the investment management process with attendant higher costs.

Various investment services track the investment performance of fund managers. These include the Pension Investment Performance Evaluation Report (PIPER) and SEI. Also, names of investment managers can be found in publications such as the *Money Market Directory* and the listing of Registered Investment Advisors (RIAs). In addition to these sources, several organizations maintain proprietary lists of investment managers along with performance figures. In fact, the committee may employ the services of pension fund consultants to identify suitable fund managers and to assist it in the selection process. Finally, names of professional investment managers can be obtained by way of referrals.

MANAGEMENT AND RELATED FEES

In addition to performance results, the search committee should carefully consider fees and other expenses charged by professional investment managers. While investment expertise is essential to the success of the fund, excessive fees and other related expenses can reduce the overall investment return.

Therefore, the compensation issue should be clearly understood. Usually, investment managers provide a fee schedule that details the cost of managing a portfolio, which is based on the size of the assets under management. The fees charged by professional managers may vary significantly. Typically, investment managers charge a fee based on the amount of money under management as well as the amount of income (i.e., interest and dividends) the portfolio receives. These fees may not cover all of the services the fund may require. For example, additional fees such as the costs of trading securities may be required. Therefore, it is important to determine exactly what services the basic fee covers. The investment manager should also be required to disclose the costs of all additional services. Finally, the fee schedule should also specify the timing of payment (e.g., quarterly, semiannual, annual) and whether these fees cover custody and safekeeping of securities services.

Table 11–1 presents a hypothetical fee schedule. This schedule provides information on a hypothetical fund's market value and the corresponding fee charged. For example, a fund with a market value of $24,000,000 would be charged an annual fee of $96,000 (i.e., $24,000,000 × 0.40%). Some fund managers will provide eleemosynary funds with discounts. Finally, these fee schedules may be negotiable.

Investment committees often overlook additional fees and expenses that are not as obvious as the ones just discussed. There can be significant additional fees if the investment manager invests in mutual funds. In addition to the management fees, the fund could incur expenses, such as front-end and back-end loads. Furthermore, 12b-1 fees charged by mutual funds for advertising and commissions paid to brokers can greatly increase the overall management cost. Unfortunately, the impact of these expenses on overall investment performance may not be apparent until after a new manager is in place.

The search committee has a responsibility to examine other costs as well. For example, the candidates should be required to

TABLE 11–1

ABC Manager, Sample Fee Schedule

Market Value of Fund	Annual Fees (%)
$500,000–$1,000,000	0.75
$1,000,000–$10,000,000	0.65
$10,000,000–$20,000,000	0.50
Above $20,000,000	0.40

furnish the committee with a commission schedule. It is not un-heard of for funds to be charged $0.25 to $0.50 or more for each se-curity share traded, even though the actual costs are a few pennies per share. For example, an investment manager may have an agreement in which it directs trades to a brokerage house in return for research services. In essence, the fund ends up paying for the investment manager's outside research without ever being aware of these arrangements.

FIRM SIZE AND OWNERSHIP

Another factor that the search committee should be aware of when developing a candidate list is the size of asset holdings the candi-date management firm accepts. Almost all investment managers specify the minimum size for assets they will manage. The invest-ment committee should determine whether the size of their fund falls above or below this minimum.

There are other size issues that should be addressed. Invest-ment committee members of smaller funds are often concerned that a money manager from a large management firm may not de-vote to them the time and individual attention that their portfolio requires. This is certainly a valid concern and should be addressed. Likewise, small management firms may also be deficient in terms of management professionals. The committee should carefully con-sider the risk if the "star performer" (i.e., the fund manager) were no longer associated with the firm. It is always important to deter-mine beforehand who will manage the fund if the designated pro-fessional manager is no longer available. Finally, the aspect of employee ownership should not be overlooked. Investment profes-sionals who have a stake in the firm can be expected to have a deeper commitment to their firm's overall success. Thus, the search committee should carefully consider these issues when the final se-lection is made.

REQUESTS FOR PROPOSALS

Once the list of investment managers has been put together, the committee contacts these firms seeking proposals. Exhibit 11–1 contains a sample request for proposal (RFP). The RFP should contain all necessary information and allow the candidates sufficient time to respond. The RFP should state the size of the fund, its goals and objectives, and any distribution requirements. Finally, the RFP should specify a deadline for receipt of the requested materials.

The RFP should explicitly identify areas the candidates must address. Candidates should be asked to provide performance information of monies under management with objectives similar to those of the fund. The candidates should provide a statement concerning their investment style, which should include its risk management and diversification strategies, methods of security selection, use of market timing, asset allocation method, and average size of its portfolio both in terms of dollars and securities held. The candidates should also indicate the framework in which purchase and/or sale of securities decisions are made. Additionally, other information such as the total funds under management, average fund balance, number of professionals employed, turnover rates, and minimum size fund accepted should be included.

One of the most important areas the RFP should address concerns the historic performance of the investment managers. In providing information on its historic performance, the investment managers will develop composites based on a number of accounts under management.

The résumés of the individual(s) responsible for managing the account should be provided. Audited financial statements should also be provided. The proposals should include the Securities and Exchange Commission's Corporate Review and Disclosure Form ADV, Part II. The RFP should inquire as to the use of outside research services and the candidate's fee schedules. Finally, each candidate should provide references from current and former clients. This information is extremely valuable in choosing the investment

EXHIBIT 11-1

REQUEST FOR PROPOSALS

Dear Investment Manager:

The Pension Investment Committee of XYZ Corporation is presently seeking proposals from investment firms to manage its pension fund. The current market value of the fund is approximately $24,000,000. A copy of the fund's Investment Policy Statement is enclosed to assist you in responding to the RFP.

In order to evaluate your proposal we request that it address the following issues:

- Your firm's investment philosophy and approach to managing XYZ Corporation's pension fund. This should include your management style, risk management techniques, diversification strategy, asset allocation methodology, degree of securities concentration, and turnover rates.

- Total funds managed on a discretionary basis. This should be categorized with regard to asset type as well as the taxable and nontaxable basis.

- Performance results including risk adjusted measures (calendar-year basis) on a 1-, 3-, 5-, 10-, and 20-year basis. These data should be presented with and without dividends reinvested. The performance figures should be provided on a gross- and net-of-fees basis. (The return presentation should conform with the standards as adopted by AIMR.)

- Performance measures during advancing and declining markets.

- Biographical information on the investment professionals in your firm. Please indicate who will have primary responsibility for the management of the fund as well as this(these) person's(s') prior investment performance record(s). This should include assets under management, average asset allocation, and annualized return statistics.

- Complete fee structure, including a separation of management fees, trading commission costs, custodial and safekeeping fees, and other relevant expenses.

- List of references.

- Three to five years of audited financial statements.

Please feel free to provide any additional material that you believe will assist the committee in its decision making process. The deadline for proposal submission is September 1, 199X.

Thank you for your efforts on behalf of the XYZ Corporation's pension fund.

Sincerely yours,

Chair, Pension Fund Search Committee

manager. The committee has a responsibility to check these references very carefully, prior to making their decision. The committee chair may delegate this task to one or more members of the search committee.

The performance time periods should be explicitly stated. For example, the candidates might be asked to provide annualized rates of return on a 1-, 3-, 5-, 10-, and 20-year basis. To avoid comparison problems, it is recommended that all performance results be measured over common periods. For example, the RFP might require candidates to use the calendar year (i.e., January to December) when reporting results. Additionally, the candidates may also be asked to provide performance results over varying market climates (i.e., bull and bear markets). The committee may also specify whether the performance figures should be with or without reinvestment of dividends.

These performance composites should be based on guidelines adopted by the Association for Investment Management and Research (AIMR). Exhibit 11–2 presents the construction and maintenance of composite guidelines contained in Section V of the AIMR's Performance Presentation Standards. As the exhibit reveals, AIMR sets forth explicit guidelines regarding how fund managers are to construct their presentation composites. The adherence to these guidelines by investment manager candidates enhances the ability of the investment committee to evaluate the relative performance fairly.

Exhibit 11–3 reports AIMR's guidelines for the presentation of composites, which are contained in Section V of AIMR's Performance Presentation Standards. The section provides additional guidelines for managers to follow when presenting composite data to potential clients.

The publication of the Performance Presentation Standards by the Association for Investment Management and Research is an important step toward ensuring that investment performance is fully disclosed. The adoption of uniform standards of comparison

EXHIBIT 11–2

ASSOCIATION FOR INVESTMENT MANAGEMENT AND RESEARCH CONSTRUCTION AND MAINTENANCE OF COMPOSITES

1. All actual, fee-paying, discretionary portfolios must be included in at least one composite. Performance records must be presented fairly and completely without intent to bias or misrepresent by excluding selected portfolios.

2. Firm composites must include only actual assets under management. Model results may be presented as supplementary information, but the model results must be identified as such and must not be linked to actual results.

3. Non-fee-paying portfolios may be included in composites if such inclusion is disclosed.

4. If investment restrictions hinder or prohibit the application of an intended investment strategy, the affected portfolio may be considered nondiscretionary. Examples of such restrictions include

   a. Tax considerations that prevent the manager from realizing profits on existing holdings.

   b. Client requirements that the portfolio include or exclude certain securities or types of securities.

   c. Minimum portfolio-size limits that exclude portfolios a manager deems too small to be representative of the manager's intended strategy. The size limit must be disclosed and adhered to rigidly, and no portfolios under the size cutoff can be considered discretionary. Composites of larger sized portfolios must not be used as representative of performance results when marketing to prospective clients whose assets are below the size cutoff.

   d. The definition of a nondiscretionary portfolio depends on a manager's particular strategy. For example, a manager may exclude a South Africa firm from the portfolio if that restriction makes its construction different from the manager's other portfolios. Another manager may choose to create a separate composite of several such portfolios. A third manager may include all such portfolios in a more broadly defined composite if the restriction does not result in holdings that are different from the other portfolios' holdings.

5. Asset weighting of the portfolio returns within a composite is required using beginning-of-period weightings (or beginning-of-period market values plus weighted cash flows, or by aggregating assets and cash flows to calculate performance as for a single portfolio). The additional presentation of equal-weighted composite returns is recommended but not required.

Exhibit 11-2   Concluded

6. New portfolios must not be added to a composite until the start of the next per-formance measurement period (month or quarter) after the portfolio comes under management or according to reasonable and consistently applied man-ager guidelines.

7. Portfolios no longer under management must be included in historical compos-ites for the periods they were under management; that is, "survivor" performance results are prohibited. They must be excluded for all periods after the last full period they were in place.

8. Portfolios must not be switched from one composite to another unless documented changes in client guidelines make this appropriate.

9. Changes in a firm's organization must not lead to an altering of composite re-sults. A change in personnel should be disclosed, but personnel changes must not be used to alter composite performance results. Performance results of a past affiliation must not be used to represent the historical record of a new affili-ation or a newly formed entity. Using the performance data from a prior firm as supplemental information is permitted as long as the past record is not linked to the results of the new affiliation. The guiding principle is that performance is the record of the firm, not of the individual.

10. Convertibles or other hybrid instruments should be treated consistently across and within composites, except when meeting client directives. Convertibles could be treated as equity instruments, unless the manager and the client have decided otherwise.

Source: Reprinted with permission from Performance Presentation Standards, Copyright 1993, Association for Investment Management and Research, Charlottesville, VA. All Rights Reserved.

is essential to the evaluation of investment performance. There-fore, the investment committee should strive to use comparable in-vestment results when evaluating performance. The adoption of the AIMR performance standards or other industry-accepted stan-dards is an important step in reaching this goal.

In short, the RFP should provide the investment committee with information critical to the search process. The committee may want to have prospective investment managers complete a questionnaire to capture much of the information in a uniform

EXHIBIT 11-3

ASSOCIATION INVESTMENT MANAGEMENT AND RESEARCH PRESENTATION OF COMPOSITES

1. Prospective clients must be advised that a list and description of all of a firm's composites are available.

2. At least a 10-year record (or the record since inception of the firm, if shorter) must be presented; presentation of a 20-year record is recommended if the company has been in existence for 20 years.

3. Retroactive compliance is recommended but not required. Section VII details the requirements for presenting performance for periods prior to 1993.

4. For any period for which compliance is claimed, the presentation of annual returns for all years is required to avoid selectivity in time periods presented. Annualized cumulative performance is recommended. Performance for periods of less than one year must not be annualized.

5. When composites include both taxable and tax-exempt securities, the manager should state the percentages of each class.

6. Managers should show both internal and external dispersion of portfolio returns in the composite. Section VIII details the recommendations for the presentation of measures of risk and dispersion.

7. Presentation of supplemental information is recommended when the manager deems this additional information to be valuable to clients. Such disclosures might include the average market capitalization of stocks held, the average quality and duration of bond holdings, and additional information on international portfolios (Section X), real estate portfolios (Section XI), and portfolios using leverage or derivative securities (Section XII). This information must not supplant the required information, and it must be accompanied by the appropriate composite returns.

Source: Reprinted with permission from Performance Presentation Standards, Copyright 1993, Association for Investment Management and Research, Charlottesville, VA. All Rights Reserved.

manner. Exhibit 11–4 contains a sample portfolio manager inquiry. This document solicits information pertaining to the company's background as well as its operational characteristics. This standardized document can be used to compare the responses of the candidates.

E X H I B I T   1 1 – 4

PORTFOLIO MANAGER INQUIRY

I. Company Information

A. Company Name

Headquarters Address

Year Founded

Branch Office Address(es)

Year(s) Opened

B. Company Ownership

Name(s) and Ownership share (%) of Principals

1.

2.

3.

4.

5.

Has Company Ownership by Principals changed in the last (circle) three or five years: _____No _____Yes   If yes, briefly explain.

If the company is a subsidiary, please name parent.

What percentage of the company is owned by employees other than those named above? _____ percent

C. Company Organization

The company is a: Registered Investment Advisor _____ ; Securities Broker/Dealer _____ ; Mutual Fund _____ ; Commercial Bank _____ ; Insurance Company _____ ; Other (specify) _____ .

What are the minimum _____ and maximum _____ account sizes accepted?

What is the average size account?

Exhibit 11–4 Continued

What is the number of accounts and dollar amounts under management per portfolio manager?

Number of Employees _____

Staff	Number	Average Years of Professional Experience
Equity portfolio managers		
Fixed-income managers		
Investment strategies		
Research analysts		
Equity traders		
Fixed-income traders		
Economists		
Operational personnel		
Compliance personnel		
Marketing personnel		
Management personnel		
Other		

II. Company Operations

Does your company use a (circle one) top-down or bottom-up approach to the investment process?

What percentages of the monies managed by your company are actively (_____ %) versus passively (_____ %) managed?

What importance does your company place on each of the following in the investment process?

	Most Important 5	4	Somewhat Important 3	2	Least Important 1
Asset Allocation					
Market Timing					
Security Selection					

Exhibit 11–4   Concluded

How are the following issues decided by your company?

	Committee	Portfolio Manager
Asset allocation mix		
Equity selection		
Fixed-income selection		
Mutual funds selection		

Does your company use outside managers to invest some of the assets your firm manages? If yes, please explain.

Does your company use derivative instruments to manage risk? If yes, please explain.

SCREENING THE CANDIDATES

The next step in the process is to evaluate the proposals submitted by the candidates. Each proposal should be screened to determine whether all requested information has been provided. In most instances, this will not be a problem. Usually, the candidates will provide additional materials, and often, the packages are quite large. Thus, the problem becomes condensing the volume of materials submitted into a workable package.

The use of a summary sheet can greatly facilitate this process. The summary sheet should identify each candidate along with information concerning his or her proposal. Exhibit 11–5 presents a sample summary sheet. Typically, this sheet would include the size of funds under management, the performance results over several periods, asset allocations, and the fee schedule. Additional information, such as the account turnover, employee turnover, and staff size may also be included in the summary sheet. This exhibit should be used as a supplement to the investment proposal packages.

E X H I B I T   1 1 – 5

SAMPLE SUMMARY SHEET

Investment Company

	ABC	DEF	GHI
Discretionary accounts ($000,000)			
Balanced	$642,987	$521,984	$451,876
Equities	195,983	103,847	232,762
Fixed income	78,964	59,725	102,863
Total	$917,934	$685,556	$787,50
Balanced account asset allocation ranges			
Equities	45–65%	40–60%	40–65%
Fixed income	35–55%	40–60%	35–60%
Equities—total return percentage (net of fees), dividends reinvested			
1 year	12.54	11.97	10.39
3 years	10.83	11.45	12.23
5 years	11.10	11.76	11.98
10 years	12.07	11.86	12.06
Fixed income—total return % (net of fees), interest reinvested			
1 year	7.83	7.76	7.39
3 years	8.43	8.32	8.18
5 years	8.88	8.67	8.41
10 years	9.02	8.49	8.54
Annual fees (based on XYZ's MV)	$96,000	$82,000	$87,000

Next, the summary sheets and supporting proposals should be evaluated by each search committee member in light of the fund's goals and objectives. During this review, each member should identify the strengths and weaknesses of the candidates. After the members have had sufficient time to study the individual packages, the entire search committee should meet to discuss the relative merits of each investment manager. The committee should then narrow the list of candidates to those that it wishes to interview. Along these lines, it would be useful to agree upon the number of candidates to be interviewed. Once an agreement has been reached, the actual selection can be accomplished through developing a consensus among search committee members. If a consensus emerges, then individual committee members may be asked to rank each candidate. If there is a disagreement regarding who is to be interviewed, the committee may expand the list of candidates. While this will increase the time requirements, it will also foster greater communication among committee members.

CANDIDATE PRESENTATIONS

Once the finalists have been identified, the committee must develop an interview schedule. The time allotted each candidate as well as the period over which the interviews will take place must be decided. The amount of time given should generally be sufficient to allow the candidates to make their presentations and committee members to ask questions. If properly prepared, a two-hour limit should be a sufficient amount of time. It is also important that all interviews be conducted over a reasonably short period of time. This will allow the committee to make comparisons while the information is fresh. A sample candidate notification letter is presented in Exhibit 11–6.

The presentations can be viewed in two parts. Typically, the presentation begins with the candidates describing their investment philosophy and management style. The presentation should touch upon their historic investment results, their procedures and policies, the fee structure for their services, and how they would manage the interviewing company's account(s).

After the candidates finish the formal presentation, the search committee should begin their questioning. It is important that search committee members decide on the types of issues to be addressed by each candidate before the meetings take place. The

E X H I B I T   1 1 – 6

INTERVIEW ANNOUNCEMENT

October 30, 199X

Mr. Investment Manager
ABC Advisors
1 Park Place
Investment City, USA

Re: Investment Presentation

Dear Mr. Manager:

This letter is to confirm the scheduled time for your presentation before the XYZ Corporation Pension Search Committee on the following date:

> December 1, 199X
> 8:00 a.m. to 10:00 a.m.
> Board Room
> XYZ Corporation

It is our understanding that Mr. Wellsworth and Mr. Smith will be making the presentation to the committee. Your presentation will be scheduled for the first hour of the meeting. The remaining time will be reserved for questions and answers.

Please telephone me if there are any changes.

Sincerely yours,

Chair, Pension Fund Search Committee

---

questions should cover both investment management and administration issues, which should lead to a more effective and organized interview process.

The committee might start by asking the managers the following question, "What accounts have you lost in the last 24 months, and why?" Several issues need to be raised during this time. The committee should determine who will ultimately be responsible for managing the fund. Sometimes, the actual individual charged with managing the fund is not one of the individuals involved in conducting the presentation. The presenters often disappear after the account has been awarded. Furthermore, it is not unusual for individuals responsible for prior performance results to no longer be affiliated with the firm. The committee has the right as well as the responsibility to insist that the person who will be managing the fund be in attendance at the interview. Finally, the committee must verify that the presentation results reflect the performance records of those who will be managing the fund.

Additional questions should be asked related to the management of the fund. Given the fund's goals and objectives, what changes if any does the candidate envision in regard to asset allocation and/or securities holdings? What performance information will be provided by the candidate, and over what period of time? How often will the candidate meet with the committee to review investment performance? What return does the candidate believe is attainable, given the fund's objectives?

After this portion of the interview is completed, the committee chair should ask the candidate if there are any questions that he or she would like to ask. This gives the candidate an opportunity to raise questions concerning issues that may have surfaced earlier in the interview. It is very important that all issues relating to the management of the portfolio be identified and openly discussed prior to the committee making its final decision.

VERIFICATION AND CHECKING OF REFERENCE

An important part of the selection process involves the verification of performance results. AIMR recommends that investment managers verify their performance results. Exhibit 11–7 reproduces the Level I and Level II verification guidelines contained in Section IX of the Performance Presentation Standards. To be in compliance with the AIMR standards, the investment results must be subjected to Level I and/or Level II verification. The AIMR guidelines require that performance claims be verified by an impartial party.

EXHIBIT 11-7

ASSOCIATION FOR INVESTMENT MANAGEMENT AND RESEARCH PERFORMANCE PRESENTATION STANDARDS

Level I and II Verification Statement

A. Level I Verification

A Level I verification attests to the fact that all of a firm's actual, discretionary, fee-paying portfolios are included in at least one composite. Examination procedures generally include verification of the following:

1. Each portfolio, including those no longer under management, is in fact either included in a composite or has been documented as being excluded for valid reasons.
2. All portfolios sharing the same guidelines are included in the same composite, and shifts from one composite to another one are based on documented client guidelines.
3. Portfolio returns within the composites are weighted by size.
4. Performance is being calculated using a time-weighted rate of return, with a minimum of quarterly valuations and accrual of income.
5. Disclosure is offered to ensure that performance has been presented accurately and in keeping with a full and fair presentation of investment results.

B. Level II Verification

A Level II verification examines both the investment management process (tests of validity and propriety of underlying shares, income, and pricing data) and the measurement of performance (computation and presentation of performance data). Examination procedures generally include verification of the following:

1. All of a firm's actual, discretionary, fee-paying portfolios are included in at least one composite (i.e., a Level I verification).
2. Performance calculations use a time-weighted return formula.
3. Asset prices.
4. Capital gains/losses.
5. Trades, on a same basis, checking the accounting trail, cost records, and actual shares or bonds still held.
6. Income streams, on a sample basis, including the timing and actual receipt of dividends, accrued interest, and the treatment of fees.
7. Cash flows are accounted for properly.

Source: Reprinted with permission from Performance Presentation Standards, Copyright 1993, Association for Investment Management and Research, Charlottesville, VA. All Rights Reserved.

The search committee should contact several references for each candidate to ascertain whether there are any issues that need to be considered prior to awarding the account. These references should be asked questions regarding their satisfaction with the candidate's performance results and their overall level of service. For example, reference accounts should be asked, "Would you hire them again?" and "Specifically, what negatives have you observed?" It is also very important to contact previous accounts to see why these accounts were terminated.

THE FINAL SELECTION

Once the verification process is completed, the committee should meet again to discuss the various merits of each candidate. The review of the presentations and supporting documents by the entire committee often leads to a consensus as to the choice of money managers. At the least, this process results in narrowing the choices. The committee can then proceed with a vote on the preferred candidate. If the search committee is a subcommittee, it recommends a candidate to the full investment committee for approval.

SWITCHING MANAGERS

It is occasionally necessary to switch fund managers at or even before their contract term expires. A number of factors can cause a desire to change fund managers: poor investment performance, higher than expected fees, changing investment objectives, and lack luster service to name a few.

Once the decision has been made to switch fund managers, the fund will enter into a transition period. During this time the new manager(s) should evaluate the current holdings of the portfolio to ascertain what changes are needed. These changes not only involve the allocation of funds among the various investment categories (i.e., equities, fixed income, and cash and equivalents) but also the allocation of actual securities within each category.

Changing the portfolio's composition involves some expenses as well. Transaction fees such as commissions will be higher than under normal circumstances. The manager should attempt to time the purchases and sales to minimize costs; nonetheless, there will most likely be significant expenses. Certainly, if the new management is to be evaluated properly, an evaluation of fund performance should be based solely upon their decisions.

The evaluators of fund performance should also recognize that there is a transition period. During this period, it will be difficult to evaluate the performance of the new manager. The committee should establish a grace period so that the new investment manager can restructure the portfolio in an orderly fashion. The new manager must carefully consider the timing of sales and purchases in relation to market fundamentals. The investment committee should recognize this important aspect when changing investment managers.

ADMINISTRATION OF CHANGE

The actual movement of the account requires substantial paperwork. Notifying the current fund manager is required to ensure a smooth transition. The committee may want to "freeze" the investment activities of the incumbent manager so that the new manager does not have to reverse transactions when the account is transferred. However, the committee must make sure that, during this process, there is constant communication between the committee and the incumbent manager. The committee must have a plan to handle investment actions that must be taken quickly during the transition period. In the final analysis, the investment committee must supervise all administrative aspects that the change in management requires.

SUMMARY

The selection of a portfolio manager(s) is the single most important decision an investment committee must make. The results of this decision are ultimately reflected in the fund's performance results. The search process for investment managers should be conducted by the full investment committee or by a subcommittee. The committee can employ the services of investment professionals or conduct the search itself.

The process begins with the establishment of the selection criteria. Next, the committee identifies individual firms whose investment philosophies and approaches match their fund's needs. RFPs from these investment professionals are then solicited. Upon receipt of the proposals, the committee members begin the screening process. Acceptable candidates are invited to make formal presentations. The committee then makes a selection from the candidates.

After the selection of a new investment manager is made, there will be a period of transition (if this is an existing fund). The committee can expect the new manager to restructure the portfolio. The new manager needs time to make the necessary purchases and sales. The committee members should be mindful of this period. The switching of managers also requires administrative coordination by the committee.

CHAPTER 12

Conducting Investment Committee Meetings

INTRODUCTION

Committee meetings are intended to provide a formal discussion of all aspects of the investment management process. Properly conducted, these meetings can ensure that the fund's investment goals and objectives are being carried out in a prudent and responsible manner. The meetings provide the setting for a wide range of discussions from investment policy issues to actual fund performance. Investment committee meetings should promote better communication among the committee members as well as between the committee and its portfolio managers. This, however, does not happen by accident; rather, it takes careful planning to conduct a successful meeting.

MEETING PREPARATION

Typically, the investment committee is charged with meeting periodically to handle administrative issues and to monitor and evaluate the performance of the investment portfolio. These meetings can take place on a monthly, quarterly, or annual basis and should at least be scheduled shortly after the measurement period's investment performance results are available. For example, if the policy statement calls for a quarterly review of performance, quarterly meetings should be scheduled during the month following the end of the quarter. The timing of these meetings should be such that they closely follow the measurement period so that corrective actions, if necessary, can be implemented, yet they should allow enough time to compile the materials dealing with the portfolio performance and market comparisons. The time and place of these meetings should ensure maximum participation by all interested parties. Exhibit 12–1 provides a sample meeting announcement letter.

There are other housekeeping items to remember in preparation for the meeting. The meeting room should be secured. Over-

EXHIBIT 12–1

XYZ CORPORATION MEETING ANNOUNCEMENT LETTER

March 20, 199X

Dear Ms. Jones:

The next meeting of the XYZ Pension Committee is scheduled as follows:

Thursday, April 18, 199X
8:00 a.m. to 10:00 a.m.
XYZ Board Room
XYZ Corporation

The agenda along with the first quarter 199X investment performance results will be mailed separately. Please feel free to contact me if you have any questions.

Sincerely yours,

Chair, Pension Investment Committee

head projectors, screens, papers, pencils, and other equipment and supplies needed during the meeting should be obtained and inspected to ensure that they are in good working order. Refreshments should be provided for all attendees. The meeting environment sets the tone for a productive meeting.

AGENDA AND MEETING MATERIALS

The meeting's agenda as well as other reference materials should be distributed to the committee members well in advance of the scheduled meeting date. Providing such information at the time of the meeting itself leads to confusion and fosters disorganization. Specifically, committee members would be required to survey the material while simultaneously listening to the proceedings. This prevents members from devoting their full attention to the issues currently being discussed by the committee.

SETTING THE AGENDA

The agenda specifies the activities to be discussed at the meeting and their sequence. The agenda covers administrative as well as performance issues to be considered during the meeting. In planning the agenda, the chair should ask the following questions: What needs to be accomplished? In what order should these items be addressed?

The committee should consider the time requirements necessary for dealing with the administrative issues when setting the agenda. Some issues can be dealt with quickly within the current committee structure. Other issues may require the formation of subcommittees. In these latter instances, the chair should carefully assign subcommittee members so that the proper balance of expertise and perspective is achieved. The reports from various subcommittees should be incorporated into the agenda.

Exhibit 12–2 presents a sample agenda. As shown in the exhibit, these meetings begin with a motion to approve the minutes

EXHIBIT 12–2

XYZ FUND MEETING AGENDA
January 21, 19XX

Item:	Responsibility
Approval of Minutes of the October 23 meeting	Chair
Administrative Issues	Chair
Report of Search Committee	Chair, Subcommittee
Investment Performance	Manager
Ratification of Purchases	Chair
Ratification of Sales	Chair
Old Business	Open
New Business	Open
Adjournment	

of the prior meeting. Keeping proper minutes provides a record of the items discussed by the committee. The next item on the agenda concerns administrative issues. These issues may involve items related to investment policy, plan administration (e.g., selecting a trustee), or they may involve the fund's investment performance. If these administrative issues can be dealt with by a committee of the whole, then discussion time should be allocated prior to or after the portfolio managers are scheduled to meet with the committee. If, for example, administrative discussions are expected to consume one hour of time, the investment managers should be invited to make their presentations at the beginning of the second hour of the meeting. If, on the other hand, the actual time devoted to these issues is unknown, it might be advisable to proceed first with the report of the fund managers. Attendance of the fund managers during these discussions is normally not encouraged. The committee may want to keep specific items that are under discussion private. Therefore, investment managers should be invited into the meeting at the conclusion of the administrative portion of the agenda or dismissed prior to that discussion.

RESPONSIBILITIES OF THE CHAIR

Conducting the investment meeting requires a special kind of knowledge and skill. Clearly, the chair needs to be familiar with the details of investment performance evaluation. However, he or she also needs the personal skills to foster an environment that promotes an open exchange of ideas and encourages communication. The chair needs to steer the committee away from unproductive uses of their time and needs to be diplomatic when seeking closure. Thus, an autocratic approach to chairing a committee is seldom successful. In contrast, a chair with a participatory philosophy, who solicits advice and opinions from all participants, is generally viewed as very effective.

INVESTMENT CONSULTING SERVICES

To properly conduct the investment committee meeting, it is important that all committee members be properly prepared. Individuals are occasionally invited to serve on investment committees because of their involvement in the community and/or because of positions held within the organization, but they are often unfamiliar with the technical aspects of investments. For these individuals, the entire process can be overwhelming. Providing support for such individuals is essential.

Investment consultants may be helpful in these situations. The investment consultants often provide market comparison data as part of their service. The investment consultant can construct a performance index that matches the goals and objectives of the fund. Investment consultants can lead the committee through the evaluation process in an organized and highly effective manner. Members can draw on the expertise of consultants to explain the interpretation of performance results. The more knowledgeable the committee members, the more successful the investment committee. Having well-prepared committee members is the key to conducting a successful meeting.

Committees often retain the services of professional portfolio consultants to evaluate the fund managers. The consultant usually conducts an in-depth analysis using proprietary models and market indexes. Such an analysis provides the committee with an independent means of evaluating the performance of the fund's manager(s). While the cost of a consultant's service varies, the benefit can be significant when the committee consists of members who are not skilled in the investment process.

Most often, the portfolio manager reviews and discusses performance results from a "top-down" perspective; that is, the discussion starts with a review of the broadest aspects of the investment environment and proceeds sequentially to narrower issues. An outline of such a top-down review is given in Exhibit 12–3.

At the end of the process, the committee should evaluate whether the portfolio achieved the desired results, and if not, why. Was the fund's shortfall (or success) due to the investments held, or was it due to asset selection? Finally, the committee must evaluate whether the manager's investment performance met the requirements outlined in the policy statement. If the manager is not properly following the investment guidelines, corrective action should be taken.

The portfolio manager's investment outlook usually follows the review of the portfolio's performance. He or she should address the overall direction of the economy as well as the expected direction of the financial markets. Does the manager expect interest rates to rise or fall? Will there be a tightening or easing of monetary conditions? What is expected in terms of inflation? How will the stock market perform? The manager should address the investment risks and other assumptions underlying his or her forecast.

The fund manager should also be asked what change, if any, is planned for the upcoming measurement period. Are there plans to dispose of any holdings? What acquisitions are planned? Will the existing asset allocation mix be altered? The committee must evaluate the planned investment strategy in light of the economic forecast. Are they consistent? The committee should reevaluate the

EXHIBIT 12-3

INVESTMENT PERFORMANCE REVIEW AND OUTLOOK

1. Economic Review and Outlooks
   - An assessment of the economy's performance in the most recent period, including an analysis of growth in real GDP, an analysis of the growth in the economy's primary sectors, information on inflation and employment, and an evaluation of the economy's actual performance relative to that forecasted.
   - A forecast of economic activity for the forthcoming period, including an assessment of the business cycle stage and newsworthy domestic and international economic trends.

2. Economic Policy and Review
   - An assessment of, and outlook for, Federal Reserve monetary policy, especially as it affects interest rates and nominal economic activity, as well as any significant developments regarding federal government spending, tax policy, regulatory policy, and international trade and exchange rate issues.

3. Market Review and Outlooks
   a. Fixed Income Markets
   - An assessment of, and outlook for, interest rates, including changes in the shape of the Treasury yield curve and spreads between Treasury securities and relevant corporate bonds.
   - A review of relevant fixed-income indexes.
   b. Equity Markets
   - An assessment of, and outlook for, corporate earnings. A review of relevant domestic and international equity market indexes.
   c. Other Markets
   - An assessment of, and outlooks for, short-term interest rates.
     A review of relevant indexes for such investments as real estate, collectibles, and commodities.

4. Fund Performance Review
   - Overall performance relative to indexes and universes.
   - Performance of equity, fixed-income, etc., components relative to indexes and universes.
   - Impact of asset allocation and security selection on overall and component performance.

5. Individual Security Review
   - Review of individual security holdings, including rationale for additions to/deletions from the fund.

asset allocation in light of changing market and economic conditions.

The committee may want to set time aside after the manager's presentation to review among themselves the investment performance results. It may be helpful to gain the perspective of the committee members concerning performance while the report is fresh in everyone's minds. This is especially true when the committee is considering the termination of a manager or is working with a newly hired one.

OLD BUSINESS

Often discussions of investment issues raised during a meeting will not be resolved at that time. Either the lack of committee time or the need for additional information can lead to postponement of issues. The "old business" portion of the meeting is reserved to revisit unresolved items from the previous meeting. The agenda should identify the issues to be discussed under this heading.

NEW BUSINESS

The "new business" portion of the meeting is designed to allow participants to discuss a wide range of issues concerning the fund. This part of the meeting can be used to solicit discussion from committee members regarding a host of topics. These may range from revisiting the goals and objectives of the fund, reviewing the adequacy of the policy document, reviewing the risk acceptance level, as well as reviewing specific investment issues.

SUMMARY

The purpose of the investment policy meeting is to carry out the committee's administrative responsibilities and to evaluate the portfolio's performance. The key to conducting a successful meeting is proper planning. The chair has the ultimate responsibility for the direction of the meeting. He or she must strive to create an open environment where a free exchange of ideas can take place.

The agenda should lay out how the sequence of events is to occur during the meeting. The meeting itself should deal with administrative issues of concern as well as the investment performance of the fund. During the earlier portion of the meeting, the committee's deliberations may take place prior to the attendance of the portfolio managers.

The main agenda item for most meetings will likely be the investment review and outlook portion. Here, investment managers present an overview of the economy and market environment and review the performance of their portfolios. During this time, committee members may ask questions concerning to the investment results and future prospects. Finally, the agenda provides for discussions on a variety of issues under the headings of old and new business.

Index